POLITICS, POLICY AND THE EUROPEAN RECESSION

This book is intended as a comparative text which presents an overview of the manner in which the major European states and the European Community have responded to the recession of the 1970s and early 1980s.

The aim, after outlining the main causes of the recession, is to describe the responses from political parties, pressure groups, political institutions and governments in individual nation-states as they have reacted to the quadrupling of oil prices, rising inflation, rising unemployment and lower growth.

Overall, a comparison of these state policies is made with a general assessment of the trends towards the creation of corporatist or neo-liberal style economic frameworks for the 1980s in advanced industrial European nation-states.

Dr Andrew Cox, the editor, is a Lecturer in the Department of Politics at the University of Hull. He has taught at the Universities of Michigan, Essex, Cambridge and Hull, and is the author (with D. H. McKay) of *The Politics of Urban Change*.

Also by Andrew Cox

THE POLITICS OF URBAN CHANGE (*with D. H. McKay*)

POLITICS, POLICY AND THE EUROPEAN RECESSION

Edited by

Andrew Cox
Lecturer in Politics
University of Hull

First published 1982 by
THE MACMILLAN PRESS LTD
London and Basingstoke
Companies and representatives throughout the world

ISBN 0 333 30577 9

Printed and bound in Great Britain
at The Pitman Press, Bath

Contents

Preface

This book was conceived as an exercise in drawing out the similarities and dissimilarities of economic policy-making in European nation-states as they responded to the oil-induced recession facing the advanced industrial countries in the 1970s. It was intended that in so doing the beginnings of a common framework might be discernible, which might point the way to renewed and sustainable economic growth. What became clear during the exercise of compiling this volume was that despite the similarities in policy response, the future of economic prosperity in individual countries was bedevilled by national idiosyncrasies of culture, economic structure and political style and institutions. As a result, the economic problems faced by nation-states may be similar but the solutions to these difficulties have and will continue to diverge. Nevertheless this writer – although this would certainly not be the position of all the contributors to this volume – would argue that while slight differences in approach are necessary, incorporationist or corporatist solutions based on consensus rather than conflict seem to offer the best solution to the economic problems of the 1980s. This book is not offered however as an attempt to force readers to reach this conclusion – they will clearly make up their own minds on their reading of the articles herein – but as the editor's considered opinion having compiled the book. However, if it does nothing more than contribute to the on-going debate over economic policies for the 1980s it will have served its purpose.

Finally my thanks must go to the contributors to this book for their speed and diligence in completing their respective chapters. Especial thanks are however due to Enid, Sally and Jan for their assistance in typing at short notice and often under trying conditions.

Hull
North Humberside A.C.

Notes on the Contributors

DAVID COATES is Senior Lecturer in Politics at the University of Leeds. His publications include *The Labour Party and the Struggle for Socialism* (1975) and *Labour in Power? A Study of the Labour Government 1974–9* (1980).

ANDREW COX is Lecturer in Politics at the University of Hull. He is the author (with D. H. McKay) of *The Politics of Urban Change*, and has written articles on economic, defence and urban problems.

KENNETH DYSON is Lecturer in Politics at the University of Liverpool. His publications include *Party, State and Bureaucracy in West Germany* (1977) and *The State Tradition in Western Europe* (1980).

NEIL ELDER is Senior Lecturer in Politics at the University of Hull. His publications include *Government in Sweden: The Executive at Work* (1970) and numerous articles on Swedish and Scandinavian government and politics.

PAUL FURLONG is Lecturer in Politics at the University of Hull, and has written on electoral politics and terrorism in Italy and on relations between the Catholic Church and the Italian Christian Democrats. He is now working on a study of the Italian Parliament.

JOSEPH HARRISON is Lecturer in Economic History at the University of Manchester. His publications include *An Economic History of Modern Spain* (1978) and articles in *Recerques*, *Hacienda Pública Española* and *Economic History Review*.

JACK HAYWARD is Professor of Politics at the University of Hull. His publications include *Private Interests and Public Policy* (1966); *The One and Indivisible French Republic* (1973); (co-editor) *Planning, Politics and Public Policy* (1975); *Planning in Europe* (1978); *State and Society in Contemporary Europe* (1979); (editor) *Trade Unions and Politics in Western Europe* (1980).

EMIL KIRCHNER is Lecturer in Government at the University of Essex. His publications include *Trade Unions as Pressure Groups in the European Community* (with Konrad Schuvaiger) and articles and contributions to books on interest groups and European integration.

BRAM PEPER is Professor of Social and Economic Policy at the University of Erasmus, Rotterdam. Professor Peper is a crown member of the Dutch Advisory Economic Council, and his publications include *The Making of Welfare Policy* (1972) and (editor) *Dutch Industrial Relations* (1973).

1 The World Recession and European Political and Economic Responses

ANDREW COX

This book seeks to outline the policy responses by the major European states to the recession which affected the advanced industrial economies after the 1973 oil crisis. Individual chapters deal with the peculiarly national, social and political responses to the problems of rising inflation, rising unemployment and declining growth, while this introductory chapter indicates the context within which European nation-states had to operate by outlining the major factors generating the recession. Having indicated how the developed world overcame these problems prior to the second oil crisis of 1978–9, it will then be possible to outline which of the European economies have responded most successfully to the recession and why.

THE NATURE OF THE WORLD RECESSION (1974–80)

Indicators of the recession

Some idea of the scope and depth of the recession which afflicted the world economy after 1974 can be gleaned from the fact that while it had always appeared to be the case in the post-war world that there was a trade-off between unemployment and inflation that would sustain high rates of growth, the impact of the quadrupling of oil prices in 1973–4 was to show that both inflation and unemployment could rise, while growth declined. This phenomena, known as *stagflation*, was the new phenomena which faced the advanced industrial economies after 1973. Table 1.1 gives a clear picture of the novel circumstances in which the OECD area found itself during the 1970s.[1] While throughout the 1960s economic growth had averaged 4.8 per cent per annum in the OECD countries, in the 1970s the average fell to a mere 3.4 per cent per annum. The depth of the fall in growth rates is further underlined however if it is appreciated that in 1972–3 growth rates were at a record annual average since the early 1950s of 7–8 per cent; rates fell swiftly in 1974 and 1975 to a mere ½ per cent and −½ per cent average respectively. Only by 1977–8 did growth rates return to a 3–3½ per cent average for the OECD area as a whole. Underlying this trend to lower growth therefore was the fact that industrial production fell by 13 per cent between 1973 and 1975 and output rose by only 40 per cent in the 1970s compared with 60 per cent in the 1960s.[2] This downward trend is further underlined by the fall in trend rates for capital fixed investment in the 1970s and the slow down in productivity increases.

The fall in growth and output after 1973 was inevitably associated with a rise in unemployment which increased by 16 per cent in OECD countries between 1974 and 1978 and is still rising in the early 1980s. From an annual average rate of 2 per cent in the 1960s the OECD unemployment figure rose quickly to 5½ per cent by the end of 1975 and, despite some decline up to 1978, by 1980 it had risen to 6 per cent, with an expected further rise to 7 per cent (or 23 million) in 1981.[3] Associated with this worsening employment position was the additional constraint for the OECD area after 1973 of having to run an overall balance-of-payments deficit. In the 1970–3 period OECD had experienced a modest cumulative surplus on current account of $7–10 billion, with the OPEC countries having a roughly balanced account and the non-oil developing countries an equivalent deficit. This allowed the OECD area to adopt relatively easy expansionary policies to stimulate growth, but after 1973 the OECD area experienced – due to falling exports and a massive increased in its imported oil bill – a combined deficit of $25–6 billion in 1974 and 1977, which added an additional constraint to expansionary policies. Finally, to make the task of economic management more difficult the unexpected happened – while output and growth stagnated inflation rose as well. The average inflation rate in the OECD had been 2.9 per cent in the 1960s, but in the 1970s it rose on average to 8.1 per cent.[4] The major increases in inflation indeed took place in 1974 and 1975 (inflation rose on average by 13.6 per cent and 11.4 per cent respectively) just as output was falling and unemployment was rising. These statistics provide an introduction to the changed economic circumstances within which the West European/OECD countries found themselves in the 1970s. Before looking at how these countries were able to overcome many of these

TABLE 1.1 Indicators of the 1970s Recession

		1962	1963	1964	1965	1966	1967	1968	1969	1970	1971	1972	1973	1974	1975	1976	1977	1978	1979
Growth of GDP (% p.a.)	OECD	5.3	4.7	6.0	5.3	5.5	3.8	5.6	4.9	3.2	3.6	5.5	6.3	0.6	−0.5	5.3	3.8	3.9	3.5
	EEC	4.4	4.2	5.8	4.2	3.6	3.3	5.3	5.9	5.0	3.5	4.0	6.0	1.7	−1.4	5.0	2.4	3.2	3.5
Change in Consumer Prices (% p.a.)	OECD	2.5	2.7	2.5	3.1	3.4	3.1	4.0	4.8	5.6	5.3	4.8	7.9	13.6	11.4	8.5	8.7	7.0	7.5
Current Balance ($ billion)	OECD	1.6	1.6	3.2	3.7	2.7	3.4	4.5	4.5	6.8	9.9	7.9	10.3	−26.0	−0.5	−19.0	−25.0	9.0	−30.0
Unemployment (%)	EEC	Average 2.1									2.6	2.5	2.5	2.9	4.4	4.9	5.3	5.6	6.0

SOURCE OECD, *Economic Outlook* (various)

difficulties by 1978 it is first of all necessary to outline the underlying factors which caused stagflation.

The causes of the world recession

While it is commonplace today to blame the quadrupling of oil prices by OPEC in 1973–4, and the subsequent doubling of prices in 1979–80, for the world recession and the stagflation experienced in the OECD countries, such an analysis only reveals half of the truth because there were already signs in the economies of the West of structural and cyclical problems which might lead to higher unemployment, higher inflation and lower growth.[5] A clearer understanding of the complex relationship between endogenous (OECD) and exogenous (OPEC) forces generating recession can be obtained if we first consider the internal problems facing the OECD prior to the quadrupling of oil prices in 1973–4.

The first point to make about the position of the OECD countries was that many of the structurally important industries – steel, shipbuilding, motor manufacture, textiles and heavy engineering – which had been the base on which these economies had prospered were experiencing, or about to experience, fundamental change. The process of change was generated by the convergence of overproduction, declining demand, low productivity, increasing international competition from newly developing countries and a move from labour based to capital intensive development. In other words, the traditional manufacturers of these products were increasingly unable to survive unless they were prepared to replace men with more efficient machinery and allow only the most efficient companies to survive in an increasingly competitive and relatively shrinking world market. Without the oil crisis therefore the need to resolve the problems of lower growth, higher unemployment and de-industrialisation would have been pressing for the West.[6] At the same time however, due to the growth of worker militancy and rising expectations of increased living standards in the developed countries throughout the 1960s, the ability of companies to shed labour or impose wage restraint on their workforce had declined.[7] Increasingly, trade unions and workers in the advanced industrial countries came to expect that increases in inflation which were externally generated (increases in food and other raw material prices) should not lead to a cut in their standards of living. The consequence of this attitude and expectation was of course that, since productivity was declining relatively and increases in wages were not being offset by gains in output and reductions in unit labour costs, either a squeeze on business profits occurred or increased inflation resulted as unearned wage rises were passed on in final prices.

Thus even before the increase in oil prices there were trends which were likely to undermine the ability of the advanced industrial economies to compete as effectively in world markets as had been the case in the past. There were also, however, problems of a more complex nature between 1970 and 1973 related to the difficulties of 'fine-tuning' the OECD economies using traditional Keynesian techniques of demand management. By 1973 the OECD countries were already experiencing high rates of inflation and were restraining demand in their economies to reduce this pressure which had been caused, largely, by their own inadequate use of demand management techniques.

In 1970–1 the OECD area experienced a cyclical downturn in economic activity much worse than anything experienced in the 1960s. This problem was exacerbated by the collapse of the international monetary system which resulted in the unsatisfactory Smithsonian agreement which tried, but failed, to bring back stability to the international monetary system.[8] The ending of fixed exchange rates against the dollar induced a wave of speculative investments in commodities and this pressure on commodity prices in 1972–3 was heightened by the somewhat unforeseen consequences of individual OECD governments' attempts to expand their economies. In order to stimulate growth rates and reflate their economies out of the 1970–1 downturn most of the major OECD countries – but especially the USA, Canada, Japan and the UK – adopted expansionary budgets to stimulate demand through fiscal policies. At the same time most of these economies slackened monetary policy, reduced interest rates and allowed a massive increase in monetary growth (from an annual average increase in monetary growth of 8 per cent in the 1960s the figure for the OECD had reached 20 per cent in 1973). The consequence of these expansionary policies was that, as opposed to the 'relay' style expansion of economies in the post-war periods of reflation, the 1972–3 period saw most of the major economies expanding in tandem; this had a massive simultaneous impact on demand for raw materials and this explains why commodity prices rose and domestic inflation rose sharply in 1972–3 (see Figure 1.1).[9]

By the middle of 1973 then the OECD countries were having to deflate their economies by adopting tighter monetary policies and they were also having difficulty in inducing workers to restrain wage demands at a time of structural change in industry and increased international competition. It is likely that the OECD would therefore have experienced slower growth and higher inflation in the 1970s compared with the 1960s without the impact of the increase in oil prices. What is however abundantly clear is that the increase in oil prices made the task of demand management inestimably more difficult and the process of economic transformation that much more problematic.

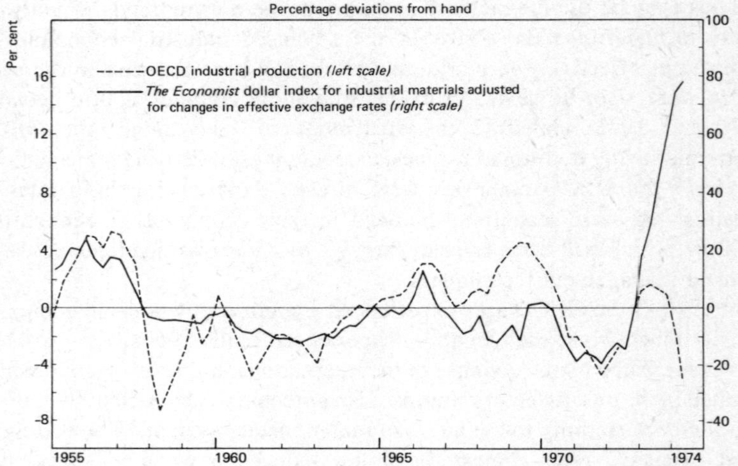

SOURCE OECD, *Economic Outlook*, no. 13 (July 1973)

FIGURE 1.1 OECD Industrial Production and Spot Prices of Industrial Materials, 1955–74

In the 1950s and 1960s the oil market had been dominated by the 'Seven Sisters' (major international oil companies)[10] and this had ensured that the price of a barrel of oil had remained stable at around $1.80. From 1970 however the control over the production and pricing of oil by the 'Seven Sisters' was gradually eroded through nationalisation of fields and the creation of new contractual relationships, as the more militant members of OPEC (Libya and Algeria) attempted to strengthen their control of what was often their only major raw material. It was not until the October 1973 Arab–Israeli conflict however that the new found strength of OPEC was realised. The ensuing increases in oil prices between October 1973 and January 1974 pushed up the price of oil from the $3 a barrel it had by then reached to $11.65.[11] This quadrupled the price of oil (see Figure 1.2) and in doing so forced the import bill for oil in the OECD up from $35 billion (1973) to $100 billion (1974), taking 2 per cent off OECD GNP immediately and forcing the OECD into a current account deficit of approximately $26 billion in 1974.[12] These developments furthermore were overlaid on an OECD economy which was being deflated throughout 1973 – causing thereby the worst recession since the second world war.

The impact of this recession was felt disproportionately in the corporate sector of the economy because workers were unprepared in 1973–4 to

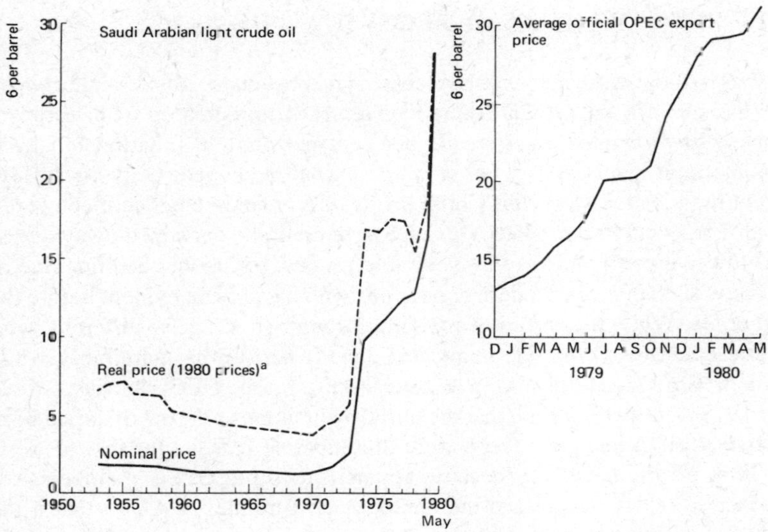

a Nominal crude oil price divided by the OECD export price of manufactures.

SOURCE OECD, *Economic Outlook*, no. 27 (July 1980) p. 115

FIGURE 1.2 The Price of Crude Oil, 1953–80

reduce their living standards to offset the massive loss in terms of trade generated by OPEC actions. Thus firms were forced either to reduce their profit levels to pay wage increases or pass these wage demands on in the form of increased consumer prices. The consequence of this was that the oil price increases directly increased consumer prices and also indirectly either reduced corporate profitability or made their position in world markets less competitive due to rising prices on finished goods. In this way the inflationary and deflationary effects of the oil price increase can be seen. Oil prices were passed on directly in consumer prices adding to inflation. The refusal of workers to reduce their living standards undermined the viability of OECD companies and reduced their ability to reinvest. Similarly, the massive swing in the terms of trade in favour of OPEC contributed to a fall in demand because the OPEC countries simply lacked the indigenous population to be able to spend their new found wealth at the same level and at the same speed as consumers in the Western economies would have done – as a result demand in the OECD area slumped and unemployment rose along with inflation.[13]

THE INITIAL PROCESS OF RECOVERY (1976–8)

By 1976 the worst effects of the recession had begun to subside and between 1976 and 1978 the OECD economies returned to increased (if historically lower) growth rates of around 3 per cent per annum; inflation fell from double digit levels to 7–8 per cent and output recovered. Only unemployment remained at worryingly high levels of around 5–6 per cent compared with 2 per cent in the 1960s; this of course could be explained away due to (a) lower growth and (b) the inevitable process of labour shedding due to structural changes in modern economies which had been evident before the oil crisis. While the record of individual countries was very different, with some countries (West Germany and Japan) performing admirably while others (Britain and Italy) were less successful, for the OECD area as a whole by 1978 it could be argued that the initial difficulties of the oil crisis had been satisfactorily managed. There were a number of reasons for this success.

First of all, it quickly became apparent to some OPEC members – in particular Saudi Arabia and the United Arab Emirates (UAE) – that if the price of oil was continually increased then the Western economies would collapse and the international consequences, not to mention the likely loss of oil revenue, that would ensue were simply not worth the risk. Since these countries control a substantial proportion of oil reserves and existing production they were able to ensure that the price of oil between 1974 and 1978 was relatively stable. Indeed these countries remained firm in their resolve even in 1976 when the more militant OPEC members created a two-tier price for oil by increasing their prices by 10 per cent instead of the 5 per cent decided upon by Saudi Arabia. The consequence of these actions was that by 1978 the *real* price of oil had declined by 10 per cent from its 1974 level, which reduced the OECD deficit and initial deflationary and inflationary impact of the 1973–4 price increases.[14]

Secondly, the major bottleneck to continued economic growth in the OECD countries had always been the actual loss of revenue to the OPEC countries which reduced domestic demand and which the OPEC countries were unable to spend quickly enough or in sufficient quantities to replace the lost demand in the West. The solution to this problem of *recycling* came through the entrepreneurial skills of the banking community. While some of the OPEC money was recycled through aid from OPEC to the non-oil developing countries, most of the recycling of OPEC revenue was undertaken by the international banking community. Between 1974 and 1978 the combined, cumulative balance of payments surplus of the OPEC countries reached $165 billion and the vast majority of this surplus was deposited (especially by those OPEC countries with small indigenous populations) in OECD banks and capital assets. The banks in the OECD then assisted the process of recycling by increasing their international lending – particularly to the non-oil developing countries – from $170 billion in 1973 to $640 billion by the end of 1979. In this way, while the indebtedness of the developing world increased, the level of demand in the world economy was indirectly stimulated, thereby assisting the OECD countries to reduce their current account deficits in 1974 and register a small surplus again in 1978.[15] This process of gradual recovery was also assisted by the decision of the financial ministers and leaders of the major OECD countries, in a series of

TABLE 1.2 OPEC Revenues and Cash Surpluses: 1973–80 ($ billion)

	1973	*1974*	*1975*	*1976*	*1977*	*1978*	*1979*[a]	*1980*[b]
Exports	42	116	107	132	145	146	212	306
Imports	21	39	58	68	84	104	102	138
Net services and transfers	−14	−17	−22	−28	−32	−37	−43	−54
Current surplus	8	59	27	36	29	5	67	114
Cumulative surplus		67	94	130	159	164	231	345
Estimated cash surplus								
invested in		57.0	35.2	37.2	33.5	13.4	53.8	
United States		11.6	9.5	12.0	9.1	1.3	8.9	
United Kingdom		21.0	4.3	4.5	3.8	−1.8	17.2	
Other countries		20.9	17.4	18.7	20.3	13.8	28.1	
International organisations		3.5	4.0	2.0	0.3	0.1	−0.4	

a Estimates
b Forecasts
SOURCE OECD, *Economic Outlook*, no. 27 (July 1980) p. 126

annual June meetings, to develop a *concerted action* programme of recovery. The idea behind this approach was to try to ensure that (a) there was no repetition of the inflationary tandem reflation of 1972–3 and (b) that those countries with low inflation and more stable balance of payments figures (Japan and West Germany) expanded first to pull the large deficit countries in the OECD out of their difficulties. The concerted action programme was finally agreed in June 1978, even though co-operative action had been attempted ever since the 1973–4 crisis.[16] These international measures were supplemented throughout the individual OECD countries by national programmes, which, while varied in design and the degree of positive state intervention as we shall see later, had certain broad similarities which contributed to the recovery between 1976–8.

It has been the case that the tax burden on oil products in the OECD has not kept pace in a proportionate sense with the increases in oil prices. In this way governments, although in varying degrees, have subsidised the use of oil by reducing the level of taxation as its price has risen. This has stimulated a higher level of economic activity than might otherwise have been the case without this tax concession. This policy similarity across the OECD has also been mirrored in the broad budgetary and monetary policies which have been pursued. While there are obviously differences in the detailed approaches of individual countries, in general the initial concern of these countries after 1973–4 was to run large public sector deficits in order to sustain economic activity by maintaining demand and also to try to solve the problems of rising unemployment. The combined public sector deficit for the OECD rose from $35 billion in 1973 to $100 billion in 1974.[17] Inflation was thus seen initially as a secondary concern, although the gradual tightening of monetary policies across the whole of the OECD after 1975 indicates that there was a growing concern with inflation once economic recovery began again after 1975. In this way, from 1976, government policies were generally restrictive on the monetary side, while slightly expansionary on the fiscal side. There were a number of obvious reasons for this apparent schizoid behaviour. While attempting to reduce demand-pull inflation generated by monetary expansion through tighter monetary policies, the governments of the OECD were worried that too much deflation might undermine the chance of economic recovery by reducing demand. This desire therefore to maintain relatively high levels of public expenditure was also necessitated by the need to intervene to support the ever increasing number of 'lame-duck' industries and firms; to create active manpower policies; and, to stimulate manufacturing investment as it declined in this period. This need for an expanded state role was also evidenced in the interventions, first through incomes and prices policies, but then increasingly through the incorporation of trade unions and employers into tripartite (social contract style) negotiations over wages and pay. In other words relative high government borrowing and expenditure was seen by many countries as a temporary cost in the pursuit of the larger goal of reduced cost-push inflation and industrial revival.[18] For those countries in the OECD which were able to implement these policies successfully, to reduce first wage demands and then public expenditure levels while shifting resources from private consumption to industrial investment (Japan and West Germany in particular), the long-term economic future appeared fairly healthy by 1978. This unfortunately took no account of the second oil crisis.

THE SECOND OIL CRISIS AND THE PROBLEMS OF THE 1980s

While some OECD countries were managing to resolve the cyclical and structural problems of the 1970s fairly satisfactorily, and while for the OECD area as a whole the position in 1978 was much brighter than it had been during the trough of the 1974–5 recession, the future of the OECD in the 1980s is as bleak as it has ever been due to the Iranian crisis sparking off a second increase in oil prices.

As intimated earlier, despite the relative success of Saudi Arabia in limiting oil price increases there was always a tension within the OPEC countries between those who saw themselves inextricably linked economically with the West and those (like Libya) who wanted to seize every opportunity to raise oil prices to increase revenue whatever the effect on the OECD economies. Throughout the 1974–8 period therefore there were continual arguments between factions in OPEC over whether prices should remain stable or whether production should be reduced now that demand had fallen in order that prices could be forced up. A stalemate ensued with some of the more militant countries unilaterally deciding to reduce production and charge higher prices on the world 'spot markets'. But when Iran stopped all exports of oil on 26 December 1978 there was a mad scramble by the OECD countries to purchase any oil available on the 'spot markets' at whatever price was charged. This panic buying arose due to fear that there would be a real shortage of oil, and prices rose even though *there was no shortage of oil due to over-production and inadequate demand*. Despite this, the panic action of the West convinced even the less militant OPEC countries that the OECD countries were prepared to pay an even higher price for their oil than that ruling, and the doubling of oil prices in a number of steps between December 1978 and May 1980 was the result. The price of a barrel of oil rose from $12.87 to approximately $31; the OECD's oil import bill rose from $140 billion in 1978 to $290 billion in 1980; inflation rose to 15 per cent plus in 1979–80; and, GNP was expected to fall by 5½ per cent in 1981. The OECD countries found themselves in much the same position as they were during 1974–5 with a second recession looming.[19]

The problem in 1980 for the OECD is however that the real position in which the developed economies find themselves is in fact much worse than it was in 1974–5. In 1974–5 the oil price increase had come on top of an economy in which growth was slowing down but from a relatively high level; in 1979–80 the second increase in oil prices (though proportionately lower than in 1973–4) occurs on an economy which has been experiencing a similar slowdown in growth but from a much lower level. In this way it may be that the recession will be deeper and longer than in the 1970s, because the base from which the OECD will be attempting to recover is much shallower than in the 1970s. Unfortunately this is not the only problem. We saw that the OECD was able to overcome the loss in its own domestic demand after

1973–4 by recycling OPEC surpluses through the international banking system to non-oil developing countries. This possibility of 'backdoor' stimulation of demand is much more problematic in the 1980s because there is a growing unwillingness by the banks to lend to the Third World countries, whose indebtedness has risen from $75 billion to $270 billion between 1972 and 1979. There is a fear that these countries will be unable to meet these debts. Secondly, in recent years due to the upward pressure on short-term interest rates in the OECD, due to restrictive monetary policies, the OPEC countries have been placing their surpluses increasingly in short-term borrowing in Eurocurrency markets, rather than into capital investments which stimulate economic growth in the long term. Finally, the success of the West Germans, the Swiss and the Japanese in selling government bonds to the OPEC countries means that there is less revenue available for recycling.[20] For all these reasons the 'backdoor' stimulation of OECD demand does not appear as easy an option as it did in the mid-1970s.

There are also perhaps more fundamental problems for the OECD economies than these primarily international constraints, because there are a number of internally generated obstacles to sustained future growth. All of the OECD countries, in part through their decision to reduce the tax on oil products, have systematically ignored the need to develop coherent energy policies. Despite government exhortations for energy conservation and some definite improvements in this field since 1974 (the final energy cost to users rose 40 per cent between 1973 and 1979 and the demand for energy has not kept pace, as it did in the past, with growth rates) the OECD area is still as dependent on imported oil in 1980 as it was in 1974.[21] OECD's indigenous energy production has only risen by 5 per cent in this period despite the supposed panacea of nuclear energy and the revival of coal production and new oil discoveries (Alaska and North Sea), at a time when energy demand from the OECD had risen by 7 per cent. Thus the OECD is still dependent for one-third of its energy supplies on imported sources, of which oil constitutes 95 per cent.[22] Given the further destabilisation of the oil market by the Iran–Iraq conflict of 1980 and the further deterioration of the effective control of the oil market by the international oil companies, the OECD countries face the 1980s without a coherent energy strategy.

This weakness is further compounded by the fact that this additional cyclical oil induced recession is to hit an OECD economy in which the structural problems generating lower growth (lack of investment, lack of competitive ability, under-consumption and over-production and rising unemployment) prior to the 1973–4 crisis have not been resolved. The manifestation of this problem is of course the rising level of unemployment which did not fall appreciably even when growth rates turned upward after

1975. Unfortunately the incidence of unemployment appears to be falling disproportionately on the young and unskilled across the OECD, and so at a time when social consensus is necessary to ensure acceptance of wage moderation and real reductions in living standards to pay for the increased cost of oil, the social and political fabric of the OECD countries may well be questioned by alienated and unemployable individuals. This pinpoints the political and economic dilemma facing the OECD: the policies which may alleviate the problems of unemployment and alienation amongst the young and ungratified expectations amongst displaced workers and those forced to accept wage moderation are only possible in the short term through higher levels of public expenditure. Unfortunately, attempts throughout the 1970s to maintain demand and to reduce social dislocation through easing the process of structural economic transformation have generated a general increase in all OECD countries of public sector borrowing.[23] It is now accepted however that this borrowing in itself contributes to inflation which in turn makes firms uncompetitive and 'crowds out' the investment that might otherwise have gone to revitalise industry.[24] This then is the dilemma of modern government: how to maintain public spending at a level that does not act as a restraint on private industry while at the same time being forced on all sides to spend public money to resolve the problems which the private sector cannot resolve – like structural unemployment, regional decline and manpower retraining and planning.

As we saw in the 1974–5 period, OECD governments initially opted for higher spending and borrowing to sustain demand and keep unemployment down; in the 1979–80 period, however, this option appears to be less attractive or possible because it is assumed that this leads to higher demand induced inflation in the long term and lower growth. The OECD countries therefore have adopted a more restrictive stance in 1979–80 and have decided to tackle inflation, rather than unemployment, by restrictive monetary policies and by reducing the burden of public expenditure. But, this approach which may or may not offer long-term growth prospects faces horrendous short-term difficulties associated with the historic rise in worker militancy and social expectations of high or higher standards of living. The problem is that the attack on inflation being adopted by the OECD countries can only work in the short-term through reducing living standards, raising unemployment, speeding regional industrial decline and transformation of industrial sectors. This being the case more advanced OECD countries have realised that there is a pressing need for social and political co-operation to maintain support for difficult economic decisions, and it is largely for this reason that there have been attempts in many OECD countries to pass permissive labour laws and to encourage worker participation in order to incorporate the potential opponents of these policies into the state's decision making structures.[25]

Unfortunately, these attempts to enmesh the trade unions and workers organisations into the state apparatus are themselves problematic because this in turn tends to alienate employers, whose own scope for autonomous action in industrial decision making is eroded; it also complicates the process of industrial transformation as workers representatives trade-off their acquiescence to change in return for higher social welfare assistance from the state. It is for this reason, plus of course due to increasing international competition, that there is a possibility of defensive import barriers being raised as an easy short-term alternative to the need to either restructure industry or displace labour. The fear for the 1980s may be therefore that, in an attempt to circumvent the harsh choices on employment, industrial restructuring and standards of living, countries may resort to protectionism which may further reduce world trade and exacerbate the present recession. Despite this general problem for the OECD as a whole it is the case that some of the European OECD countries are in a more favourable position in the early 1980s mainly because they have been able to overcome some, if not all, of the international and domestic problems that have been outlined by their political and economic responses to the two recessions.

EUROPEAN RESPONSES TO THE RECESSION

While the OECD countries were generally able to overcome the problems posed by the 1974–5 recession successfully, as the further crisis generated by the second oil crisis indicates, the basic structural economic problems which were in evidence before the oil crisis have not been adequately resolved by all, or even most, of the OECD countries. Nevertheless, some European countries – in particular West Germany, Sweden and to a lesser extent France and the Netherlands – have been able to tackle some if not all of the endogenous and exogenous problems outlined above. The relative success of these countries in tackling the problems of growth, unemployment, balance of payments, capital investment and inflation are outlined in summary form in Tables 1.3–1.7. These tables also outline the failure of the British, Italians and Spanish to resolve the underlying economic difficulties of the 1970s.

It is clear from these basic statistics, as well as from the analyses of each of these countries' individual economic and political responses, to which the remainder of this book is devoted, that only some European states are able to view the 1980s with confidence. Interestingly enough, as the analyses in this

TABLE 1.3 Growth of Real GDP at Market Prices: OECD and Seven Major European Countries

	1970	*1971*	*1972*	*1973*	*1974*	*1975*	*1976*	*1977*	*1978*	*1979*	*1980*[a]
Total OECD	3.2	3.6	5.5	6.3	0.6	−0.5	5.3	3.8	3.9	3.5	1.2
West Germany	6.0	3.2	3.7	4.9	0.5	−1.8	5.2	2.7	3.5	4.4	2.0
Sweden	5.3	−0.2	1.6	3.4	4.2	0.8	1.3	−2.7	2.4	3.8	3.0
Netherlands	6.7	4.3	3.4	5.7	3.5	−1.0	5.3	2.8	2.4	2.6	0.2
France	5.7	5.4	5.9	5.4	3.2	0.2	5.0	2.8	3.3	3.2	2.0
Britain	2.3	2.8	2.4	8.0	−1.5	−1.0	3.7	1.3	3.5	1.7	−2.2
Italy	5.3	1.6	3.2	7.0	4.1	−3.6	5.9	2.0	2.6	4.9	3.5
Spain	4.1	5.0	8.1	7.9	5.7	1.1	3.0	2.6	3.1	1.4	1.5

a Estimate
SOURCE OECD, *Economic Outlook* (various)

TABLE 1.4 Unemployment Rates: OECD and Seven Major Countries (% of total labour force, seasonally adjusted)

	1970	*1971*	*1972*	*1973*	*1974*	*1975*	*1976*	*1977*	*1978*	*1979*	*1980*[a]
Total OECD	N/A	N/A	N/A	3.0	3.3	5.1	5.3	5.3	5.2	5.1	5.2
West Germany	0.5	0.7	1.0	0.9	2.7	4.8	3.6	3.6	3.5	3.2	2.8
Sweden	0.9	1.5	1.7	2.5	2.0	1.6	1.6	1.8	2.2	2.1	1.8
Netherlands	1.4	1.8	3.0	2.3	3.3	4.7	5.1	4.9	5.0	5.1	N/A
France	1.7	2.1	2.3	2.6	2.3	3.8	4.4	4.9	5.2	5.9	6.0
Britain	2.3	3.0	3.4	2.8	2.5	3.9	5.5	6.1	6.1	5.8	6.0
Italy	3.2	3.2	3.7	3.5	2.9	5.9	6.6	7.1	7.2	7.6	7.8
Spain	1.5	2.0	3.0	2.2	3.2	4.0	5.0	5.5	7.3	9.0	10.9

a Estimate
SOURCE OECD, *Economic Outlook* (various)

TABLE 1.5 Current Balances: OECD and Seven Major European Countries ($ billion)[a]

	1970	*1971*	*1972*	*1973*	*1974*	*1975*	*1976*	*1977*	*1978*	*1979*	*1980*[b]
Total OECD	6.8	9.9	7.9	10.3	−26.0	−0.5	−19.0	−24.6	10.3	−37.4	−81.0
West Germany	0.8	0.8	0.8	4.6	9.8	3.4	3.4	4.2	8.7	−5.7	−16.9
Sweden	−0.2	0.2	0.2	1.2	−0.9	−1.6	−2.0	−1.7	−1.4	−2.9	−3.6
Netherlands	−0.5	−0.1	1.2	2.3	2.2	1.9	2.7	0.6	−1.3	−2.5	−1.6
France	0.1	0.5	0.2	−0.6	−5.9	−0.1	−6.1	−3.3	3.7	1.5	−4.0
Britain	1.8	2.8	0.5	−2.2	−7.9	−3.5	−2.8	2.5	6.4	5.2	−2.7
Italy	1.3	1.9	2.0	−2.6	−8.0	−0.7	−2.8	2.5	6.4	5.2	−2.7
Spain	0.1	0.8	0.5	0.5	−3.2	−3.4	−4.2	−2.1	1.6	0.6	−3.4

a Goods, services and all transfer payments
b Estimate
SOURCE OECD, *Economic Outlook* (various)

TABLE 1.6 Consumer Prices: OECD and Seven Major European Countries (% changes from previous year)

	1970	*1971*	*1972*	*1973*	*1974*	*1975*	*1976*	*1977*	*1978*	*1979*	*1980*[a]
Total	5.6	5.3	4.8	7.9	13.6	11.4	8.5	8.7	7.0	8.5	11.2
West Germany	3.4	5.3	5.5	6.9	7.0	6.0	4.5	3.7	2.7	4.1	5.0
Sweden	7.0	7.4	6.0	6.7	9.9	9.8	10.3	11.4	10.0	7.2	13.0
Netherlands	3.6	7.5	7.8	8.0	9.6	10.2	8.8	6.4	4.1	4.2	6.2
France	4.8	5.5	6.2	7.3	13.7	11.8	9.6	9.4	9.3	10.7	13.2
Britain	6.4	9.4	7.1	9.2	16.0	24.2	16.5	15.8	8.7	12.0	18.7
Italy	5.0	4.8	5.7	10.8	19.1	17.0	16.8	17.0	12.1	14.8	20.5
Spain	5.7	8.3	8.3	11.4	15.7	16.9	17.7	24.5	19.8	15.7	17.0

a Estimate
SOURCE OECD, *Economic Outlook* (various)

TABLE 1.7 Capital Formation and Fixed Investment: Seven Major European Countries (% changes from previous year)

	1970	*1971*	*1972*	*1973*	*1974*	*1975*	*1976*	*1977*	*1978*	*1979*	*1980*[a]
West Germany	1.5	4.5	3.5	6.0	−7.9	−4.1	4.7	4.0	6.3	8.5	5.7
Sweden	3.5	−2.5	5.9	−0.2	1.1	−1.5	−1.6	−1.8	−6.0	5.4	5.5
Netherlands	8.3	1.7	−1.3	4.5	−4.2	−4.0	−1.9	10.8	3.1	−0.5	2.0
France	7.5	5.1	7.1	5.8	3.2	−3.4	4.5	−1.3	0.7	2.0	2.0
Britain	1.3	1.0	1.1	4.1	−2.5	−1.3	−4.3	−2.1	1.6	−3.2	−5.0
Italy	3.4	−5.2	3.0	8.2	4.2	−13.0	2.3	0.0	−0.1	4.5	4.2
Spain	3.8	−1.9	13.5	14.3	4.4	−3.4	−3.1	−2.2	−4.0	0.0	2.0

a Estimate
SOURCE OECD, *Economic Outlook* (various)

book reveal, the reasons for this optimism lie as much in the success of political processes as in economic policies because the problems facing European states in the 1980s are as much political as economic. Only those nations – like West Germany and Sweden in particular – that have been able to resolve or mitigate the effects of the political difficulties of the recession (lack of social consensus, ungratified social and economic expectations, demands for greater political involvement and participation of labour, and the need to incorporate conflicting and outmoded group and sectional interests) have been able to tackle the basic structural and cyclical economic problems. States which have failed to arrive at political and social consensus over the sharing of economic burdens and which have pursued polarised/ideological policies have tended to experience economic and political failure. Britain and Italy and to a lesser extent Spain, with its peculiar political problems of transition from despotic authoritarianism to liberal democracy in the 1970s, fall into this latter category.

As the chapters in this volume indicate, while there is no one blueprint for economic recovery and prosperity that European states must adopt, there does seem to be a correlation between these countries which have developed neo-corporatist/incorporationist solutions and relative economic prosperity and success.[26] While these forms of intervention and incorporation cannot of themselves ensure economic growth (witness the more successful record of the less corporatist West German economy when compared with the more corporatist Swedish, Dutch and French economies), it does seem to be the case that, given the need in the late 1970s and early 1980s to resolve economic problems by reducing social and economic expectations and extending burden sharing across all sectors of the society, those countries which refuse to adopt this approach face insurmountable political problems on top of economic constraints. Thus countries like Britain which have to face the adversarial political forces of capital and labour as well as party policies which limit the possibility of consensus; countries like Italy with a fundamental division between left and right and a state structure which is basically corrupt and discredited; and countries like Spain, having to undertake a fundamental political transition to oust and replace existing elites to generate modernisation and growth, have had political obstacles to overcome which have generally militated against the resolution of economic crises. This is not to say that the more corporatist countries have not experienced political problems: this they surely have and will continue to do. The point here is however that such countries are less hamstrung by the need to find consensus and political harmony over economic goals, which allows for concerted and consistent action to deal with economic problems. The force of this conclusion is seen if we consider for a moment the individual records of the seven major European countries discussed in this volume.

West Germany

As Tables 1.3–1.7 indicate West Germany has experienced the highest growth rate per annum of the seven countries analysed since the 1974–5 recession. This record is remarkable given that West Germany's growth rate before 1973–4 was below the OECD average and indicates the resilience and strength of this economy. Figures for unemployment (consistently below the OECD average with only Sweden having a better performance over the decade), balance of payments (showing a strong surplus until 1979), inflation (the lowest over the decade for these seven countries), and fixed investment (consistently higher average growth rates than the other seven countries) all underscore the fact that the West Germany economy has been the most capable and resilient in withstanding the shocks of the two oil price rises. This is not to say that West Germany has not and does not experience difficulties – for example the strength of the mark has hit the competitiveness of exports, the average growth rate is lower than in the 1960s, structural and regional unemployment and de-industrialisation has set in and unit labour costs have been rising as productivity has been falling – but that in relation to other European countries West Germany has tackled these problems most competently.

The reasons for this success are many as Dyson indicates in this volume. The relatively new industrial infrastructure created by post-war reconstruction and the close relationship between the banking and industrial sectors in Germany are clearly important factors behind the German economic success but, as Dyson shows, post-war political and institutional arrangements have been of immense importance in generating consensus on economic goals and the role of the state. In particular the fact of a SDP/FDP coalition government being in office in the 1970s representing labour and business interests in government, assisted up to 1977 by a Concerted Action programme (incorporating business, labour, financial institutions and the government and bureaucracy) has ensured that the state has been able to orchestrate a package of measures aimed at economic recovery without generating ideological conflicts of interest. Interestingly, institutional arrangements have assisted the SDP/FDP government because the Bundesbank has been constitutionally responsible for imposing relatively restrictive monetary policies after 1972. This has meant that much of the opprobrium for financial stringency and public expenditure cuts has fallen on the Bundesbank rather than on the government, which has ensured a greater degree of co-operation with the government. This co-operation has been assisted by the fact that all sectional economic interests support the state because there is consensus that the state should intervene boldly and positively in three areas in the German economy. The state intervenes to overcome bottlenecks in the market (like energy); to support and subsidise and develop high technology industries (like microprocessors); and to resolve intractable problems (through the use of regional policies and active manpower policies to solve regional and structural problems).[27] Thus, there is no conflict in Germany over the need for the state to intervene to purchase equity in declining staple industries, or to encourage mergers and underwrite expensive research and development costs because both business and labour recognise the need for state action to generate economic growth.

Despite this consensus on the state's role and the acceptance of neo-corporatist consultations between business, labour and government throughout the 1970s the West German political and economic system also faces a number of difficulties. Since 1975, the effects of the oil crisis have been to reduce the growth rate in the economy and exacerbate the problem of unemployment and question the earlier assumption that state spending could rise to support those most in need. Since 1975 the SPD/FDP coalition, despite pursuing mildly reflationary measures to ease Germany out of the recession, has had to reduce expectations about public expenditure and consumption and emphasise the need for public expenditure on capital infrastructure investment. This has meant of course a desire also to reduce wage demands and maintain the competitive position of German exports in an increasingly competitive world market. The consequence of this has been the demise of Concerted Action in 1977 as the trade unions became disillusioned by the rejection of social reforms in favour of increased aid for business and profits at the expense of wages and social expenditure. Worker militancy and strikes have therefore grown in number, especially in areas experiencing de-industrialisation and structural or regional decline (like the Ruhr). Despite this, wage bargaining (as the inflation record indicates) is still moderate and there is consensus about the need for a positive, if limited, state role in the economy. For this reason, plus the willingness by both sides of industry to negotiate and solve their problems in a spirit of compromise with and through the state, West Germany can face the 1980s with more optimism than most other OECD countries.

Sweden

As the tables indicate Sweden, perhaps the most well developed corporatist economy, has also resolved many of the problems of the world recession, if less successfully than West Germany. Sweden entered the recession later than most other OECD countries and its growth rates did not decline until 1975–7. Since then however Sweden's growth rates have been (like West Germany) well above the OECD average and in 1979–80 only Italy has had a better rate of growth. Sweden has also had the lowest rate of unemployment of these countries throughout the decade. Against this success Sweden has been less successful in maintaining a balance of payments surplus due to high unit labour costs and declining demand for exports in the recession. Inflation has also been problematic: after 1975 inflation was running in double figures, except for 1979; although the overall record was much better than Britain, Italy and Spain and was comparable with France. Fixed investment also declined every year after 1974; although a definite improvement comparable to that in West Germany was recorded in 1979 and 1980.

Thus Sweden while having a worrying problem of inflation and balance-of-payments problems has performed relatively well in investment, unemployment and growth. Undoubtedly, as Elder shows, part of the reason for this success lies in the historic attachment to corporatist political structures which allow for mutual discussion of interests and goals between all sectors of society. In this relationship the state's role is essentially one of orchestration rather than dictation because 90 per cent of industry is in private hands. The state's role is to encourage dialogue between all sectors of industry in advisory boards and to encourage centralised wage bargaining agreements. Moderation in these agreements has been assured historically due to the state's accepting a large social welfare obligation which is indicated in inflation-proofed social welfare benefits, active manpower policies, regional policies and the state takeover of declining firms and industries for rationalisation and modernisation (steel, textiles and shipbuilding). This social-welfare role also explains why the Social Democratic government pursued reflationary policies in the immediate aftermath of the oil crisis. Unfortunately part of the price for this was statutory wage restraint which alienated the trade unions and resulted in 1976 in the defeat for the Social Democratic government for the first time since the 1930s. The strength of corporatist structures in Sweden has however been indicated by the fact that the new Centre–Conservative coalition has not reneged on commitments to help the unemployed and has continued to intervene to assist declining industries and sectors. Wage restraint has however also been necessary and in 1980 Sweden experienced its worst post-war record of strikes before the government imposed wage restraint on the trade unions and employers.

These developments indicate that, while corporatist structures assisted in the growth of the Swedish economy in the 1950s, 1960s and to a lesser extent in the 1970s, there is no guarantee this structure will operate as effectively in the future. The continuity of labour quiescence has always been bought by high social-welfare expenditure, a rising living standard and low unemployment. While governments after 1973–4 have been able to ensure low unemployment they have not been able significantly to reduce inflation or maintain as consistently a level of growth, and unemployment has only been reduced at the cost of a massive increase in public expenditure and higher taxation. This latter development is problematic because Swedish corporatism has always been premised on a highly profitable private sector which is now experiencing 'crowding out' by the public sector and reduced investment. The resolution of these problems in the short-term can only occur through reduced public (social welfare) spending or falling wage rates, which may further erode the vitality of consensus which has underpinned the

Swedish economy. Despite these problems the strength of corporatist structures should ensure a relatively easy acceptance of the need to reduce living standards in the short-term.[28]

The Netherlands

Sweden has performed relatively successfully since the 1973–4 recession and the same may be said of the Netherlands, the country which comes closest to mirroring Sweden's corporatist political and economic relationships. Overall however the Netherlands has probably experienced more problems than Sweden and faces the 1980s with less certainty about continued economic success.

Due to the fortuitous discovery of natural gas in the 1960s and relatively low wage rates bargained through national wage agreements in corporatist institutions, growth rates in the Netherlands were well above the OECD average up to 1975; since then however these rates have declined below West Germany, France and Italy. Unemployment has followed a similar pattern: being around the OECD average and comparable with Swedish rates until 1974, since then unemployment rates have risen in line with the declining economies of Britain, Italy and Spain. The balance of payments has also moved into deficit since 1978 indicating the problems that the Netherlands is bound to face in the 1980s as natural gas runs out. Fixed investment has also experienced a decline, although there was a modest recovery in the latter part of the decade. This recovery is still well below trends in West Germany, Sweden and Italy however. Finally, the Netherlands has experienced some success in reducing inflation which was at the OECD average between 1970 and 1976 but which has fallen since then. Only West Germany has a better inflation record.

The Netherlands therefore face the 1980s with great difficulties associated with rising unemployment and balance of payments problems. Nevertheless in one area – in particular inflation – there has been a positive record of success. Undoubtedly, the role of corporatist bargaining and compromise, with centrally negotiated wage policies between labour and business has contributed here to moderation in wage demands. Furthermore when the government has had to intervene in the determination of wage rates this has been accepted by all sides due to the consensual nature of Dutch corporatist relationships. Indeed part of the acceptance of wage restraint after 1973 arose due to the government accepting that the corollary would be high public expenditure on unemployment, job protection and social welfare. This *social contact* approach with burdens being placed more heavily on the more prosperous sectors of the community created its own problems, particularly over wage differentials, and in 1977 the Labour government was replaced by a Conservative–Christian Democratic coalition committed to further reductions in wage rates and the burden of public expenditure. As a result there has been growing labour unrest and increased tension within corporatist institutions in the Netherlands as Peper indicates. Nevertheless, the strength of corporatist institutions is indicated by the fact that, despite cuts in public spending tighter monetary policy and a rejection of workers' demands for a greater say in industry, the trade unions have accepted wage restraint below the level of inflation at the end of the decade. In this sense despite the relatively intractable economic difficulties facing the Netherlands – deindustrialisation, increasing unemployment, declining natural gas reserves, lack of export competitiveness and low productive investment exacerbated by high public spending – these will not be compounded by adversarial political conflict.

France

Like the Netherlands the French economy in the 1980s is likely to be beset by relatively intractable problems. Despite this and notwithstanding the lack of well developed corporatist structures to incorporate labour, the record of this country in the 1970s has been similar to that of the Netherlands in that, while it has not performed as well as Sweden and West Germany, it has been far more successful than Britain, Italy or Spain. Clearly, as Hayward argues in this volume, this has not been due simply to the policies pursued in response to the oil crisis, but has been due more to the underlying problems experienced by the French before 1973 and the responses already developed to deal with these.

The intractable problems facing the French after 1980 are likely to be those experienced at the end of the 1970s. While growth rates have been reasonable, with only West Germany and Spain having better records over the decade, these rates are lower than France has been used to. Similarly, despite attempts to alleviate unemployment the record in France is much worse than West Germany, Sweden and the Netherlands, although better than Britain, Italy and Spain. The balance of payments has also experienced deficits throughout the 1970s on current account, bar for the 1978–9 period. This record compares unfavourably with West Germany, Sweden, Netherlands and to a lesser extent Britain. Since 1975 inflation in France has risen above OECD averages and remains in double figures at the end of the decade. Despite this fixed investment has shown a degree of resilience only surpassed by West Germany. Overall then France faces the future with lower growth potential, higher unemployment and rising inflation, but France while not being able to overcome these problems with the same success as West Germany or Sweden has still performed better than Britain, Italy and Spain.

The explanation for this relative success lies in part in the ability of French governments to support industrial concentration and state intervention to underwrite productive and high-technology investment and development through the neo-corporatist, indicative planning system created since the Second World War. This dirigiste system premised on close co-operation between business and bureaucracy in the state, for positive intervention to modernise and subsidise profitable investment, was the hallmark of French planning. This approach adopted up to the Seventh Plan was not fully corporatist however because it excluded labour. But this was not a major problem for the government because the labour movement in France is weak and divided and not in a position to resist state or private-sector imposed policies for wage restraint. Happily, for the state, up to the late 1970s most worker militancy could be bought off with increased living standards and relatively rising social expenditure. Unfortunately, one of the major problems facing French governments at the end of the 1970s was the fact that lower growth made it less possible to continue expansionary budgets and from 1976 (but particularly from 1978) a more deflationary monetarist policy stance was adopted in France. Less doctrinaire than in Britain under Thatcher, nonetheless the dirigiste, indicative planning approach has given way to more laissez-faire national policies, with only limited ad hoc intervention by the state to assist 'lame duck' and high-technology industries. Whether this approach will continue under the more expansionist rhetoric of Mitterrand after his election in May 1981 is as yet uncertain.

France therefore stands at a political/economic crossroads because the 1980s will pose peculiar problems for France of reduced living standards which may well heighten labour militancy, at a time when traditional centres of intervention in the economy are being questioned and dismantled, which will further compound the existing conflicts between central administration and local and regional levels of government. The 1980s may well therefore see increased intra-bureaucratic conflicts and rising worker militancy as inflation rather than unemployment becomes the major concern of government.

Britain

Turning from relatively successful states to those that have experienced immense difficulties in reacting both to the underlying structural problems of the pre-recession period, as well as to the impact of the recession itself, Britain's record has been disastrous when compared with her closest competitors in Europe. Apart from 1973, Britain's growth rates over the decade have always been below the OECD average. Prior to the oil crisis Britain's growth rates were comparable with Italy; now Britain records the worst growth rate of all the seven countries in this volume. Unemployment has also gone from bad to worse and Britain's rates have been consistently worse than the OECD average; since the oil-induced recession only Italy and Spain have worse records. This weak position has been underlined in the current account of balance of payments which has been in deficit and continually balanced by invisible earnings and, from 1977, oil exports have masked a deteriorating export performance which in the 1980s (given the oil and interest rate induced strength of the pound) will probably be worse. Fixed investment has fallen in every year since 1973; again the worst record of the seven countries analysed. Finally, the record for inflation has also been abysmal, with only Italy and Spain having a worse record at the end of the decade.

All indicators for economic performance are bad in Britain and this pinpoints the fact that Britain has been unable to solve the economic problems that have questioned the long-term viability of the economy. There has been no reform of the antiquated industrial base of the economy; there is a lack of capital and high-technology investment; outmoded and defensive labour practices are debilitating; there is a divorce between the interests of the City and the productive base of the economy; there has been a continual rise in expectations of increased living standards and wages without increased productivity and profitability; and, an ever increasing burden of rising public expenditure on a declining private economic base. As Coates shows in his discussion of these problems, in large measure the failure to resolve these problems (which were apparent before the oil crisis and not caused by it) has been due to political stalemate and inertia rather than through economic myopia. British governments throughout the 1970s and particularly since 1972 have pursued ever increasing neo-corporatist solutions which have mirrored the state interventionist policies in other European countries. Unfortunately, due to the adversarial nature of political life in Britain and the defensive strength of both labour, business and financial interests to resist state modernisation and rationalisation of the financial and industrial base, it has been impossible for any government to make centrist, neo-corporatist, policies work in office. Britain has therefore oscillated between neo-liberal monetarist solutions and failed corporatist prescriptions, forcing the British economy into a permanent downward spiral. The recent electoral victory of an even more ideologically and adversarially based Conservative government, bent on pursuing monetarist policies which ignore the true problems facing the industrial base of the economy, further underlines the political failure which exacerbates Britain's declining economic situation.

Italy

In one sense Italy has experienced a similar political failure to Britain and an analogous economic decline. Nevertheless, in so far as the Italian economy has prospered despite the corruption and debilitating effects of Italian political and administrative life, it might be argued that the underlying problems facing Italy are not, in economic terms at least, as great as those in Britain. Despite this somewhat optimistic conclusion there is no doubt that on most indicators the 1970s have been problem years for the Italian economy.

Growth in Italy has been extremely variable year on year and though for five years of the decade it has fallen below the OECD average, when it has been growing quickly annual rates have exceeded the OECD average substantially. Interestingly, since 1978–9 after the effects of the oil recession Italian growth has been the highest of the seven countries analysed here – including West Germany. This indicates the resilience of the private market economy in Italy despite the political and economic disabilities it has to labour under through the activities of the client-based state.[29] On other indicators the Italian record has been poor. Public expenditure has been forced to rise to accommodate client interests and maintain the existing Christian-Democratic/Centre coalitions in power. This 'timeless budget', as Furlong terms it, has generated a debilitating deficit of 18½ per cent GNP for public expenditure, which has not been aided by the massive growth in the black-market economy and by officially condoned tax evasion on a massive scale. This failure to raise revenue has been a major problem especially after 1975 when the Italian government reflated the economy to solve the problem of oil-induced stagflation. Unhappily, this reflationary policy has not really had the desired effect in stimulating exports as the continuing deficit on balance of payments and recurrent lira crises indicate. Similarly, fixed capital investment in Italy has been declining relative to public expenditure as a share of GNP and unemployment rates have risen from around the OECD average in 1973–4 to the worst record of the seven countries studied here – bar Spain. Finally, since 1973 inflation in Italy has only been surpassed by the record in Spain; even Britain has had a better inflation record.

Undoubtedly, as in Britain, one of the major factors explaining this poor economic record has been the failure to develop sufficiently coherent and socially and economically consensual political and administrative responses to the structural and cyclical problems of the 1970s. Like Britain Italy has all the manifestations of a politically *blocked* society: the Communist party cannot take office to mobilise positive state intervention and corporatist incorporation of labour and business; the Christian-Democrats can govern but cannot question the economic and political roles of those groups which give them support but which are often inimical to economic advance – like the agricultural and small business interests. Thus Italy has, according to Furlong, a partial pluralistic corporatism premised on clientelism rather than modernisation, in which political and administrative institutions are seen increasingly as corrupt and devoid of legitimacy. It is not surprising that political violence and terrorism is rife in this country. Nor is it surprising that IMF interventions and a strong role for the Bank of Italy have been necessary to attempt to resolve the expenditure profligacy of a political system without economic purpose or direction.

Spain

In considering the economic performance of the final country analysed in this volume it is as well to remember that Spain, while obviously suffering severe economic difficulties in the latter half of the 1970s, has also experienced a political inability to react forcefully due to the need to solve the difficult problem of the political transition from Francoism to a liberal democratic/Parliamentary form of political activity first. This has conditioned and delimited the scope for action of all of the post-Franco governments and has made the job of fighting recession that much more difficult. Despite this, because Spain's economic miracle has been premised on foreign tourism, foreign investment, the receipts from Spanish workers abroad and the availability of cheap oil imports, it is likely that in the 1980s Spain will be one of the West's problem economies. Furthermore, Spain will also face the difficulty of meeting the social, political and economic expectations which the transition to liberal democracy may well have engendered in the people, the trade unions and the radical political parties and separatist regions.

For all these political reasons Spain will have problems in the 1980s, but economic indicators also point to acute difficulties. Between 1961 and 1973 Spain had the highest growth rates of any country in the West at an average of 7.3 per cent per annum. In 1975 this came abruptly to an end and since then growth rates have been no better than those in Britain and worse than those in France, Sweden and West Germany. Unemployment in Spain is now running at 10 per cent of the labour force as returning migrant workers swell the numbers hit by the recession; since 1977–8 Spain has had the worst unemployment record of the seven countries analysed. The balance of payments after 1973 also went into fundamental deficit, mainly due to the acute oil dependency of the Spanish economy. Even the small surpluses recorded at the end of the decade were quickly eroded once the second oil price increase was passed on in 1979–80. Only in one area has Spain performed reasonably well and that is in the amount of fixed capital investment, which showed a remarkable resilience after the political transition was complete in 1978. The underlying indicators show however that this rate of increase is still nowhere near as high as the rates recorded at the beginning of the decade before the oil crisis. Finally, Spain has faced a major inflation problem due to relatively favourable wage settlements to buy off labour under Franco and, later, under the period of political transition. This problem, which has seen Spain move into double-figure inflation since 1973, has been exacerbated by the inflationary effects of oil-price increases on an oil-dependent economy.

Spain, then, experiences slightly different problems to those of the other two nations – Britain and Italy – which are problem economies. Britain and Italy were experiencing structural economic problems prior to the oil crisis and this merely complicated dilemmas which the immobilism of their respective political systems compounded. Spain however has been the one country which has suffered severely from the oil crisis. It was not so much that political problems in Spain have made economic modernisation difficult (although, as Harrison shows, it certainly made it difficult for governments to concentrate specifically on economic problems); it was more that the oil crisis knocked the props which had supported economic growth out from under the Spanish economy. Thus with the ending of cheap oil, the loss of job opportunities for migrant workers due to the recession and the similar effect this had on tourism to Spain, the props which had sustained high economic growth and rising living standards had gone. Spain therefore faces the 1980s with many of its political difficulties resolved; but the economic problems which are likely to be experienced may well ensure that political cleavages over workers' rights, regional autonomy and rising living standards and an expanded interventionist state role may well surface again in the 1980s.

This clearly indicates a fact which is true for all advanced industrial countries: there can be no sustainable economic growth without political and social consensus and harmony: yet the absence of economic growth makes the realisation of this consensus and harmony impossible. This is the catch-22 situation which declining countries find themselves in at the beginning of the 1980s. Unfortunately, as the papers in this volume indicate, the move towards tight fiscal and monetary policies across the OECD which has developed at the end of the 1970s, is not likely to generate the social consensus needed to accommodate reduced living standards – standards which are required in the short term to solve the stagflationary effects of the second oil crisis. This dilemma will however face all of the OECD countries, not just those in which the relative decline in living standards will be most acute.

CONCLUSIONS

It is clear from this general introduction to the responses of the major European nations to the economic difficulties of the 1970s that they fall into at least three broad categories: relatively prosperous nations (West Germany and Sweden); nations at a political and economic crossroads (Netherlands and France); and, problem nations (Britain, Italy and Spain). Interestingly enough, as the contributions to this volume indicate, while it is the case that the two oil crises have exacerbated the problems of individual countries, only Spain can be regarded as a nation which is able to blame the oil crisis for destroying the conditions on which its economic growth had been based. Thus, for the remaining six nations examined in this volume, while the oil crises made the economic problems which had to be faced that much more acute, in practice these economies would have faced problems in the 1970s anyway due to increased international competition, declining export markets, low productive investment and rising social and economic expectations amongst the population which contributed to lower productivity and higher unit labour costs. There is no doubt that the oil crisis has made these problems that much more difficult to resolve than they would have been, but while adding a large import-bill burden to economic management, the underlying problems of rationalising regional and structural inefficiencies, moderating wage demands and channelling more expenditure into investment are no different now than they would have been without the oil crisis. In this sense the political response and ability to generate consensus on economic burden sharing and the handling of economic transformation has been of crucial importance. In this way, it seems to have been the case that those nations which have developed incorporatist approaches to the recession have fared much better than those nations in which fundamental political cleavages remain to be resolved. This is not to argue of course that incorporationist states do not experience their own problems – of rising expectations, high public-expenditure burdens and the internalisation of conflicts, and a declining legitimacy for state institutions – but that the alternatives of authoritarian or clientelist elitism or adversarial party politics do not seem to assist at all in the resolution of basic economic conundrums.

Interestingly, Kirchner's discussion of the European Community supports this general conclusion. As Kirchner argues, while the EC has moved to extend the customs union liberalisation of trade, which was one of the basic goals behind the creation of the Community after the Second World War, the logic of the economic problems facing the Community in the 1970s and 1980s is pushing the EC towards more incorporationist/neo-corporatist solutions. Thus the latter half of the 1970s has seen the EC moving towards intervention to modernise and rationalise inefficient sectors of industry – like steel, textiles and shipbuilding – and search for integrative burden-sharing arrangements like workers' participation and a common energy policy. Unfortunately, however, as Kirchner further indicates, these corporatist solutions have not always been successful because of the independent attitudes of individual nations to the economic recession.

Here then is the fundamental dilemma facing the EC: individual nations facing declining economic prospects and the need to develop their own incorporationist economic solutions nationally, must face difficulties in accepting more fundamental corporatist solutions through supra-national institutions. This has meant so far that European-wide solutions to the recession of the 1970s and 1980s have proved illusory and no more glaring example of this failure has been the inability of the countries of the EC to arrive at a workable energy policy. This failure is compounded by the similar inability of these nations and the OECD area as a whole to reduce significantly their dependence on imported oil, which makes their freedom of economic manouevre that much more problematic. Furthermore, this relatively autonomous action has been mirrored in the move to tighter monetarist policies in all of these countries since 1978, as each economy attempts to solve its balance of payments and inflationary problems by deflationary policies. Without any doubt this approach, mirrored as it is in the USA, can only further depress demand across the Western economies and, in the medium term, exacerbate the recession. Unless an approach to the similar problems being experienced by these nations can be found by far greater co-operation and burden sharing without tandem deflationary policies then it may well be that the 1980s will witness the development of three tier economic development in the EC and OECD. Within these three tiers there will presumably be countries like West Germany and Sweden which have been able to generate sufficient consensus and harmony politically and socially to resolve difficult economic problems of structural transformation through positive state and private sector co-operation to sustain relatively high levels of economic growth. At a secondary level we may see countries like France and the Netherlands which due to economic or political constraints (declining natural energy sources or inability to gratify rising social expectations generating debilitating political and economic conflicts respectively) have relatively limited growth potentials. Finally will come countries like Spain, Britain and Italy which either lack basic economic resources (like energy) or have apparently irreconcilable political and social tensions which militate against consistent and positive economic performance.

Clearly the message for the declining economies is that, unless they can generate the incorporationist and consensual relationships between business, finance and labour which has been generated in the relatively prosperous nations, then the prospects for the 1980s are bleak.

NOTES AND REFERENCES

1. The OECD countries include United States, Japan, Germany, France, United Kingdom, Italy, Canada, Australia, New Zealand, Austria, Belgium, Denmark, Finland, Greece, Iceland, Ireland, Luxembourg. Netherlands, Norway, Portugal, Spain, Sweden, Switzerland, and Turkey.
2. 'The OPEC decade', *The Economist*, 29 December 1979, p. 40; and OECD, *Economic Outlook,* no. 26 (December 1979) p. 6.
3. OECD, *Economic Outlook*, no. 26, p. 6; and OECD, *Economic Outlook*, no. 25 (July 1979) pp. 18–19.
4. *The Economist*, 29 December 1979, pp. 40–2.
5. OECD, *Economic Outlook*, no. 14 (December 1973) pp. 5–6.
6. *The Economist*, 29 December 1979, pp. 39–40.
7. See Solomon Barkin *et al.* (ed.), *Worker Militancy and its Consequences, 1965–1975* (New York: Praeger, 1975).
8. Richard W. Sterling, *Macropolitics: International Relations in Global Society* (New York: Alfred A. Knopf, 1974) pp. 526–34.
9. OECD, *Economic Outlook*, no. 13 (July 1973) pp. 14–16; and OECD, *Economic Outlook*, no. 27 (July 1980) p. 121.
10. The Seven Sisters are BP, Texaco, Exxon, Gulf, Shell, Mobil and Socal. See Anthony Sampson, *The Seven Sisters* (London: Corgi, 1977).
11. OECD, *Economic Outlook*, no. 27, pp. 121–2.
12. Ibid., pp. 115, 121.
13. Ibid.

14. Ibid., pp. 115–24.
15. *The Economist*, 29 December 1979, pp. 44–5.
16. OECD, *Economic Outlook*, no. 24 (December 1978) pp. vii–x.
17. OECD, *Economic Outlook*, no. 27, p. 121.
18. OECD, *Economic Outlook*, no. 19 (July 1976) pp. 6, 29–31.
19. OECD, *Economic Outlook*, no. 27, pp. 115–23.
20. Ibid., pp. 126–7.
21. Ibid., p. 118.
22. Ibid., pp. 118–19.
23. On this general problem see James O'Connor, *The Fiscal Crisis of the State* (New York: St Martin's Press, 1973).
24. This general problem is discussed at length in OECD, *Economic Outlook*, no. 26 and no. 27 *passim*.
25. These trends are discussed in G. Lehmbruch and P. Schmitter, *Trends Towards Corporatist Intermediation* (London: Sage, 1980).
26. Ibid. By corporatist we mean simply that the state intervenes to control and regulate an essentially privately owned economy, in which private profit is encouraged but the state's role in providing for social welfarism and modernisation is accepted by business and financial interests. These two interests are incorporated into the decision-making structures of the state, alongside trade union/labour representatives who are given a co-equal place in decision-making in return for co-operative behaviour on wages and labour relations. For an interesting introduction to these trends see R. J. Harrison, *Pluralism and Corporatism: the Political Evolution of Modern Democracies* (London: Allen & Unwin, 1980).
27. Joachim Hirsch, 'Developments in the political system of West Germany since 1945', in Richard Scase (ed.), *The State in Western Europe* (London: Croom Helm, 1980) pp. 122–3.
28. Casten Von Otter, 'Swedish welfare capitalism: the role of the state', in Hirsch, op. cit., pp. 155–7.
29. Carlo Donolo, 'Social change and transformation of the state in Italy', in Hirsch, op. cit., pp. 165–6.

2 The Politics of Economic Recession in Western Germany

KENNETH DYSON

From a comparative perspective West German political arrangement displayed remarkable adaptability and resilience in the face of the economic uncertainty and tension that the country experienced after 1973. Adaptability was encouraged by a complex, diffuse system of economic policy making whose organising theme was delegation and dialogue. At a political level it was assisted by a federal coalition government of Social Democrats (SPD) and Free Democrats (FDP) which from 1969 onwards ensured representation of worker, managerial and employer interests. The comparatively minor economic crisis of 1965–6 had produced a Grand Coalition of the Christian Democratic Union/Christian Social Union (CDU/CSU) with the SPD, and the economic recession of 1966–7 had helped generate support for a neo-Nazi political party as well as the rise of Extra-Parliamentary Opposition. A new resilience was apparent in the complete failure of extremist political opposition of right or left to make significant electoral headway in the more deep-seated recession of the 1970s.

In two periods, 1974–5 and 1977–8, doubts began to be expressed about the capacity of political arrangements to cope – in the first instance, with the consequence for employment and growth of the oil crisis of 1973; in the second, with the failure to maintain an economic expansion that would be sufficient to lead Western Germany securely out of recession. The period 1974–5 saw economic stagnation, rising inflation and mounting unemployment; a new ideological debate inside the SPD; Willy Brandt's resignation as Chancellor (following, but not directly caused by, a major public-service strike); and the consolidation of the CDU/CSU's majority in the upper chamber (Bundesrat). The peirod 1977–8 was characterised by the demise of the *Konzertierte Aktion* (concerted action) of government, unions, employers and the Bundesbank; by the year of the big strikes (1978) when the spirit of social partnership seemed threatened; by the danger to exports from the sharply falling value of the dollar and the subsequent deterioration in relations with the United States; and by the setback to the federal government's energy programme from the anti-nuclear demonstrations. Even so the SPD/FDP coalition was re-elected in 1976, albeit with a much reduced majority; and in 1979–80 Western Germany adapted extremely smoothly to the second major oil-induced inflation. Economic activity remained brisk, and the coalition was again re-elected in 1980 with an increased majority.

The period after 1973 was one of great strains, of frequent puzzlement amongst economic policymakers and, occasionally, of anger and resentment.[1] There were strains between the federal government and the SPD over the poverty of reforms as very few specifically SPD policies found their way into the statute book; between SPD and FDP ministers over economic priorities and the measures to be adopted; within both SPD and FDP over the nuclear issue; between unions and employers over wages, technological change and worker participation; and between the federal government and the Bundesbank over the timing and scale of adjustment of monetary policy. Economics ministers were puzzled by the failure of reflationary programmes to produce the anticipated effects on the unemployment figures. By 1978 it was clear that recovery, whether by tax cuts or by public expenditure, was unlikely to do much to relieve unemployment. Anger and resentment were evident over the government's reversal of its electoral promise of 1976 to continue the indexing of pensions to wage rises;[2] over the militant tactics and repressive responses that were apparent in the nuclear demonstrations of 1976–7; over the employers' decision to submit the codetermination (worker participation) law to the Federal Constitutional Court; and over the sharp increase in the practice of lockouts by employers as a response to strikes. Despite the new language of political conflict a highly differentiated, interwoven network of economic actors displayed a remarkable adaptability. Conduct suggested a continuing mutual forbearance in the interests of maintaining an economic order which, however deficient in detail, proved mutually advantageous and seemed to deserve to survive.

Before exploring the detailed developments in the economy and looking at the specific problems of economic management the general context of ideas and actors will be examined.

MINISTERS, POLICIES AND INSTITUTIONS

In contrast to his predecessor Brandt who presided over an economic debate with whose technical fiscal and monetary details he was unfamiliar,

Chancellor Helmut Schmidt acted as an economic supremo.[3] Schmidt's first declaration of policy in 1974 pledged his government to concentration. Concentration meant for Schmidt priority to an economic management that would create stability and opportunities for growth. He worked in close cooperation with his FDP Economics Ministers (Hans Friderichs, from late 1977 Graf Otto Lambsdorff) and gave active and detailed support to the budgetary discipline that was imposed by his successors (SPD Finance Ministers Hans Apel and Hans Matthöfer, who tended to appear as his State Secretaries). To the irritation of some cabinet colleagues and of the parliamentary party an economic policy cabinet dominated the formulation of government economic policy. Its members were the Chancellor, Hans-Dietrich Genscher (as leader of the FDP), the Economics, Finance and Labour Ministers, and the President of the Bundesbank. In addition Schmidt drew on an informal circle of elite advisers who were drawn from the worlds of banking and industry.[4] He pursued a strategy of continuous close personal contact to leading figures throughout the economy. The purpose was not just to gain a detailed grasp of a constantly changing economic situation and to acquire a sense of the possible but also to bring to bear on elite decision-makers a global perspective. Schmidt conceived of politics as an activity of safeguarding and improving the economic basis of the state in order to prevent the re-emergence of the sort of material and moral evils that had haunted recent German history.[5] Hence he practised a businesslike approach to politics, one which emphasised the importance both of technical knowledge in practical problem solving and of discipline. Ministers were encouraged to specialise in their own particular tasks and general theoretical discussions in cabinet were discouraged. Under Schmidt's Chancellorship the characteristics of political leadership were economic experience and expertise; emphasis on international economic statesmanship with Germany playing a leading role in the Western economic summits; skills of crisis management rather than long-term strategic visions; a sense of the possible; and contacts and cooperation with those possessing economic and financial power in business (over investment policy), banking (over interest rate and exchange-rate policies) and organised labour (over wages and technological change).

Schmidt's political style was functional to the effective management of government business under conditions of impending economic crisis and was difficult to dislodge in the context of the political and economic pressures that accompanied recession. Nevertheless, it was associated with problems of identity and vitality for the SPD. A gap emerged between SPD party policy and governmnent policy that was presided over by a highly popular Chancellor on whom the party seemed dependent for electoral success. Within the SPD there was a less rosy view of the record of the government. By the late 1970s the mayor of Hamburg (Schmidt's home state) was speaking of a 'spiritual deficit' as resignation spread through the SPD. Volker Hauff, the Federal Research Minister, emphasised the need to motivate through goals and values other than the economic. In November 1977 the SPD districts of Lower Rhine, South Bavaria and South Hesse attacked 'the lack of direction' and 'neglect of programmatic work' of the party. They were joined in the next year by Bremen, Hamburg and Schleswig-Holstein. Loss of young voters to the Green parties in local and state elections were seen as symptomatic of these failures. The green parties offered themselves as a normal alternative to the *Atomstaat* of the established parties and pledged a new priority to neutrality, non-violence and quality of the environment. Party intellectuals like Peter Glotz and Erhard Eppler sought to reactivate party discussion from outside Bonn. Indeed the post-1974 phenomenon of a reversal of the flight of able SPD politicians and officials from state capitals to Bonn that had occurred since 1969 was to be explained in part by the frustration of the discipline of power in Bonn. The absence of an offensive reform strategy in line with SPD party policy could of course be understood in structural terms rather than just in terms of Schmidt's 'limited' political conception and 'authoritarian' style. The SPD had to govern in coalition with the FDP which provided two successive powerful Economics Ministers who were seen as close to the employers' interests and whose influence was a source of irritation both to the SPD and to the unions.[6] Moreover, the consolidation of the CDU/CSU majority in the Bundesrat meant a dual majority at the federal level; the upper chamber of state government could veto any legislation that affected the territorial, financial or administrative interests of the states. In the arbitration committee of Bundestag and Bundesrat representatives various reforms, like the 1975 tax reform, were so amended that their specifically SPD content was heavily reduced. Of course, the SPD Bundestag party was not without influence: for example, it contained influential lobbies for coal (one of whose members was Adolf Schmidt, chairman of IG *Bergbau*), the Saar and the Weser.

West German policy style in economic management emphasised dialogue in order to generate confidence and stable, realistic expectations and to foster a global perspective, both internationally and at home, and expertise (*Sachlichkeit*) in order to ensure the relevance and objectivity of that dialogue. A sense that these two qualities were lacking in so powerful a partner as the United States after 1976 shocked West German political leadership and played a part in the deteriorating US/German relations of the late 1970s. Dialogue in a spirit of objectivity was the animating spirit of the collaborative 'power-sharing' that characterised German economic policymaking and it could function because of the widespread political agreement on the character of the economic order.

The language of German political economy displayed some interesting features. Whereas the English-language term 'economic system' suggested a close association with the idea of equilibrium, the German term *Wirtschaftsordnung* (economic order) manifested a characteristically German connection between law and economy and the role of legal categories in economic debate. This connection found its best expression in the related term *Wirtschaftsverfassung* (economic constitution). *Wirtschaftsverfassung* referred to the legal basis of the economic system, to the constitutional provisions, legislation, regulations and court judgements which related to the organisation and functioning of the economy. The importance of law in economic policy did not just reside in the extent to which issues like lock-outs, codetermination and the implementation of the nuclear programme were transferred to the courts for legal resolution. As is generally true of politics in a Roman law country, legal categories were part of the texture of political life. The term economic order suggested a requirement to relate conduct in a rationalist manner to economic 'first principles' and to those of the social market economy.[7] Second, an effective functioning of the economic order was seen to depend on an acknowledgement of interdependence, in other words on a spirit of social partnership (*Sozialpartnerschaft*). In addition, the term 'stability' expressed a fundamental principle of the social market economy that was the precondition of attainment of specific goals of economic policy: a stable structure of relative prices was essential to investment in real growth and permanent employment. Social partnership and stability have been central terms in the German language of political economy: the first supported neo-corporatist ideas of collaboration in economic policy, the second was associated with the monetarist view of inflation.

At the heart of classic neo-liberal thought about the social market economy was the idea of an independent, neutral force that could take a detached view and create the objective conditions for stability. This idea found its expression in the law of 1957 which established the Bundesbank and laid down its statutory requirement to safeguard the currency. Its autonomous exercise of this key function was only to be understood against the recent historical background of two disasterous hyper-inflations. However, the 1960s saw the growth of Keynesian thought, its political expression by the SPD Economics Minister Schiller after 1966, and its embodiment in the new policy instruments that were created by the law on stability and growth of 1967. Besides facilitating deficit budgeting to counteract the sort of recession that had been experienced in 1966–7, new instruments of collaboration were established: the *Konjunkturrat* and the *Finanzplanungsrat* to coordinate the economic policy assumptions and spending plans of federal, state and local authorities,[8] and *Konzertierte Aktion* (concerted action) to coordinate the assumptions of public authorities, trade unions and employers with reference to the attainment of the so-called 'magic square' of goals that were laid down in the new law (price stability, high level of employment and external balance with continuous economic growth). The purpose of these new instruments was enlightenment. Continuous mutual information would enable rational and objective decisions in terms of the public interest so that an effective 'global steering' of macro-economic aggregates could be achieved with a minimum of direct government intervention in individual markets. As we shall see, after 1972 under Schmidt's direction there was a shift back towards monetary policy as stabilisation returned to top priority. Whilst the Bundesbank acquired a leading role in economic policy, Schmidt took a detailed interest in its activities and enjoyed notably close personal relations with its successive presidents – Klasen, Emminger and his former State Secretary Pöhl. Nevertheless, the central characteristic of German economic policy remained a flexible 'strategy of the middle way' that embraced Keynesian and monetarist elements and rejected a dogmatic approach that could threaten the social consensus which was seen as the key condition of an effective economic policy. There was tension between both elements, but each was derived from, or rationalised with reference to, the larger concept of the social market economy.

The system of economic policymaking was well adapted to a dispersal of the heavy load of responsibility that is involved in the management of a modern economy. A complex system that relied so heavily on the maintenance of distinct spheres of action and delegation of decision was heavily dependent on cooperative dialogue for its effective functioning. As this division of labour combined with the presence of competing party interests and ideologies, the system could be expected to generate some intense politicking. Even so, the system was held together by a basic concept, the social market economy, and by a common language of political economy that emphasised collaboration.

One element of the economic policymaking system was government policy for long-term improvement of conditions for growth: for example, identifying bottlenecks (like energy) and easing structural adjustment by stimulating innovation (as in micro-electronics). SPD ministers saw an active structural policy as one of their major contributions. In particular, the creation of the Research and Technology Ministry in 1972 expressed a recognition of the importance of state support in the development and introduction of new technologies. Technocratically minded SPD ministers like Horst Ehmke and Volker Hauff pursued the idea of modernisation of the economy through an active, anticipatory technology policy. The activities of this new 'structural ministry' aroused suspicions: of imperialism as its able expert staff extended their interests into the sectoral and environmental concerns of FDP Economics and Interior Ministers; and of favouritism as 80 per cent of its assistance went to fifteen groups of firms (notably to Siemens). This area of expenditure became a major priority when Matthöfer shifted from the Research to the Finance Ministry.

A second element of the system of economic policymaking was the encouragement of responsible collective bargaining. The importance of attitudes in both sides of industry to effective economic management was well understood, and social partnership, particularly in the form of *Konzertierte Aktion*, was undoubtedly helped by SPD participation in government. However, *Konzertierte Aktion* did not arrive at binding decisions and was primarily an occasion for the government to present 'orientation' data to the unions and employers so that they would be better informed about the consequences of their prospective policies. In fact wage agreements kept within government figures only during recession periods like 1967–8 and 1975–6.[9] The trade unions resented the narrow scope of its subject matter, and the withdrawal in 1977 was eventually the cause of its collapse. Nevertheless, there was a continuing recognition that the principle of *Tarifautonomie*, of autonomy of price and wage determination from public regulation, was dependent on some measure of social partnership, of collaboration with reference to the public interest.[10] If *Tarifautonomie* was a stronger theme in Western Germany than in that other haven of neo-corporatist politics, Austria, and suggested the danger of centralisation of economic decision-making, social partnership was more firmly established than in Britain.

Third, in line with the government's determination that monetary policy should carry the main burden of stabilisation, the Bundesbank assumed the key role in the fight against inflation. For the purpose of enlightenment of the *Tarifpartner* Schmidt encouraged the Bundesbank to publish annually its monetary target. As the central bank was not subject to the directives of the government when exercising its power to safeguard the currency, there was scope for conflict between the two centres of economic decision-making. However, both institutions sought to work closely together.[11] On the one hand, the bank looked to the government to provide a consensus for policy and recognised the importance for the success of its monetary policy of the government's decisions on exchange-rate policy and the size and financing of its deficit. On the other, the government realised that the bank's authority gave it considerable room for manoeuvre to safeguard what it saw as the longer term requirements of stability against political expediency. The Bundesbank was criticised primarily for doing its job too well: for prolonging and deepening the 1973–4 recession, for throttling recovery in 1976 and for threatening economic expansion again in 1979 by restrictive monetary measures. These measures were the consequence in part of repeated failure to achieve monetary targets and in part of the inflow of 'hot' money. Two new constraints to central bank policy emerged from the mid 1970s: the rapid growth of the budget deficit and the mark's role as the world's second reserve currency. The Bundesbank was noticeably seceptical about Schmidt's major initiative to bring an element of stability into the world's currency markets, the European Monetary System which came into operation in March 1979. The central bank not only persuaded the Chancellor to reduce the number of participants in the system but also reserved for itself the right to suspend interventions in currency markets unilaterally if support of the EMS threatened its duty to safeguard the currency.

A fourth element which cannot be ignored in an account of German economic management is the universal banking system which, as we shall see, has meant a large role for bankers in industry and the emergence of an industrial-banking oligarchy. Government was insulated to a greater degree than in Britain from the complex and detailed problem of monitoring and responding to the problems of major companies. The banks served as an 'early-warning' system which identified weaknesses in industry and on occasion mounted rescue operations.[12]

Finally, regular expert reports were issued by the five economic research institutes and notably by the Council of Economic Advisers (*Sachverständigenrat*) which had a marked impact on the level of intellectual sophistication in economic argument.[13] Their role was to provide neutral, authoritative advice about the measures which were needed to achieve the goals of economic policy outlined in the law of 1967.

The overall picture is one of a variety of economic actors whose autonomous activities are perceived to be interdependent. For example, the stabilisation policies of the Bundesbank are seen as essential to the effectiveness of the long-term structural policies of the government, whilst the effectiveness of stabilisation is viewed as dependent on cooperation and consent. The system continued to operate without polarisation owing to the conversion of the SPD in its Bad Godesberg programme of 1959 to the concept of the social market economy and owing to the style of political leadership that was pursued by the SPD Chancellor.[14] In the next two

TABLE 2.1 West German Economic Indicators (1970–9)

	GNP (% change on previous year)	Cost of living index (% change on previous year)	Unemployment		Strikes and lockouts		Productivity in manufacturing industry (% change on previous year)
			Figure (thousands)	% of employed wage and salary earners	Days lost (thousands)	% of work force affected (excepting soldiers and Beamte)	
1970	5.9	3.3	148,846	0.7	93	0.5	4.5
1971	3.3	5.2	185,072	0.8	4,484	22.0	6.1
1972	3.6	5.6	246,433	1.1	66	0.3	8.2
1973	4.9	7.0	273,498	1.2	563	2.3	6.8
1974	0.4	7.0	582,481	2.6	1,051	5.2	4.2
1975	−1.9	6.0	1,074,277	4.7	69	0.4	5.2
1976	5.1	4.3	1,060,336	4.6	534	2.8	8.0
1977	2.6	3.7	1,029,995	4.5	24	0.1	4.3
1978	3.5	2.7	992,948	4.3	4,290	22.4	4.1
1979	4.4	4.1	876,137	3.8	483	N/A	N/A

SOURCE Deutsche Bundesbank, *Monthly Report* (various); Federal Economics Ministry.

sections the strains to which this policymaking system was subjected will be examined.

DEVELOPMENTS IN THE ECONOMY, 1973–80

West German economic development presented a complex picture. On the one hand, there were grounds for concern about growth and employment; on the other, extraordinary successes were achieved in the management of inflation, in productvity and in export performance.[15] For example, from 1974 to 1978 the rate of inflation declined steadily from 7 per cent to 2.7 per cent. An average productivity increase in manufacturing industry of 5.2 per cent per annum in the 1970s was only slightly below the average of 5.5 per cent per annum in the 1960s. Perhaps the most worrying sign was the long-term decline in the rate of growth: net national product rose on average by 7 per cent in the 1950s, 4 per cent in the 1960s and just over 2.2 per cent between 1970 and 1977. In the 1970s growth was notably erratic, and confusion was compounded by repeatedly erroneous economic forecasts. After an abysmal performance in 1974 and 1975 growth of GNP varied from a heady 5.1 per cent in 1976 to a disappointing 2.6 per cent in 1977 and a surprise 3.5 per cent in 1978 and 4.4 per cent in 1979. Investment rates of 25 per cent of GNP in the 1950s were stabilised during the next decade, but their decline in the 1970s suggested a rising average age of plant and machinery. Nevertheless, in comparative terms investment figures remained sufficiently good for Germany to remain the outstanding industrial power of Western Europe. Fixed capital formation as a percentage of GNP rose steadily from 20.8 per cent in 1977 to 22.9 per cent in 1979. In 1975 Germany's gross fixed capital investment accounted for 31 per cent of the EC total and represented 29 per cent more new investment than in France. Like other West European societies, however, West Germany experienced de-industrialisation. Industry's share of GNP dropped from 54 per cent in 1970 to 48 per cent in 1978. Even so this share was remarkably high by international standards. Whereas industry's share of GNP was 41 per cent in Britain and France in 1975, the figure for Germany was 51 per cent.

Exports, which accounted for 27 per cent of GNP in 1978, were crucial to the economy and provided its major stimulus. West Germany continued to dominate European markets with nearly half of its total exports going to the EC. In addition, so successful was the export drive on OPEC markets that till 1978 West Germany had a trade surplus with the oil-producing countries. There was, nevertheless, a decline in Germany's international price competitiveness. After 1970 her exports became less competitive in terms of unit wage costs than those of the USA and Britain (but became more competitive than those of France and Italy). However, Germany remained the world's leading exporter of capital goods and the international leader in plant construction with a market share of 50 per cent.[16] The machinery and industrial plant exports which make up more than half the total were relatively price-inelastic, and in this area German industry proved notably adaptive. If exports were hit by the appreciation of the mark, the steady decline of domestic inflation provided support. To the aggravation of other countries the payments surplus rose to 41 billion DM in 1978 (although in price-adjusted terms it actually declined), but the rising costs of imported materials and import penetration sent it into deficit in 1979. One major change was the rapid expansion of foreign direct investment, notably by the chemical and electro-mechanical industries in the desire to be nearer the market. After 1973 West Germany became for the first time a net exporter of industrial capital. Nevertheless, in 1977 foreign industrial investment amounted to only 4.6 per cent of total capital spending at home.

Unemployment remained an intractable problem and a politically sensitive issue especially in the SPD. It was a central issue in the Bavarian and Hesse state elections of 1974 when the SPD suffered severe reversals. In the period 1975–7 unemployment averaged over one million; indeed, in 1975 an unemployment rate of 4.7 per cent exceeded one of 4.4 per cent in Britain. There were of course regional variations: for example, in 1977 only 2 per cent unemployment in some parts of Baden-Würtemberg and over 8 per cent in the Saar, Ostfriesland and the Bavarian forest (with a peak of 18.3 per cent in Passau). Spatial variations were, however, less dramatic than in Britain, France or Italy. Consequently, regional policy did not have the same political importance.[17] Jobs were lost on a large scale: 1.6 million between 1970 and 1976 (428,000 in construction alone). An increase of jobs in services and public administration did little to offset the huge losses in industry. At the same time there was the prospect till 1985 of a growing number of people on the labour market owing to demographic factors. As some 11 per cent of school-leavers of fifteen years of age in 1974 did not possess the qualifications to take up an apprenticeship, a problem of employment for unskilled youth presented itself. In addition to high unemployment a sharp decline occurred in the number of foreign workers from 2.6 million (12 per cent of the labour force) in 1973 to 1.85 million in 1977–8. This decline followed a period of rapid expansion between 1968 and 1972 especially in the car, iron and steel, and chemical industries.

The political problem of unemployment was complex. First, the anger in the SPD about the global figure was ventilated in cabinet by successive Labour ministers who wanted greater reflation and more attention to labour market policy. These political pressures continued to be resisted by FDP economics ministers who remained committed to the view that the market economy was sufficiently resilient to emerge successfully from recession. The solution was to be provided by the market once tax cuts increased profits enough to encourage investment in jobs. However, as early as 1975 the Labour Ministry was worried about the problem of structural unemployment, about those who were too poorly educated (in 1977 every second unemployed person had not completed occupational training), handicapped in some way (approximately one-third) or old (one in eight were over 55) to be helped by global reflationary measures or by investment in rationalisation. They threatened to form a new proletariat of unemployed. SPD policymakers, especially in the Bundestag, began to see unemployment as a social problem that could only be resolved by such expensive structural measures as more and better training, longer holidays, a shorter working week and earlier retirement. They were supported in 1979 by the Munich Institute of Economic Research which argued that otherwise a growth figure of over 6 per cent would be needed to have a significant effect on unemployment. In fact, and in comparison to other countries like Britain that had traditionally relied on regional policy, the long experience and huge financial resources of the autonomous *Bundesanstalt für Arbeit* (founded in 1952) created a strong basis for an active labour market policy. Another controversial proposal was community service. In 1977 the Labour Ministry developed more ambitious employment programmes which provided some half billion marks in the form of federal subsidies (mainly to local authorities) to stimulate community service. However, when profit rates revived after 1977 as the share of wages and salaries in GNP began finally to drop and employers began to hire, some of the force of the structuralists' case was lost. By 1979 the rate of unemployment (as a percentage of the labour force) had dropped to the lowest in the EC: 3.4 per cent compared to 5.3 per cent in Britain and 6.1 per cent in France. The number of foreign workers had begun once again to expand.

Second, scepticism existed about the significance of the global figure. For example, Hesse's Economics Minister (FDP) argued that the unemployment figure told little about the real availability of labour. He suspected on the basis of surveys that only about half of the registered unemployed in Hesse were genuinely seeking employment. Approximately 20 per cent of the unemployed were difficult to place because they wanted part-time work. Surveys at local employment exchanges showed that many of the unemployed, especially women seeking part-time work, were not interested in a job. Indeed it was difficult to fill jobs in mining, foundries, food processing and hotels. Economic growth was being held back by pressing shortages of certain types of skilled worker, for example in electronics, especially where new plants were opening (like Mercedes in Bremen). The prognoses of the *Bundesanstalt für Arbeit* about labour shortages had proved all too often incorrect. It was training technicians and then paying them for a second time as unemployed skilled workers. Unemployment and shortage of labour were a parallel problem. In 1978 the conference of state economics ministers concluded that there was not a problem of mass, long-term or youth unemployment. Genuine unemployment was 10–25 per cent lower than the official statistics. In many districts, like the Sauerland and Rhine/Main, vacancies exceeded unemployment.

Third, political attention began to focus increasingly on 'shirkers' or 'parasites' amongst the unemployed, on those who were alleged to be taking advantage of generous social provisions. To the irritation of the unions the Labour Minister Herbert Ehrenberg responded in 1978 by introducing controversial legislation which sought to make it more difficult for an unemployed person to turn a job down as unattractive. The problem was to identify the real shirker from those who were simply too inadequately educated or in too poor health to cope with technical jobs and whom selective employers were increasingly unprepared to accept.

Two regions that were already plagued by an excessively narrow and vulnerable economic structure emerged as industrial crisis areas in the 1970s. The Saar had failed to diversify its economy from a dependency on coal and steel before the crisis of 1973. By 1977 it had an unemployment rate of 7.2 per cent (the federal average was 4.8 per cent) and one vacancy for every fourteen unemployed (with a federal average of one for every four). Its coal and steel industries were in urgent need of rationalisation in order to overcome the disadvantages of divided ownership and small scale. The major political and economic problem was the Ruhr, Europe's largest industrial region. The Ruhr had in fact been a crisis region since the mid 1960s and between 1967 and 1977 lost well over 100,000 jobs. It had changed from a German industrial model to an area of acute structural weakness and deprivation, one that was losing out economically and environmentally to other regions and becoming increasingly costly to support (with, for example, huge subsidies of some five billion marks a year to the coal industry). There were more unemployed in the Ruhr than in any other area of the Federal Republic. In 1978 almost all the Ruhr cities belonged to the twenty labour districts with the highest unemployment rates in the country. One-quarter of the unemployed had been without a job for more than a year. Moreover, since 1961 the Ruhr had been an area of rapid population-loss at an increasing rate (of 40,000 a year after 1975). Between 1965 and 1978 the Ruhr lost 330,000 people, many of whom were the better qualified and higher-earning workers. Those left behind were the old, larger families and foreigners, in short the ones who were most likely to be thrown back onto the social services. There was a danger that some Ruhr cities would turn into centres of social crisis. Certain city areas, like Duisburg-Hamborg, and areas that were adjacent to closed mines were in acute economic, physical and social decline. Compared to the rest of North-Rhine Westphalia the Ruhr had poorer medical services, higher infant mortality, more remedial children, fewer children going on to university and, of course, serious problems of air pollution. Some one-third of the unemployed had health problems. Local authorities were forced to beg for federal aid. Their social expenditures rose, whilst their tax revenues dropped as businesses ran into trouble (for example, a city like Duisburg was heavily dependent for its revenue on the success of the steel giant Thyssen).

The SPD/FDP government of North-Rhine Westphalia saw the Ruhr as beset by 'post-industrial' problems that had been generated by a narrow and rigid economic structure. Although coal and steel were no longer the motors of the economy, some 40 per cent of jobs in the Ruhr depended on coal. The service sector was very undeveloped and did not even account for 20 per cent of jobs. With exceptions like the location of the Opel works at Bochum there had been little success in diversification. When local authorities attracted firms, they tended to come from other Ruhr cities. Pollution, a shortage of land and a lack of attractive housing did not excite outside interest. According to some observers, the long tradition of state aid to the Ruhr (going back to the paternalism of the Prussian state) had helped to fossilise the economic structure. Market problems had been met not by encouragement of adaptation of the economic structure but by cartelisation, as in 1893 and again in 1968 (when Schiller forced the mines which were threatened by cheap imported coal into the new Ruhrkohle AG). The importance of the Ruhr problem was accentuated by the political significance of the region to the SPD in federal, as well as the state, elections. A 'fighting group Ruhr' was formed within the SPD Bundestag party to press for greater federal aid. However, despite the same coalition arrangement in Düsseldorf as in Bonn (in 1980 the SPD gained an overall majority in North-Rhine Westphalia), proposals to provide aid generated growing tension between the state and federal governments. One focus of these tensions was energy policy. Riemer (FDP), the state's Economics Minister, opposed the proposals of his party colleague, Lambsdorff, to develop nuclear power in favour of giving top priority to an expansion of coal-fired power stations in the Ruhr. The FDP Economics Minister in Bonn was sceptical about the value of spending taxpayers' money on a prosperous electricity-supply industry. After 1973 federal priorities did of course shift to both nuclear and coal as sources of energy. However, growing public subsidies to the coal industry and a huge increase in coal stocks led to a recognition by 1978 that nuclear energy would be much cheaper. Bonn's research programme was directed to nuclear technology rather than coal technology. Belief that higher oil prices would lead to a renaissance of the Ruhr began to fade. Conflict between the state and federal governments came to a head over the one-billion-mark Ruhr Aid Programme of 1979; the federal government began to complain about the failure of the state government to produce satisfactory practical proposals to combat unemployment.

One of the major anxieties about German industry at the onset of the recession was the effect of a falling investment rate since the end of the 1950s on the age of machinery and plant. From the early 1970s investment focused strongly on rationalisation and labour substitution. Hence, even firms that were expanding in 1975–6, like Daimler-Benz (motor vehicles) and Deutsche Babcock (industrial plants), were doing so with the same or a reduced labour force. Recession had even sharper effects on investment and employment in other sectors. In 1974 the chemical giants like Hoechst had record profits as a result of a price explosion. However, during the years 1977–8, when the mark was appreciating and prices were depressed, they experienced poor turnover and profits. Between 1970 and 1978 the chemical industry shed over 40,000 jobs. A more dramatic victim of recession and of high interest rates was the construction industry. In 1974 10,000 dwellings were standing empty. Schmidt and Friderichs were convinced of the need for contraction of the industry and even opposed the proposal of the Housing Ministry to channel more public expenditure into social housing where a shortage did exist. Giant construction firms like Hochtief and Holzmann compensated for domestic stagnation and the decline in public sector orders by pushing up exports, especially to the oil states. The period 1973–7 saw over 3,600 bankruptcies and the loss of more than 350,000 jobs in the industry. The strain of contraction was apparent within the *Hauptverband der Deutschen Bauindustrie*. Its president was attacked as the representative of the construction giants which benefited at the expense of smaller firms from the association's intimate relations with the Housing Ministry. Nevertheless, lower interest rates and new public sector orders (the Bonn programme for future investment channelled four billion marks into construction in 1978) caused a boom in 1978 that outpaced overall economic growth. Even then, in real terms construction was below the level of 1972.

The German steel industry entered the recession with a reputation as the largest, most efficient European producer. In 1974 it accounted for 34.2 per cent of EC capacity and was the biggest EC exporter. With worldwide recession and the crisis in construction and motor vehicles the steel industry entered a four-year crisis period from 1975 to 1978. Profits were halved in 1974–5 and 1975–6, and the industry went heavily into the red in 1976–7. Firms like Klöckner and Thyssen were badly affected. By 1978 there were fears that the industry was losing ground to other European states whose steel firms benefited from huge government subsidies. The turnabout occurred on the Rhine and in the Ruhr in 1979 when there was the best post-war production of steel (with the exception of the two record years of 1973–4). The major problem was that the firms were unable to make full and speedy use of spare capacity because of heavy shedding of manpower in past years. However, the steel crisis in the Saar was protracted. To the anger of other steel producers it was proposed in 1980 to create a union of steel firms in the Saar. In return the modern furnaces of this new steel giant were to be assisted by 1.3 billion marks of public aid.

The strain of contraction had its effect on that strongly unified and politically powerful industrial lobby, the Association of the Iron and Steel Industry. Its leading members (representing firms like Krupp and Thyssen) met monthly in the private exclusive 'steel club'. Two changes began to divide its members. First, there was a new competition for state aid, for example for shares of the federal government's steel research programme which expanded rapidly. One major source of irritation was the large financial support that was offered by the federal government and the Saar government to the Luxembourg firm Arbed to help it acquire and develop the Saar steel works. Second, the club was joined by two SPD members, former public servants: Pieper, the new head of the federal government's own Salzgitter, and Rohwedder (ex-State Secretary in the Federal Economics Ministry) at Hoesch. When Hoesch became a recipient of large state aid for its investment, the other steel bosses became suspicious of their privileged contacts in Bonn. What united the steel managers was their reluctance to accept the EC's steel cartel of 1977, a voluntary restriction of production in order to avoid ruinous price competition. When in 1980 after a period of heavy losses steel quotas threatened to cut short the steel boom and produce short-time working, the German producers agreed to withdraw from the arrangement.

The car industry achieved also a remarkable turnaround. Whereas Volkswagen had been axing 20,000 jobs in 1975, the industry as a whole was experiencing an investment boom by 1980. Investment was double that of 1977. Nevertheless, investment in new automated technology at home and in new plants overseas threatened to displace workers. In addition, car firms competed intensely for generous state aid to their investment. In their search to create more jobs state governments sought to attract car firms by favourable credits, grants and the provision of sites. For example, the

Bremen government paid some 250 million marks to attract Diamler-Benz. For Opels' new works at Kaiserslauten the government of Rhineland-Palatinate was bearing about one quarter of the cost. But as far as the trade unions were concerned, state governments were competing to help car firms to rationalise jobs away.

The greatest single pressure on the banks came from AEG, the second largest company in the electronics industry. With 176,000 employees (in 1973) it threatened to provide the most spectacular bankruptcy in the history of the Federal Republic. Between 1968 and 1974 AEG's shares lost most of their value; after 1973 no dividends were paid. There were two rescue bids. In 1975 Walter Cipa was appointed to launch a housecleaning programme. However, his authoritarian style irritated bank and employee representatives on the supervisory board. Debts grew to seven billion marks in 1980 against the background of an annual turnover of less than three times that sum. Led by AEG's major shareholder, Dresdner Bank, the banks combined to launch a major rescue operation. In 1980 Hans Friderichs, now chairman of the Dresdner Bank, became chairman of the supervisory board and nominated a new chief executive. Nevertheless the continuing crisis of morale and leadership at AEG was not typical of the electronics industry. The great success, notably in exports, of its larger rival Siemens was in large part the consequence of a massive research and development programme in the past and of its greater disengagement from consumer goods.

Recession brought about some significant changes in the ownership of industry. One development was the purchase of shares in leading companies by oil states. Kuwait acquired 14 per cent of Daimler-Benz shares in 1974, 30 per cent of the shares of the steel firm Willy Korf in 1975 (in a secret deal that was not reported to the Federal Cartel Office till 1978) and 10 per cent of the shares of Metallgesellschaft. In 1977 Iran took over 25 per cent of the capital of Krupp. Indeed the increase of the banks' shareholdings in industry was justified by reference to the need to limit this process of foreign acquisition. There was also a spectacular increase in the concentration of industry. The number of fusions rose from 242 in 1973 to 554 in 1977. In 1977 the fifty firms with the largest turnover were involved in fusions 336 times. Faced by recession, many small firms and banks were seeking protection under the umbrella of larger companies which in turn used the opportunity to extend their market power. By 1978 the hundred largest firms (in terms of turnover) controlled a quarter of the industrial market. In the chemical industry the ten largest firms accounted for 40 per cent of turnover. 1978 saw some spectacular and controversial fusions: Flick-Gerling, Commerzbank-Fichtel and Sachs and, above all, the great Veba-BP deal which was turned down by the Federal Cartel Office but later approved by

Lambsdorff on grounds of safeguarding energy supply. Although the Cartel Office's powers had been strengthened in 1973 and the Economics Ministry official who designed its new powers was later appointed its president, only two of 773 mergers between 1973 and 1977 were prohibited. Complaints about the ineffectiveness of the Federal Cartel Office as a safeguard against monopoly power involved not just fusions but also control of the misuse of market power. Although the Cartel Office and the oil companies were repeatedly in dispute about whether petrol price increases constituted such a misuse, no attempt was made to take out an order against them. Not only was it difficult to prove misuse but also the result, as in the case of the pharmaceutical company Hoffmann-La Roche, could be protracted court proceedings before an order could take effect. In 1979 Lambsdorff introduced legislation to force companies to pay back any gains that had been made from misuse of market power.

The banks had their problems. Recession brought default on interest repayments, the collapse of the Herstatt bank in 1974, AEG's mounting deficit and major bankruptcies like that of the construction giant, Beton, and Monierbau. Overall, however, the recession brought high profits to the banks and a sharp increase in the value of their shares – as a result of increased profits from international transactions, of high interest rates and of commissions for issuing loans on behalf of public authorities. By acting as the principal absorbers of government securities the banks enabled a smooth non-inflationary financing of the public deficit and earned the goodwill of government. They were also able to consolidate their economic power. Under the German system of universal banking the practice of commercial and investment banking was united under one roof. The extraordinary network of bank involvement in industry was extended, in part as a protective measure against foreign acquisitions, and remained an important source of bank profits. The banks' power over industry derived from three sources: large bank shareholdings, much of which were procured after both world wars when outstanding credits were converted into bank-held shares and bonds to assist reconstruction (for example, the Dresdner Bank had shareholdings of over 25 per cent in more than fifteen firms including Metallgesellschaft, Hapag-Lloyd and Kaufhof, whilst the Deutsche Bank was heavily involved in Daimler-Benz and Philipp Holzmann);[18] exercise of proxy rights for shares (in fact most shares) that they have on deposit from customers; and seats on the supervisory boards of companies. The result was a network of reciprocal influence in which, on the one hand, industry had ready access to funds and, on the other, the banks were able to exert financial discipline in industry. Industrial rescue operations, as in the case of AEG, took on a different character from those in Britain. Through overlapping shareholding and interlocking directorships the banks provided an efficient and private system of 'early-warning' and control that was more insulated than in Britain from the public political arena. The economic power of the banks was a subject of criticism and not just from unionists who feared its effects on jobs. Even Lambsdorff expressed a wish to see bank holdings reduced to a maximum of 15 per cent. There were also growing worries about accountability for worldwide operations. As West Germany's importance as a trading nation increased, a rapid expansion of German banks abroad occurred during the 1970s.

The most dramatic change in banking was in the role of the twelve state central banks. Their original tasks had been to act as the banks of state governments and local authorities and to serve as the clearing houses for savings banks. From the late 1960s they emerged quickly as universal credit institutions which, as state central banks, were spared fear of bankruptcy. Under ambitious, entrepreneurial managers like Ludwig Poullain at the Westdeutsche Landesbank and Wilhelm Hankel at the Hessische Landesbank they enjoyed an extraordinary expansion into new controversial areas (like industrial credit and shareholding, credit for construction, involvement in foreign banks and speculation in foreign exchange), and they opened up branches abroad. The Hessische Landesbank grew to be the second largest state bank and the fifth largest bank. With this expansion the top jobs in these institutions became the best paid in the public service and attracted an influx of former ministers and civil servants to occupy them. There were also scandals that involved Poullain and Hankel and led to a concern on the part of local authorities and savings banks to bring the state banks under a tighter control.

The development of nuclear power provided the most dramatic political issue that was brought to a head by the oil crisis. In 1974 the federal government put forward new targets for its development. Up to 1977 the major parties and the trade unions were agreed on the need to exploit the peaceful uses of atomic energy in order to guarantee future energy supplies, growth and employment. Even then growing alarm in the political parties at the local and regional levels about the strength of citizen protest produced some disagreement about how best to realise the nuclear programme. Nuclear power was not an issue in the 1976 federal election. However, the great demonstrations and occupations of sites for prospective nuclear power stations in the winter of 1976–7, followed by the electoral successes of the Green lists in some state elections, confronted the political parties, notably the SPD/FDP coalition, with a serious political problem.[19] The product of citizen action at Brokdorf and Wyhl was a political and administrative stalemate in the construction of atomic power stations. Schmidt (who appealed to the support of the trade unions) and Lambsdorff continued to favour the rapid development of atomic energy. Both shared a pessimistic scenario of mounting energy shortages. A complex combination of ideological sympathy for the ecological concerns of the so-called Greens, of disillusion with the appeal of the economism of political leadership and of electoral anxiety created new problems of unifying the governing parties, especially the SPD. SPD and FDP party congresses, which were shocked by the repressive measures of the CDU government to secure the Brokdorf site, were concerned to toughen the criteria that had to be fulfilled before construction could begin.

The nuclear issue caused also federal/state conflicts, especially between the SPD/FDP coalitions in Bonn and Düsseldorf over the relative priorities of coal and nuclear energy. In late 1978 a spectacular showdown occurred in the FDP over the fast-breeder reactor. The dispute between the FDP economics ministers in Bonn and Düsseldorf about this proposal was followed by the threat of all four FDP ministers to resign from the Bonn cabinet if they were not supported by their parliamentary colleagues. As is typical of public policy issues in the Federal Republic, judges were elevated to a key role in its resolution. The administrative courts blocked the final approval of atomic power stations until adequate facilities had been provided for the disposal of atomic waste. This criterion proved to be the stumbling block of the whole nuclear programme. The federal government had planned to construct a concentrated 'atomic park' in Lower Saxony. At Gorleben the largest atomic project in the world was to offer facilities for waste reprocessing and underground disposal. However, in 1978 Ernst Albrecht, the CDU Minister-President of Lower Saxony, rejected this proposal in the face of mounting popular resistance and doubts about its safety as a disposal site. There was now the prospect of an ever growing tonnage of atomic waste without adequate facilities for disposal. At the end of 1977 the blockage of the nuclear programme meant the loss of over 1.6 billion marks per annum in construction orders and, to the irritation of the unions, of more than 20,000 jobs. Whereas a French nuclear plant could be completed on the basis of an original authorization, German plants needed a step-by-step approval that lengthened lead-times in construction to eight to ten years. In addition, the threat that was posed by the formation of the new Green Party early in 1980 to contest the federal election led to even greater hesitation within the SPD about future atomic power stations. The SPD's energy commission (supported by Hauff) proposed drastic energy savings, including speed restrictions on autobahns, and higher coal subsidies. However, Lambsdorff's rejection of *dirigiste* measures and interference with market forces underlined the party political stalemate over energy policy.

INDUSTRIAL RELATIONS

The spirit of social partnership that has long been regarded as a central feature of Germany's well-organised system of industrial relations was put under great strain by protracted recession, unemployment, threats to living standards and the displacement of jobs by technological change. Painful readjustment to rapidly changing circumstances, in the context of a new uncertainty about economic prospects, generated the sort of pressures that were likely to disrupt industrial relations. At one level, relations between the federal government and the unions were helped by the extent to which union officials were members of the SPD. Unlike in Britain individual unions were not affiliated to the SPD, and the German Trade Union Federation (DGB), to which the seventeen industrial unions belonged, was pledged to party political neutrality. Nevertheless, ten out of eleven officials on the executive of the giant matalworkers' union (IG Metall, the largest union in the Western world) were SPD members. At another level, as the long steel strike of 1978–9 revealed, there was a danger that unions could lose control of their members. A widespread sentiment that union leaders were out of touch with the specific day-to-day problems at factory level began to work its way through into the calculations of those leaders. Between 1969 and 1979 there were eight major strikes, including in 1978 the first (and successful) dockworkers' strike in 55 years. The effective strike in the public service by ÖTV (the Public Services Federation), which was the cause of great political embarrassment to Brandt's government, was above all about wages. From 1976 onwards, however, the issues that dominated in strikes broadened. The bitterness of the national printers' strike of 1976 was the product of the rapid displacement of jobs (of 18 per cent since 1970) by new technology and the union's determination to arrive at an agreement with the employers about the social consequences of technological change. Similarly the effects of micro-electronics were at the heart of the printers' strike and of the metalworkers' strike in Baden-Württemberg in early 1978.

The broadening of the agenda of industrial relations was the product of two causes. First, wage bargaining was subjected to new pressures. Increasing energy prices, appreciation of the mark, high unit labour costs and the combined call of the economic establishment for wage restraint reduced the room for manoeuvre in the distribution of resources and encouraged employer associations into new forms of solidarity (including elargement of strike funds and resort to the lockout as a counterveiling power to the tactical use of the strike weapon). Second, the unions hoped to lessen the effects of technological changes on employment, even perhaps to induce greater employment, by the proposal for a 35-hour working week. By 1978

IG Metall officials, backed by a resolution of thier congress, were pressing for this proposal as a matter of principle both for the trade union movement as a whole and for the unemployed. The proposal was put to its first major test in the seven-week steel strikes of 1978–9, the second longest strike in the history of the Federal Republic and the first strike in the industry since 1928.[20] The background was a sharp loss of jobs in the steel industry (30,000 in the prosperous period 1970–4 and 41,000 between 1974 and 1978). Grass-roots pressure for the 35-hour week was so strong that in 1978 the DGB Congress had voted for the proposal against the wishes of the DGB's higher officials. In 1978 the three big strikes of printers, metalworkers and steelworkers illustrated the threat to the moderation of union leadership from the basis. The aggressive language that accompanied these strikes (with references, for example, to the relations between the old steel barons and the Nazis and to the use of lockouts in the dark days of the Weimar Republic) suggested a deterioration in the climate of industrial relations and cast doubt on the image of Schmidt as a crisis manager who could handle the unions because of his close contacts to them.

Sozialpartnerschaft, a system of orderly, cooperative negotiation between the 'social partners', was put under strain by political factors as well as by the effects of the micro-electronics revolution. First, there was union irritation over the paucity of political reforms by the SPD/FDP government, notably over the failures to achieve full parity representation of employer and worker members on the supervisory boards of corporations and to tackle structural unemployment by a major reform of vocational education. After 1976 the DGB and the SPD working group on employee affairs were disillusioned by the failure of the new Labour Minister, Ehrenberg, to represent employee interests as effectively as his predecessor Walter Arendt appeared to do.[21] They were particularly aggrieved by his proposal of 1978 to restrict the terms on which the unemployed could continue to receive benefits. The trade unions wanted an active, comprehensive labour market policy that sought to create or preserve sufficient jobs to meet the supply of labour, whereas Ehrenberg advocated a market approach according to which the supply of labour had to adjust to the demand for it. In 1979 Ehrenberg attempted to heal the wounds by replacing a retired CDU division head in his ministry by a Social Democrat, Wolfgang Bodenbender, who was particularly close to the unions. Second, after 1976 the unions were anxious about the government's proposal to end the indexing of pensions in order to restore financial regularity to pension insurance. In 1978 IG Metall threatened to mobilise its members against this change of policy. Finally, the employers referral of the codetermination law to the Federal Constitutional Court angered the unions and was the immediate cause of their withdrawal from *Konzertierte Aktion*.

The unions saw in this action an attempt by the employers to put a stop to social development through the courts.

The nature of developments in the economy aggravated industrial relations. On the one hand, the employers feared that union wage policy was no longer adequately orientated to the larger requirement of the economic system as it had been in 1967 when wage increase of 4.3 per cent average were well below a productivity rise of 7.6 per cent. Whereas productivity gains had exceeded the increase of real wages in the 1950s, the reverse was the case in the 1970s. The employers' associations hammered home the consequences – in the short run, an upward pressure on prices; in the medium term (and apparent in 1974–5), an unwillingness to invest with effects on growth and prospects for real wages; and, in the long run, unemployment. A symptom of the new malaise was the rising proportion of wages in the national income (up from 61.7 per cent at the end of the 1960s to 65 per cent in 1975). The employers were also encouraged to greater solidarity and toughness in the 1970s by the fear of divide-and-rule tactics of the unions to exploit the increasing tension between boom sectors (like car firms, their suppliers and parts of the electronics industry) and slump sectors (like steel, iron foundries, shipbuilding and docks) and between profitable and less profitable firms in these sectors. A political revitalisation of the employers was further inspired by the idea that the ideological sympathy between unions and the government and codetermination threatened to create a *Gewerkschaftsstaat* (trade-union state). Under Hanns-Martin Schleyer's direction the Federation of German Employers' Associations (BDA) formulated a new basic programme and sought to achieve greater solidarity during annual wage rounds. On the other hand, the trade unions, which had accepted wage restraint in line with the combined recommendations of the government, the Council of Economic Advisers, the economic research institutes and the Bundesbank, and had resisted strong grass-roots pressure, became disillusioned by 1977 with the failure of this moderation to have significant effect on unemployment figure. In the view of some unionists, notably in the printers' and metalworkers' unions, high wage awards were one way of inducing greater demand and thereby creating a better environment for investment. They rejected the connection between high wage awards and unemployment. The weight of institutional opinion was, however, firmly against such a policy. Instead the unions pressed for new forms of cooperation in industry to deal with structural change (including full parity representation on supervisory boards and selective corporatism to deal with problems in particular sectors), for the shorter working week, for a governmental role in investment planning and for the rapid exploitation of nuclear energy.

There was also a change in the political economy of industrial relations. From 1949 to 1963, when Ludwig Erhard was Economics Minister (he was then Chancellor till 1966), government had sought to stabilise expectations, create confidence about economic development and keep intervention to a minimum. In the absence of comprehensive or detailed economic guidance, unions had negotiated a variety of wage agreements which were oriented to the particular circumstances of individual regions and sectors. Schiller's 'enlightened' economic policy after 1967 was a turning point. Through *Konzertierte Aktion* the federal government sought to provide information of assistance to both sides of industry in the form of annual projections which showed what rate of wage increase would be compatible with full employment and price stability. Prognoses assumed a new importance as instruments of economic policy. One consequence was that different unions orientated themselves to a single figure and paid less attention to the diverse conditions of regions and sectors. Furthermore, prognoses could have inflationary implications, they tended to be on the optimistic side and to be seen as hurdles to be cleared in negotiations rather than as outer limits. The 'realistic' figure was in fact determined by the 'wage leaders' (IG Metall and ÖTV) at the beginning of the wage round. Another consequence was a more academic character of economic debate. Unions recruited large new research staffs direct from the universities and thereby opened themselves up to a greater extent than before to the left-wing ideological currents that had been sweeping the universities. Left-wing ideologists made a notable impact on the education (GEW) and printers' unions. Their influence on the style, language and even content of union policy was largely exercised through union publications.

There were signs of new tensions and frictions within the unions. The unions have traditionally emphasised the themes of unity and solidarity; they see organisational concentration in the hands of the leadership as essential to effective bargaining. Regional tactics are informally coordinated at central headquarters which maintain large staffs of trained economists. The impression of unanimity is reinforced through central control of personnel policy (for example, IG Metall's ten district leaders who handle the wage negotiations are appointed by the executive and not elected by the district conference) and of official publications, through the practice of holding congresses only about once every three years, and through the dependence of many local branches on financial help from the centre. The IG Metall Congress is an occasion for expressions of solidarity rather than for open debate and controversy. Emphasis is on long reports, approval of the policy of the executive and ceremonial. Over one in five of the delegates are full-time union officials in the pay of the executive. The chairman has never been contested for re-election, and only twice have there been contests for election to the executive. Despite the emphasis on unanimity, divisions within unions became increasingly obvious. Eugen Loderer, who replaced the powerful Otto Brunner as head of IG Metall, did not have the same grip on officials and on wages negotiations. There was greater opposition within the executive, and district chiefs, like the influential and controversial Franz Steinkühler in Stuttgart, grew to a new power. Similarly, after the death of Herbert Schwiedel in 1976 the printers' union was without an integrative 'strong-man' figure; its negotiating committees were greatly expanded to improve their representative character. The union movement experienced new pressures for democratisation which threatened the traditional independence of central officials and central control of bargaining. These pressures were accompanied and reinforced by a professionalisation of the unions that suggested a change in the distribution of power. A rapid increase in the number of full-time officials at district and central levels encouraged a more abstract theoretical outlook. Correspondingly, a decrease in the number of honorary officials implied a loss of detailed local contacts and knowledge and of concern for offering individual help.

The deterioration in the character of industrial relations needs to be kept in perspective. Although the number of days lost through strikes in the 1970s was nearly three times that in the 1960s, the figure for the 1950s was much higher. Even after 1976 moderation remained the principal characteristic of union behaviour. Harsh words in public were accompanied by negotiation and accommodation in private at the top. In fact the most dramatic change came from the employers who resorted on a new grand scale to the practice of the lockout. Days lost by lockouts rose from 73,000 in 1950–9 and 1,347,000 in 1960–9 to 5,185,000 between 1970 and March 1978. The great controversy over the lockout gained momentum in 1978 when support of 200,000 members (80,000 on strike and 120,000 locked out) in Baden-Würtemberg cost IG Metall half of its annual income. According to the unions, the lockout was an arbitrary, repressive measure that augmented the advantages already enjoyed by employers. In the view of the employers, and of the Federal Labour Court in judgements of 1955 and 1971, it was essential to the proper functioning of *Tarifautonomie* that employers should have an equivalent weapon to that of the strike. The great lockouts of 1978 were in part a strategic response to the employers' perception of their limited room for manoeuvre in the context of low growth and an appreciating mark; and in part a tactical response to selective regional strikes (with full nationwide strikes there would have been little point in lockouts). Both IG Metall and the printers' union sent their locked-out colleagues to court to seek compensation, and in a judgement of 1980 the Federal Labour Court developed a new criterion of reasonableness according to which the printers' lockout had been unreasonable and justified compensation.

The political circumstance of SPD participation in government helped to reduce the extent of threat to social partnership. Individual unions supported the SPD/FDP coalition with varying degrees of enthusiasm. The most loyal support came from the miners', chemical workers' and construction workers' unions, whereas ÖTV, the metalworkers and the printers expressed on occasion their irritation at the failure of political action over tax, pension and vocational education policies and over democratisation of industry. As the DGB had no effective coordinating power, Schmidt laid emphasis on frequent meetings with the powerful leaders of its seventeen industrial unions to discuss economic policy and such issues as pension reform. Although *Konzertierte Aktion* failed to function after 1977, Schmidt continued an informal practice of collaboration with the accent on political education of union leaders into global realities. If the unions remained formally independent of political parties, they were far from politically neutral in their pursuit of union aims. Consequently, CDU politicians like Kurt Biedenkopf and other commentators began to question whether the unions would be prepared to cooperate as closely with a CDU/CSU government.[22]

CONCLUSION

The West German government's policy response to the threat of economic recession that had been generated by changes in the international economy in the 1970s was conditioned by the differentiated and liberal institutional structure of the economy at home. In particular, and as a response to distrust of state economic power after the experience of the Third Reich, much reliance was placed on two institutions: the central bank for the attainment of economic stability, and the big commercial banks as the major focus of relationships with industry for assisting the adaptation of industry to changes in the market. State and bank power was matched to privately formulated and competitive market strategy oriented to the requirements of industrial efficiency and product development. Domestically, the commercial banks, as market-oriented institutions themselves, ensured that the strategies and structures of industry were sensitive to the working of the market in which they developed their own particular expertise. Internationally, the German government and banks sought to breathe new life into transnational institutions and arrangements in order to ensure stabilisation of the international economy and to open or maintain access to foreign markets. In other words, German economic policy did not consciously seek to impose the state's will on the market and to insulate firms from the market's constraints. The differentiated character of the economic policymaking system was the counterpart of the focus on sensitivity to market in domestic policy and on the constraints of interdependence and the need for dialogue and adaptation in international economic policy.

Government's economic policy was based on the premise that the problems of stability and growth had economic causes and could not be effectively tackled, and indeed were likely to be aggravated by addressing their political symptoms. This premise was reflected in government's insulation from the political pressures of industry by the commercial banks in the field of industrial policy and in the central bank's insulation from reflationary political pressures in the realm of currency management. The banks acted as major initiators and organisers of industrial activity so that industrial policy remained somewhat screened from the general arena of politics. Outside the SPD left and technocrats the conception of an activist, entrepreneurial role for the state had little support, except when the structural problems of industry were perceived to be too great for the banks to handle alone (as in such cases as the Ruhr coal industry in the 1960s and the Saar steel industry and the shipbuilding industry in the 1970s). The premise of the economic cause of industrial problems was widely shared; distributional struggles, which involved the exercise of power in the economic system, were constrained by the primacy that was attached by actors within industry itself to the attainment of the economic goals of stability and growth.

An economic policymaking system as differentiated as that of West Germany suggests considerable limitations on party government in economic policymaking. The making of economic policy displayed a curious ambiguity. One characteristic of the system of economic management was the pervasiveness of party identification not only amongst senior officials in the economic ministries but also as a criterion in appointments to the council of the Bundesbank. Most notably, in 1979 Karl Otto Pöhl (SPD), a former journalist, State Secretary in Bonn's Finance Ministry and confidant of Schmidt, became president of the Bundesbank. More generally, the growing importance of partisans in positions of authority suggested the *Parteienstaat* (party state) character of the Federal Republic. Successive economic policy programmes were designed with great attention to party political symmetry – aid to the lower paid to meet SPD concern about social justice and aid to the employers to meet FDP concern for the logic of the social market economy.[23] Electoral considerations also influenced economic policy formulation. The attempt of the coalition parties to adopt distinctive profiles before an election, as in 1979–80, could exacerbate problems of making policy for energy, pensions, taxation and the public debt.[24] Public subsidies were often designed to attract voters or at least to appease party feeling. Expenditure on agriculture, particularly on social policies for farmers, was greatly expanded by an FDP Agriculture Minister. The Ruhr aid programme was launched in time for the local authority and state elections of 1979 and 1980 in North-Rhine Westphalia, whilst a new and generous programme of aid to the shipping industry appeared before the Schleswig-Holstein election of 1979.

To the sensitive observer the balance of party political power was clearly significant for the evolution of economic policy. The term consensus, when applied to German economic policy, is liable to detract attention from differing party political perspectives. For instance, within the social-liberal coalition SPD ministers like Ehrenberg tended to prefer a Keynesian response of a sharp injection of demand in order to offset recessionary tendencies; by contrast Friderichs and later Lambsdorff sought to concentrate on a longer-term improvement of the conditions of supply in the name of competitiveness. Furthermore, SPD politicians, including Schmidt, held a more instrumental conception of the market economy. The term social market economy did not even appear in the SPD's election programme of 1980. As in its framework programme OR '85 the party emphasised an 'active, anticipatory structural policy' that was centred on the Research Ministry. The disputes between Hauff's 'SPD ministry' and Lambsdorff's 'market economy ministry' over energy and structural policy surfaced in the 1980 election campaign, in which Lambsdorff came to personify the principles of the market economic order. Following the FDP's electoral success in increasing its share of the vote in 1980 from 7.9 per cent to 10.6 per cent (whilst the SPD stabilised its share) Lambsdorff was in an even stronger position to contain the ambitions of the Research Ministry and was expected to become the central party-political figure in economic management.

At the same time professional public-service values remained paramount in economic policy making and were safeguarded by the growing percentage of public officials in the membership of the major parties.[25] The government was not notably constrained by detailed alternative economic policies of the coalition parties although its economics ministers offered contrasting perspectives. This situation was not fundamentally changed by the SPD's new medium-term programme 1975–85. The parties hesitated to be very specific in the face both of their self-conception as 'catch-all' parties (*Volksparteien*) which deliberately opened themselves to attract a maximum of support and of the prevailing conception of social partnership which emphasised cooperation.[26] Schmidt sacrificed SPD party policy not only to the exigencies of coalition (as over vocational education and codetermination) and the need (as with the 1975 tax reform) to get the agreement of the Bundesrat but also to his view of the autonomy and priority of government. He was assisted by SPD Finance Ministers like Apel and Matthöfer who were progressive technocrats and backed Schmidt's attempt to educate party and country into the logic of economic argument. There was also the autonomous role of the Bundesbank which, as in its controversial restrictive measures of January 1979, was prepared to withstand criticism from Bonn. The Bundesbank's policy leadership stemmed from a combination of intellectual and legal authority that confirmed its strategic importance. Its authority flowed from the perception at political and administrative levels of the priority of stabilisation and of the significance of monetary policy to stabilisation and from the legal authority of the central bank to act to safeguard the currency. Another source of expertise in economic policymaking was provided by interest groups. Certain interests had notably close cooperative relations with government ministries that overrode party considerations – the nuclear industry with the Research Ministry, the oil industry with the Economics Ministry and the *Beamtenbund* with the Interior Ministry. In particular, the Federal Association of German Banks and the Federation of German Industry (BDI) had intimate contacts to the Economics and Finance Ministries. The head of the currency policy division of the Finance Ministry had previously been on the payroll of the banks' association, whilst the Director-General of the BDI for many years was Fritz Neef, former State Secretary in the Economics Ministry (he was replaced by a former State Secretary in the Defence Ministries). Interests were also able to offer their expertise and exert their influence in parliament. In the Bundestag 70.3 per cent of the members of the committee on labour and social policy were union members and 77.7 per cent of the members of the agriculture committee were farmers.

The dictates of party policy were sacrificed to the need to tie together a loosely structured, yet clearly identifiable system of economic policymaking through negotiation and accommodation. Partisan arguments were firmly presented and argued in the context of a perceived interdependence which suggested the value of mutual forbearance. An economic expertise that paid great attention to the logic of the economic order carried a great deal of influence in the deliberations of interests as well as of the government and bundesbank. Accordingly, economic problem-solving took on a technically rational character. It was pervaded by a functional rather than ideological spirit that subordinated specific goals to the larger requirements of an effective functioning of the whole economy. The nature of German economic argument is only to be understood against the background of an intellectual tradition of political economy that has given key place to the concept state.[27] This tradition has fostered public-regarding attitudes, a deep sense of interdependency and social responsibility even in the exercise of private economic power. No longer is the concept state simply identified with a public bureaucracy which seeks to realise certain inherent public purposes in the face of political opposition and market constraints. It is used to imply a shared responsibility for maintaining a particular moral framework for economic activity.

Generalisations about the future of Germany's economic-policy arrangements must inevitably be tentative and provisional. In the 1970s, as in the two previous decades, West Germany's economic policy arrangements have been tied together by shared assumptions. These assumptions are rooted in historical experiences of inflation and of the political and economic dislocation which inflation can induce. Consequently, there has been a cultural support for the central bank's stabilisation policies and for union wage restraint, both of which have supported each other. There are, nevertheless, threats to the harmony and stability of the economic policymaking system, threats which have already surfaced in the 1970s. Problems of cooperation could be aggravated, for example, by changes within the system of collective bargaining as a result of intransigence of the employers (in the unlikely event of an overall majority for the SPD) or of rank-and-file dissent within the unions; by the effects of a change in political power on the climate of industrial relations (if, for example, a right-wing CDU/CSU government which distrusted the neutrality and party-political independence of the unions was elected to office); or by a perception that the central bank's overreaction was producing unbearable costs in terms of growth and unemployment. Perhaps even more significantly, in the longer run it is possible that anti-inflationary cultural attitudes will erode in importance as time, political security and experience of new economic problems displace the primacy that has been attached to price stability in German economic calculations.

NOTES AND REFERENCES

1. The detailed politics of economic management after 1973 are discussed in K. H. F. Dyson, 'The Politics of Non-Planning in West Germany', *West European Politics* (1981).
2. On the effects of recession on social policy, the pensions issue which haunted the 1976–80 legislative period, and Wehner's abortive 'social policy offensive' of the SPD, see Dyson, op. cit.

3. This section appears in a modified form in Dyson, op. cit.
4. Members of this circle included bankers like Jürgen Ponto (a terrorist victim in 1977) of the Dresdner Bank and Wilfried Guth of the Deutsche Bank and industrialists like Berthold Beitz (Krupp), Herbert Grünewald (Bayer), Hans Merkle (Bosch) and Bernhard Plettner (Siemens). The influence of bankers was not new; Adenauer had relied, perhaps to an even greater degree, on the advice of bankers like Hermann Abs (Deutsche Bank) and Robert Pferdmenges.
5. On Schmidt's conception of political leadership see Peter Glotz, *Die Innenausstattung der Macht: Politisches Tagebuch 1976–8* (Munich: Steinhausen, 1980).
6. This irritation came to a head over the SPD's abortive proposal for a reform of vocational education to relieve youth unemployment. Economics Minister Friderichs vetoed the proposal in cabinet.
7. The background of the social market economy was the desire to re-establish the idea of a distinction between state and society after the 'total state' of the Third Reich. The state's purpose was to provide the basic economic order, the moral framework of economic policy, within which the economic process could unfold automatically. Its functions were to ensure economic stability by safeguarding the currency and to maintain competition and participation in the economic process by policies for small firms, anti-monopoly policy and incentives for saving. *Ad hoc* intervention in the economic process was to be avoided in order to secure the autonomy of economic activity as the chief function of civil society. The social market economy achieved depoliticisation in two senses: a restriction of the scope of political rule by market decision and an autonomous central bank to reduce the influence of politicking on currency management. See A. Müller-Armack, 'Die Anfänge der Sozialen Marktwirtschaft', in R. Löwenthal and H.-P. Schwarz (eds), *Die Zweite Republic* (Stuttgart: Seewald, 1974).
8. During the recession of the 1970s the Counter-Cyclical Advisory Council and the Financial Planning Council did not in fact prove effective forums for a coordinated fiscal policy of the three levels of government. During the 1970s it proved difficult to realise federal expenditure programmes in the interests of economic recovery. State governments and local authorities had an abiding suspicion of deficit budgeting, held back expenditure during recession and failed to take up federal aid. From a Keynesian perspective federal expenditure programmes were compensating for the pro-cyclical policies at state and local levels. For details of the problems of realising federal reflationary programmes see Dyson, op. cit.
9. G. Lehmbruch and W. Lang, 'Die Konzertierte Aktion', *Der Bürger Im Staat* (September 1977) p. 207.
10. Hanns-Martin Schleyer, *Unternehmerpolitik* (Stuttgart: Seewald, 1978) p. 74.
11. H. Bockelmann, 'The Role of the Bundesbank', address to ASGP conference Liverpool 1979, and K. Dyson, 'The Ambiguous Politics of Western Germany', *European Journal of Political Research*, no. 7 (1979) pp. 375–96.
12. An excellent example was provided in 1967 when the banks mounted a major rescue operation for the ailing Krupp empire which in effect passed into their hands.

13. The Council of Economic Advisers, the so-called 'five wise men', dates from legislation of 1963. It was established as an authoritative institution whose members were appointed for five years by the Federal President and were expected to assist an objectification (*Versachlichung*) of wages policy through its yearly reports. In contrast to its American equivalent the Council's function was to advise all those responsible for economic policy decisions and not just the government. In its early reports it advocated *Konzertiene Aktion*. By and large the Council has adopted a critical view of government policy and served to stimulate a more sophisticated economic discussion. Its reports are submitted to the Bundestag and the Bundesrat and the government is legally obliged to offer a reply to them.
14. In the words of the Bad Godesberg programme: 'free competition and the free initiative of entrepreneurs are important elements of Social Democratic economic policy . . . the Social Democratic Party is in favour of the free market wherever real competition exists. But whenever markets are dominated by individuals or groups, various measures are required to preserve the freedom of the economy. As much competition as possible – as much planning as necessary.'
15. The source of the figures contained in this section is the excellent monthly reports of the Deutsche Bundesbank and the monthly reviews of the Federal Economics Ministry.
16. The spearhead of this German advance into world markets has been engineering firms which are generally subsidiaries of large manufacturing groups (Lurgi of Metallgesellschaft, Kraftwerk Union of Siemens, Thyssen Rheinstahl Technik, Krupp Koppers, Nannesmann Demag, and so on). Their huge industrial projects are generously financed by the banks, and the government's programme of export insurance usually guarantees nine-tenths of the amount.
17. Regional policy was initially a responsibility of the states and had little importance as a federal issue. As the result of a constitutional amendment of 1969 (Article 91a, i) improvement of the regional economic structure became one of three new joint tasks (*Gemeinschaftsaufgaben*). In return for providing one half of the costs incurred by the states the federal government acquired the right to participate through a new joint federal/state committee in the planning of regional policy. There are 21 action programmes covering 59 per cent of the area of the Federal Republic.
18. A 25.1 per cent holding provides banks with blocking power over managerial decisions.
19. For a useful discussion see H. Kitschelt, *Kernenergiepolitik* (Frankfurt: Campus, 1980).
20. The result of the steel strike was longer holidays rather than a reduction in the working week.
21. Arendt had formerly been president of the miners' union (IG Bergbau). In the same year (1969) that Arendt became Federal Labour and Social Minister the vice-president of his union, Heinz Oskar Vetter, was elected president of the DGB. After such close personal relations it was a shock to the DGB when Ehrenberg was appointed Labour Minister in 1977 without consultation of the unions.
22. K. Biedenkopf and R. von Voss (eds), *Staatsfuhrung, Verbandsmacht und*

Innere Souveränität (Stuttgart: Bonn Aktuell, 1977).

23. For details see Dyson, op. cit.
24. A major development in economic management was the huge increase in the size of the public debt. The decisive change came in 1974–5 when the debt was more than trebled. A higher debt was incurred in 1974 than in the first four years of the government combined. In 1980 it was already higher than the federal budget. On the politics of the public debt see Dyson, op. cit.
25. On the concept of the 'party state' (Parteienstaat) and its practical expression in the penetration of party members into the major public institutions see K. Dyson, *Party, State, and Bureaucracy in Western Germany* (Beverly Hills: Sage, 1977).
26. W. Paterson, 'Problems of Party Government in West Germany: A British Perspective' in H. Döring and G. Smith (eds), *Party Government and Political Culture in Western Germany* (London: Macmillan, 1982).
27. The implications of the continental European state tradition for political economy are discussed in K. Dyson, *The State Tradition in Western Europe* (Oxford: Martin Robertson, 1981).

3 Continuity and Innovation in Sweden in the 1970s

NEIL ELDER

Sweden, Denmark and Norway are unique in Western Europe in the degree of dominance enjoyed in their political systems by Social Democratic and Labour parties since the early 1930s. Among these three Scandinavian states that dominance was most marked in Sweden, where the Social Democrats held office almost without interruption from 1932 until 1976. A powerful factor in their initial success was the positive nature of their response to the crisis of the Great Depression. Instead of the fiscal orthodoxy and book-balancing exercises adopted, for example, by the Labour government of the time in Britain, the Social Democrats in Sweden put into practice the pre-Keynesian demand stimulation prescriptions of Wicksell and the Stockholm School of Economists. They thus offered hope at a time of depression. But the crucial factor in their success was that, as was the case elsewhere in Scandinavia during this period, they entered into partnership with the Agrarians in a Red–Green coalition on the basis of aid for the primary sector of the economy together with an expansion of welfare facilities. This horse-trading (Swedish, 'cow-trading') deal was a matter of the harmonisation of interests, scarcely of ideology, and both sides were experienced in hard bargaining through their comprehensive union, marketing and co-operative organisations.

THE POST-WAR ECONOMIC SUCCESS OF SWEDISH CORPORATISM

If the degree of corporatism in a state be measured in terms of the degree of comprehensiveness of recruitment to the major interest organisations in its industrial and economic life, then Sweden by the 1960s could probably claim to be the most corporatist of all advanced industrial states. By 1967 some 90–5 per cent of blue-collar industrial workers, for example, belonged to unions affiliated to LO (Landsorganisationen – the nearest Swedish equivalent to the TUC). This was, it may be noted in passing, in the absence of closed-shop legislation, never felt to be necessary in Sweden. Similarly over 90 per cent of white-collar workers in the public sector and approximately 70 per cent in the private sector were affiliated to the umbrella organisation for salaried staff, the TCO.[1] Coverage was similarly impressive on the employers' side, at least among the larger firms belonging to the Federation of Swedish Employers (SAF). The same held true of farmers' organisations, with 90 per cent of farmers working landholdings of 10 hectares and more being members of RLF the NFU equivalent. Finally – although the list could be extended – some 70 per cent of those in employment with university and technical high school qualifications were enrolled in SACO, roughly translatable as the Central Association of Swedish Professional Workers.

It would of course be simplistic merely to play the numbers game, however, in order to assess the extent of corporatism. It is more important to try to assess the *weight* of organised interest groups in the determination and application of public policy. By this criterion, too, Sweden scores very highly in comparative ranking in the pre-1970s post-war era. Four points may be briefiy made in this connexion.

In the first place, it had become something of a tradition that the state should keep out of the collective-bargaining process which was of decisive importance for settling the pattern of wages and incomes for periods of one, two or three years at a stretch (one year being the most common period of validity for an agreement). The origins of this tradition can be traced back to the epochal Saltsjöbaden Agreement of 1938 between both sides of industry, reinforced and underpinned since 1956 by centralised framework agreements setting the norms for individual union and local settlements both in the public and private sectors. Wage-drift might on occasion push particular settlements markedly above the norm, but in general the nature of the collective-bargaining arrangements in Sweden made it simpler than in many other countries to reach well-founded investment decisions. Highly centralised and self-disciplined organisations on either side of the labour market helped ensure that commitments once entered into would not be reneged upon. The commitments themselves had the character of legal contracts with financial penalties for wildcat strikes, and they were backed up by agreements designed to safeguard essential national and social interests as well as the interests of third parties to disputes. All this was made easier to bring about by the fact that there were, and are, fewer than two dozen trade unions all told affiliated to the LO, and that these are organised on an industrial rather than on a craft basis.

Second, a considerable influence has been exerted on economic policy by the research economists attached to the LO Secretariat, and especially by Gosta Rehn and Rudolf Meidner. This influence has been decisive in the evolution of a sophisticated and far-reaching labour market policy. Naturally it has been assisted by the long tenure in office of a Social Democratic government, but at the same time it has a number of features which have ensured the continuation and, indeed, the expansion of the policy under the succeeding non-socialist regimes after 1976. More, however, will be said of this later. Meantime it should be mentioned that the influence of LO's research department has also been exerted in support of other policies to good, although less uniquely important, effect. Among such policies may be reckoned the steady expansion of the public sector on the services side and the increased collectivisation of savings resources.

The third and fourth factors are less peculiar to Sweden, at least if attention is concentrated on the essence and not the form of the matter. They relate to the degree of (a) institutionalised and (b) non-institutionalised association of the major interest organisations in the genesis and execution of public policy, and in particular of public policy on the economic front. Institutionalised association covers in part arrangements of a type generally familiar in Western industrialised states. Thus, for example, the major groups have representation on a National Economic Council and the heads of their research departments sit on a departmental research council providing the NEC with the necessary background information and evaluation service. Less familiarly, it has long been standard practice in Sweden to circulate draft legislative proposals on 'remiss' to the major interest groups and administrative agencies affected for formal open comment. This practice follows on from an earlier stage in the policymaking process at which it is customary to set up a commission of enquiry to consider a matter: here again the major interest groups have often been represented on the commission of enquiry, although rather less frequently towards the end of the 1960s. On the other hand, though, this same decade saw a considerable increase in the number of interest-group representatives serving on the boards of the decentralised and administrative agencies.

The formal nature of these institutional arrangements, with their association of the major groups as open and independent actors in the policymaking process, is unusual. It is, however, an open question whether the groups are thereby given a greater weight in the shaping of policy than is the case with a system of numerous advisory councils and committees meeting on a regular basis to consider questions of relevance to the groups represented on them and supplemented by departmental committees, again with group representation, to consider specific projects for reform. But perhaps the most striking single example of institutionalised group association in Sweden occurs once more in the field of labour market policy. Here the Labour Market Board (arbetsmarknadsstyrelsen – AMS) must rank as one of the most important and influential of the decentralised administrative agencies, with significant discretionary powers over the detailed application of a large budget. The chairman of this board and his deputy are government appointees; the peak union and employers' organisations (LO and SAF) provide three members apiece, the salaried staffs have two, and in addition one member each represents the agricultural interest, the association of professional workers, and women in the labour market.

Finally, the non-institutionalised association of the major interest groups in policy formulation may be briefly dealt with. This is a question of periodic consultations on economic matters on an *ad hoc* basis between the government and top-level representatives of the organisations. Thus from 1949 to 1955 there were 'Thursday Club' meetings to seek to promote economic growth and stimulate exports. Four years later began a series of annual conferences in the autumn at Harpsund, which might be described as the Swedish equivalent of Chequers. This period of so-called 'Harpsund democracy' came to an end in 1964 amid complaints from the non-socialist opposition parties that Parliament was being by-passed – the classic objection on principle to corporatist trends. Then, in the 1970s, followed the differently constituted sessions at Haga Castle just outside Stockholm, but of these, more anon.

However, the major interest organisations in Sweden have not been involved in the kind of concertation of policy on the grand scale associated, for example, with French economic planning. Swedish governments have preferred to operate through fiscal and monetary controls in combination with special devices to maintain employment levels and counter-cyclical fluctuations. The Social Democratic governments have supported a free-enterprise market economy on the production side with the private sector accounting for over 90 per cent of the total. At the same time they have laid stress on an equitable distribution of the product through transfer payments and steeply progressive taxation, and they have steadily expanded the public sector on the services and welfare side. The pattern of policy in this respect has been decidedly Galbraithian rather than Marxist.

The basic congruence of underlying attitudes between both sides of industry on the nature and structure of the economy was one factor of importance in the generally favourable economic development of Sweden before the 1970s. Industrial relations were not seen in zero-sum terms, though naturally this did not preclude hard and tough bargaining, sometimes stretching over many months, when the collective agreements fell due for renewal. Steady economic growth in turn no doubt smoothed the course of wage negotiations: GNP increased in the post-war years to 1971 at an average annual rate of 3.3 per cent as compared with an interwar average of 2.5 per cent.[2] By 1972 Sweden could show an annual growth rate over the previous century second only to that of Japan and a per capita income some 40 per cent higher than the Western European average and very nearly as high as that of the USA. The concentration of the Social Democrats in the immediate post-war period on maintaining full employment and then, from the late 1950s, on the stimulation of economic growth implied a substantial degree of harmony of interest between government and employers' organisations. The government was also able to count on the general support of a trade-union movement that was virtually undivided ideologically – or perhaps it would be more accurate to say, in its pragmatic approach.

But Swedish prosperity did not depend on a single cause. The good fortune of the country in escaping the ravages of war must be accounted a contributory factor. Much was owed, too, to a comparatively high quality of technology and management. A large proportion of managers have engineering or scientific qualifications, and engineering and science have long enjoyed high social status. Technical high schools of university standard sprang up in the major cities comparatively early in the nineteenth century, and Swedish inventions such as the ball-bearing have quite frequently provided an impetus for industrial expansion and a growth in overseas trade. Furthermore, a comparatively sophisticated private banking system, in which the Wallenberg dynasty have played a prominent role from the start, has helped to provide a financial infrastructure for economic growth.

Sweden's share of world population is 0.2 per cent, of world production just over 1 per cent, and of world trade 1.8 per cent. Engineering products account for almost a half of what is sold abroad. The country has the most multinational industrial development in the world if the criterion is the scale of productive operations abroad in relation to the size of the domestic economy. In per capita terms, the international operations of Swedish companies are exceeded only by the Netherlands and Switzerland. Much of the activity is accounted for by firms such as SKF, Volvo, Saab, ASEA, Atlas Copco, Alfa-Laval, Electrolux and L. M. Eriksson. Roughly a half of Swedish industrial output is exported, and in the technologically advanced sectors the proportion is close to two-thirds.

This openness to world markets inevitably carries with it a certain vulnerability, and against this background the importance of labour market and counter-cyclical measures on the domestic front is enhanced. The LO strategy on the labour market was to squeeze the workforce out of areas showing low profits and consequently depressed wage-levels and to encourage a vigorous labour mobility into growth sectors by retraining schemes, financial incentives, the provision of new housing stock, etc. In part this strategy was designed to support a 'solidary' wages policy involving the reduction of wage-differentials: for this reason LO favoured highly centralised wage bargaining. In part also the aim was to reconcile full employment and price stability, in combination with a policy of restricting consumer demand through indirect taxation. Between 1956 and 1971 the appropriations for the Labour Market Board multiplied fivefold to 2,000 million Swedish crowns.

Perhaps the most original measure adopted in counter-cyclical strategy was the scheme for investment reserve funds which began to become a significant factor from the mid-1950s onwards. The essence of this was that firms could choose to set aside 40 per cent of their pre-tax profits for reserve funding and obtain relief from profits tax when the funds were later used for investment, provided that the investment was made at a time determined by the authorities. This device could be seen as a classic example of Social Democratic government regulation to reduce the frictions of a free market economy without doing violence to its spirit.

The first signs of strain in the Swedish economy started to appear in the mid-1960s and, partly as an indirect result of this but partly on other grounds, relations between the government and the employers' associations began to cool. Sweden's share of exports in the world market showed a falling off for the first time and the unemployment rate rose slightly. Underlying these developments was a decline in the competitiveness of Swedish raw materials (iron ore, timber) and of the traditional industries based upon those raw materials.

The Social Democrats in office reacted with a variety of measures, but they based these in large part upon the findings of an LO working party that had called in 1961 for greater governmental control of important investment decisions in the private sector. First, they expanded labour market resources and at the same time adopted a notably more selective approach both in the use of these and in the release of investment funds in the interests of economic 'fine-tuning'. In part this reflected a growing preoccupation with regional policy: firms were now induced to increase investment in the development area of Northern Sweden, thus putting into reverse the earlier policy designed to increase labour mobility southwards. Second, in 1967 the Social Democrats set up the Swedish Investment Bank, designed to channel the rapidly mounting pensions funds – which by 1971 accounted for a quarter of total assets in the capital market – into medium- and long-term investment projects. Third, one year later they created a new Ministry of

Industry together with a council on industrial policy, representative of both sides of industry, to advise on structural adjustments, etc. New boards were also brought into existence to promote research and development (STU), to help launch industries in development areas (SVETAB) and to encourage product innovation (SUAB). The burst of activity was marked by some notable failures in attempts by the state to provide dynamic direct management for an assortment of industrial concerns: friction with the entrepreneurial community increased in consequence.[3]

This friction was compounded by a radicalisation of Social Democratic policy that was simultaneously taking place under the combined influences of generational change, New Left thinking and, though to a much lesser degree, the growing political significance of the Communist Left party. The main thrust of this radicalisation was towards the realisation of a greater measure of 'industrial democracy'. Fuel for the trend was provided by the report in 1968 of a commission of enquiry that demonstrated a highly concentrated degree of control in the private sector of industry together with wide disparities of income within society. One of the main effects, indeed, of the drive from LO's side for a 'solidary' wages policy appeared to be the forcing on of industrial mergers by the pressure exerted on weaker firms, with a resultant concentration of profitability in the most expansive areas. The effects of the campaign for industrial democracy may be summarised as, first, to put through a series of enactments which culminated in the 1976 Co-Determination Law and effectively tilted the balance of power at the workplace towards the unions; and second, to contribute towards the appearance in 1975 of a scheme for worker funds which has more corporatist implications than anything resulting from the world recession of the 1970s. These developments, and especially the second, will be referred to shortly.

THE OIL CRISIS AND THE SWEDISH RESPONSE

The impact of the general economic recession and the quadrupling of oil prices in 1973 was slower to make itself felt in Sweden than in other countries. The Social Democrat government made every effort to bridge the recessionary period elsewhere in the world, mostly by the use of traditional instruments of economic policy not implying any tendency towards an increase in corporatism. Employment levels, for example, were successfully maintained by the usual combination of labour market and investment fund methods. Thus in 1975–6, at a period of weak demand and much spare capacity, at least a quarter of manufacturing investment was financed from funds previously set aside. Sweden suffered smaller cyclical fluctuations than most of her trading partners, and this proportion of investment would probably never have been made without policy intervention.[4] These measures to tide over the hard times were reinforced by subsidies for stockpiling and by the stimulation of domestic demand so as to compensate for the shortfall in demand from abroad. Inevitably the latter policy helped cause the trade balance to move rapidly into the red – from a surplus in 1973 to a deficit of 3½ billion Swedish crowns in 1974.

Another factor which provided a cushion against the initial effects of recession was the international boom in raw material prices in 1973–4 which meant that production, investment and profits continued to rise in Sweden in 1974, in contrast to the trend elsewhere. One reaction from the government side was to tax windfall profits and earmark the revenues from these for use by trade unions in improving working conditions – a rather characteristic balancing out measure. But the bridge was to prove to have too short a span, since the recession was deeper and of longer duration than had been expected.

Inflationary pressures could not be avoided and, from 1973 onwards, had the effect of eroding the autonomy of the parties in collective bargaining negotiations. They began, reinforced by large increases in local taxation, by negating the income-tax concessions passed through by the Social Democrats in 1970. Powerful pressures built up for large wage-increases in order to counteract the drastic incidence of inflation on the steeply progressive tax-scales. In order to counter the threatening upward spiral of wages and taxes, the government was forced, as Elvander put it,[5] into an unofficial incomes policy. In the process, it sought to concert action with the non-socialist parties in opposition as well as with the major interest organisations.

The outcome was a series of meetings at Haga Castle between 1973 and 1975, resulting in agreements to reduce direct taxation and to increase employers' contributions, both in the private and public sectors, for national-insurance purposes in return for a promise of wage-restraint. The parliamentary situation at this period was unique, with the single-chamber Riksdag equally divided between socialist and non-socialists. But since the Social Democrats could not expect Communist Left support in this kind of package deal, they had to seek cooperation elsewhere. They got it from the Liberals (1974 and 1975) and the Centre Party (1975 only): neither of these were anxious to advance the date of the next elections before the September 1976 schedule. The Conservatives preferred to play profile politics outside Haga altogether.

In the event, a wage settlement was reached in 1975 to cover a two-year period and not a single year, but at a level which increased wage costs by some 40 per cent between 1975 and 1977 (employers' contributions included). Largely, though not entirely, in consequence, Sweden lost over a fifth of her share in world export markets during this period.[6]

The general election of September 1976 saw the Social Democrats removed from office for the first time in well over a generation, to be replaced by a tripartite non-socialist coalition of Liberals, Centre Party and Conservatives under the premiership of Torbjörn Fälldin of the Centre Party. The margin of victory was extremely narrow but the event was sufficiently momentous to make the headlines in the Western press. Two years later, this coalition fell apart upon the nuclear-power issue, to be succeeded by a very weak Liberal minority government which saw out the period remaining until the mandatory elections in September 1979. These elections produced a majority of one in Parliament for the three non-socialist parties, whereat a second tripartite administration was formed under Fälldin. So Sweden has remained under new management since the Social Democrats were ousted.

The new management inherited simultaneously the worst of the domestic recession and a wage agreement which was both costly and due to expire in Spring 1977. 1976 saw the worst trade deficit of the post-war period, at 5.2 billion Swedish crowns, and 1977, at 4.9 billion, was not much better in this respect. The inflationary trend moved steadily upwards: consumer prices increased by 6.7 per cent in 1973, 9.9 per cent in 1974, 9.8 per cent in 1975, 10.3 per cent in 1976 and 11.5 per cent in 1977. Industrial production started falling below the OECD average in 1976 and GDP, which had still managed to average a 3.8 per cent annual increase from 1965–70, only showed a 0.3 per cent annual increase from 1974–7. Faced with such adverse circumstances, the chances of the non-socialist government winning the co-operation of the workforce in the matter of wage restraint appeared at least to some observers to be slim.

In the event, the unions showed notable forebearance in the wage negotiations of the later 1970s and thereby contributed significantly to a revival in the competitiveness of Swedish exports. A number of factors may be suggested by way of explanation. In the first place, the non-socialist governments gave a continuing high priority to the maintenance of employment levels, using the same mechanisms as their predecessors in office. Taking the period 1970–8, expenditure on labour-market measures increased fivefold, and within that category expenditure on training schemes increased seven and a half times. Much of this latter went, however, on in-firm training designed to reduce lay-offs under the first Fälldin administration, although policy shifted more in the direction of promoting recruitment to industry in 1979. Low unemployment helps consensus management of the economy, and the Swedish achievement in this respect compares favourably with performance elsewhere (see Table 3.1).

TABLE 3.1 Unemployment rate on Sweden, 1976–9

	1976	*1977*	*1978*	*1979*
Unemployment rate (% of workforce)	1.6	1.8	2.2	2.1
Persons affected by labour market measures (% of workforce)[a]	2.6	2.8	3.3	3.5

a i.e. training schemes, public works programmes, sheltered employment
SOURCE OECD, *Economic Survey: Sweden* (Paris, April 1980) p. 12

Second, and in close alliance with the foregoing measures, the successive non-socialist governments continued the pre-1976 policy of extensive state aid to the hardest-hit sectors of industry combined with takeovers to promote structural change and slimming-down programmes. Expenditure on industrial support increased from 60 million Swedish crowns in 1970 to 10½ billion in 1979. The process of taking over the largest shipyards was pushed through to completion, and in 1977 the three biggest steel-producing concerns were merged into Swedish Steel, with half the assets in the possession of the State Holding Company (Statsföretag AB, set up in 1969 to manage all state-run enterprises). Similar steps were taken in respect of two sizeable enterprises in the area of forest products. Policy towards investment continued to be concerned primarily with picking up the pieces: the bulk of state support went into the depressed sectors – glassware, textiles, clothing, but especially, of course, shipbuilding, iron and steel, and forest products. Adaptation was further promoted: an increased concentration on specialised steel-making, the switching of some shipyard capacity to bridge construction, prefabricated factory work, the manufacture of offshore platforms, and so on. At the same time, labour-market policy, as mentioned above, encouraged in-firm training to avoid some lay-offs and the greater part of the wages bill was subsidised by the state for redundant labour temporarily on the payroll. The weak Liberal government of 1978–9 it only commanded one-ninth of the seats in Parliament – thus won Social Democratic support for a two-year guarantee against lay-offs for workers at two shipyards.

In these respects the traditional lines of policy were largely preserved and the severance of close bonds between the labour movement and the government did not make a great deal of difference to the situation. There were, of course, differences of nuance. The non-socialist administrations have shown a greater readiness than their predecessors to help smaller firms. They have also moved steadily away from selective towards general interventions on the labour market front. But the avoidance of a high level of unemployment remained a top political priority. In the process, it should be stressed, there has been a continuing steady drift of labour from the private into the public sector. Sweden in the 1970s had in fact the fastest growing public sector of any OECD country: government outlays as a percentage of GNP moved from 20.1 in 1960 to 58.9 in 1977. Similarly, the total tax burden was the highest of any OECD country – 53.4 per cent of GNP in 1977, compared with an average for the organisation as whole of 36.2 per cent.[7]

Taxation policy continued to be used as an instrument to influence the course of wage negotiations, although concertation with the opposition disappeared after 1976 and some significant shifts of direction occurred as a result of the change of regime. Both in 1977 and 1978 a comparatively expansive fiscal policy was adopted, with income-tax cuts initially along much the same lines as those proposed by the Social Democrats, although with greater reliefs given in the middle-income brackets. The main shifts of direction came in the phasing out of the employers' payroll tax, abolished finally in mid-1978, and the introduction at the end of the decade of automatic indexation for personal taxation as a shield against inflationary pressures. The first of these changes was designed in part to help restrain prices and in part to help arrest the drift of labour into the public sector. The second, although unpopular with LO because it widened differentials and thereby damaged efforts towards a 'solidary' wages policy, was nevertheless intended to reduce the pressure for higher wages.

In the event, the wage-rounds of 1977 and 1978 both ended in modest settlements. In addition to the factors already mentioned, militancy was discouraged by the high level of stocks held by firms as a result of earlier financial inducements. Both sides also showed an appreciation of the need to restore the competitiveness of Swedish exports and to bring down the rate of inflation. The 1977 negotiations were marked by an outbreak of white-collar militancy and by much bitterness between SAF and LO on account of an attempt by the employers' organisation to have sickness benefits reduced. This attempt, however, required legislative action to succeed and the government was not prepared to lend its assistance. The 1978 round, by way of contrast, went without a hitch and the agreements reached contained a safeguard against inflationary pressures which in effect prolonged their validity until late 1979, when the negotiations for the 1979–80 round began.

Successive devaluations of currency in 1977 and declining manufacturing unit labour costs stimulated a recovery of export shares, turning heavy trade balance deficits in 1976 and 1977 into a healthy favourable balance of 5.2 billion Swedish crowns in 1978. At the same time consumer prices fell from their peak level of annual increase of 11.5 per cent in 1977 to 10.1 per cent in

1978 and 7.2 per cent in 1979. The long period of weak economic growth also showed signs of coming to an end in 1979, with GDP rising by 3.8 per cent as against 2.4 per cent the previous year. On the debit side, continued heavy budget deficits reached a level of some 10 per cent of GDP in 1979, necessitating a sharp rise in indirect taxation in the autumn of that year. Private industrial investment fell in 1979 for the fifth successive year, despite the inducements made available by official policy. It seems likely that the climate in this respect was affected by a fear of further oil price rises. Worst of all, of course, such rises did occur in mid-1979, helping to push up the rate of inflation again towards double figures and to cause a large external deficit to reappear.

These developments created a difficult situation for the 1980 wage round, which eventually broke down early in May to result in the worst labour troubles in the country's history – not excepting the general strike of 1909. 700,000 workers were locked out by firms belonging to SAF, a further 100,000 were brought out on indefinite strikes by the LO side. After ten days of acute social and economic dislocation, the conflict ended when the government made an unprecedented direct intervention to induce the employers to accept a mediation offer to which LO had already agreed.

Why did the collective-bargaining machinery break down in 1980 after weathering difficult situations in 1977 and 1978? The statistics of inflation published in the course of the negotiating phase by the Central Statistical Office showed an increase of over 5 per cent since December, but this was only marginally worse than had been the case three years earlier. The arguments for restraint in view of the impact upon Swedish exports and the domestic cost of living continued to be as cogent as ever. However, a number of points may be made. The situation was complicated in 1980 by the fact that account had been deferred until the current negotiating round of the impact of earlier price rises above the threshold for renegotiation agreed in 1978. Again, the employers, desperate to increase Swedish market shares by pushing down relative costs, were only reluctantly willing to go as far as the first bid of a mere 2.3 per cent put forward by the official mediators. Increasing financial stringency caused the government (Fälldin II) to cut back sharply on the rate of increase of public expenditure, and, while labour market measures continued to be well funded, the payment of a slice of equalisation grant to local-government authorities was, for example, deferred. A tacit incomes policy was probably becoming more difficult to manage with local-government requisitions tending to counterbalance the benefits of state income-tax remissions. In any case the divergence of tax-policy from previous practice made for growing strains between LO and the non-socialist coalition. In the event the conflict was settled on the basis of the second bid from the mediators – 6.8 per cent for the private sector and 7.3 per cent for the public. The initial request from LO's side had been for 13 per cent – roughly in line with the new annual rate of inflation.

THE OIL CRISIS AND THE PROBLEMS OF NUCLEAR ENERGY

Sweden has the third highest consumption of energy per head in the OECD – after Canada and the USA (1979 figures). Much of her industry is fuel-intensive – paper and pulp, iron and steel – and the climate in winter helps to explain the high usage. Roughly a fifth of the supply comes from hydro power, just over a tenth from nuclear power – which generates a quarter of the electricity used. Oil dependence is the highest in the world, in the sense that oil accounts for some 70 per cent of fuel imports, the highest per capita level in the world. Despite this dependence, programmes to expand nuclear-power capacity, such as that contained in the minority Liberal government's bill of March 1979 to meet a fifth of energy consumption from this source by 1990, have met with the fiercest opposition on environmental and safety grounds, and from 1973 onwards throughout the rest of the decade the nuclear issue moved to the forefront of the political debate. Its impact requires a closer, although necessarily far from leisurely, scrutiny.

The hitherto prevailing inter-party consensus on the desirability of an extensive programme for the construction of nuclear-power stations for peaceful purposes was broken in 1973 when the Centre Party and the Communist Left Party (VPK) came out in opposition to the completion of any plants beyond the five already in operation, and then called for the phasing-out of these five. A decision to refrain from the use of nuclear power for military purposes, it may be added in passing, had long been accepted on all sides in line with Sweden's steady support for non-proliferation and nuclear disarmament treaties. Furthermore, Swedish reserves of uranium ore were left unexploited in the ground, although she is estimated to have 70–80 per cent of Europe's extractable resources, equivalent to approximately 15 per cent of world reserves. The then existing programme of nuclear-power stations envisaged a total of 11.

In a major parliamentary debate on energy policy in 1975 the Conservatives backed the Social Democrats in increasing the number of stations to 13, the Liberals opted for 11 to cut down the risk of alienating their prospective allies in the Centre Party, and the Centre and Communist Left maintained an opposition of principle to the whole programme. The running was made on the opposition side by Fälldin, the Centre Party's leader, who had formed his ideas on the issue while serving on the Nature Conservancy Board and under the influence of American and Swedish nuclear physicists disquieted by the levels of risk involved. The usual Left–Right bipolarity of the political scene in Sweden was thus sharply cross-cut and the nuclear issue was one reason for the ousting of the Social Democrats from office in September 1976.

The Centre Party thereupon found itself in office – or rather, chose to take up office – in combination with two parties which held a diametrically opposed viewpoint to it on the issue which had helped to bring them all to power. Before the coalition could even be finalised, the Centre was obliged to accept the activation with nuclear fuel of the sixth station in the programme. The price for this was, in brief, a general agreement to phase out the whole operation if the level of risk after thorough expert investigation proved unacceptably high. Accordingly a Law on the Conditions for Activating (future) Nuclear Power Stations was passed in April 1977. But the issue was a canker for the coalition, sapping its strength from within. Declining levels of support for the Centre Party were indicated by the opinion polls, and two years after the formation of the coalition the Centre Party took the lead in what was viewed by many as a mercy-killing. They wanted a referendum on the nuclear question which their partners were unwilling to concede. The establishment of several commissions of enquiry could not dispel the impression that the partners would never agree because, to borrow Sydney Smith's aphorism, they were arguing from different premises.[8]

The minority Liberal government which followed brought in an energy bill in March 1979 providing for twelve reactors. Very soon afterwards, the incident at Harrisburg caused the Social Democratic opposition to do a U-turn and call for a referendum on the issue: the Liberals readily acquiesced. The nuclear question was in danger of bringing about voter drift, if not worse, from those parties in favour of the programme: a referendum would remove it from the political agenda with minimum political fall-out. Accordingly the referendum was fixed for March 1980, by which time the Fälldin II administration was in office. The Centre Party agreed to abide by the result, in the sense that it felt that it could stay on in office with a clear conscience even if the result went against its preferred line.

This was in fact what happened. *Three* alternatives were put to the voters. *All* were cast in terms of phasing out the nuclear programme, but Lines 1 (Conservative) and 2 (Liberal *and* Social Democrat) envisaged the completion of the building programme of 12 reactors – the same as in the Liberal bill of Spring 1979 – while Line 3 (Centre and Communist) would have stopped the fuelling of any more in the programme. Lines 1 and 2, moreover, put it that nuclear power should be terminated at a practicable pace, having regard to the amount of electric power that would be needed in order to maintain employment and the standard of living. The difference between Lines 1 and 2 was that the latter wanted the state and the municipalities to be in charge of the production and distribution of electric power, instead of the mixed-economy arrangements presently prevailing. At the end of the day Lines 1 and 2 received 58.2 per cent of the votes cast, divided 18.9 per cent and 39.3 per cent respectively, while Line 3 had 38.5 per cent. The balance of 3.3 per cent was accounted for by blank papers. This outcome was sufficient to enable the activation programme to carry on. Participation, it may be added, was markedly below the level at general elections – 74.3 per cent voted – and there were clearly a number of Social Democratic, Liberal and Conservatives supporters who followed Line 3, although not enough to swing the result.

THE FUTURE: STATE CORPORATISM OR WORKERS CORPORATISM?

Nuclear power was one of the main issues in the electoral campaign that led to the Social Democratic defeat in 1976. The other was the issue of worker funds which, in its original formulation at least, had more corporatist implications than any economic policy pursued by successive governments throughout the decade to combat the effects of economic recession. The original draft plan, evolved in 1975 by Rudolf Meidner of the LO Secretariat and usually referred to by his name, was enthusiastically endorsed by LO at a congress in the summer of 1976 and then stalled on by Olof Palme and the Social Democratic Party. At the time of the election in September 1976, therefore, the labour movement gave forth an uncertain sound on the issue, while the non-socialist parties campaigned fiercely in opposition to what they regarded as 'blue and yellow socialism' (after the colours of the Swedish national flag). Gunnar Nilsson, the chairman of LO, was in no doubt that all this contributed to the electoral defeat when he subsequently reflected while on holiday in Italy on what had happened, and electoral analysis has lent support to his view.[9] Contrary to expectation, the funds question was not an issue in the 1979 electoral campaign; it was shelved by both LO and the Social Democrats until *joint* studies had been completed. But it is certain to be at the centre of political controversy in the 1980s.

The genesis of this issue antedated the economic recession, but the recession has had an impact upon its evolution. The immediate cause can be traced to resolutions passed at the 1971 LO Congress calling for the siphoning off of excess profits from the most expansive sectors of the economy into institutions not under private control, if possible so as to increase worker influence over firms. Three separate motives can be disentangled here: first, a desire to combat an increasing inequality and concentration of economic power in the private sector; second, and in close alliance with this, a desire to press ahead again with the 'solidary' wages policy; and third, the pursuit of 'economic democracy'. As the recession began to bite, another motive began to feature more prominently: a wish to stimulate investment through collective saving.

A brief comment should perhaps be made at this point about the pursuit of 'economic democracy'. Steady pressure began to be exerted from 1970 onwards towards this end by both LO and TCO, the peak white-collar organisation. It sprang in part from growing worker resistance to plant closures for reasons of industrial rationalisation and to the heavy pressures in favour of labour mobility. It resulted in the use of legislative power to determine questions previously left for settlement to the collective bargaining process or to the discretion of the employer. Thus, statutes passed in 1974 greatly increased job security, for example. A series of enactments put worker/employee representatives on the boards of companies in the private and public sectors and also on the boards of administrative agencies. Finally, a sweeping Co-Determination Law of 1976 not only ended the monopoly of employers to direct work allocations and to hire and fire labour but made the nature and type of production a negotiable issue between unions and management and gave the union side the decisive voice in interpreting agreements reached. All these measures were put through before the Social Democrats left office: none of them met with opposition, except on details, from the non-socialist side.

The original Meidner funds scheme would have carried this shift in the power-balance so far onward as to raise the question of whether or not a mixed economy was to survive in Sweden at all. In bare essentials, it proposed that a fifth of the net profits of firms with over 50 employees should be allocated each year to a central fund run by the unions and their peak organisations, both white- and blue-collar. The yield on the funds was to be used, inter alia, to purchase shares. Via share-purchase, worker representatives would eventually reach a majority position at share-holders' meetings.

It is not surprising that this radical project should have put the cat among the pigeons. For one thing, it raised the question of whether the unions or the government should have the power to regulate capital formation and, ultimately, economic policy. The process of reworking the scheme has been long and convoluted and cannot be explored in the present context, but a final decision is scheduled to be taken by LO and the Social Democrats acting in concert in 1981. Meantime no fewer than seven different *provisional* projects have been submitted to a commission of enquiry in the field by the main political parties and interest organisations in the labour market. The one which has the joint approval of LO and the Social Democrats maintains the principles of centralised union-administered funds and the earmarking of profits but weakens the provisions implying a fundamental shift of control in the economy and links the yield on shares held to the strengthening of the national pensions funds. The non-socialist parties each have their own scheme, but all oppose centralised union-run funds and the earmarking of profits for them. Clearly the whole question, with all its implications for the growth of corporatism in Sweden, is set to be in the forefront of the 1982 electoral campaign.

CONCLUSIONS: THE SWEDISH ECONOMY IN THE 1980s

What, in conclusion, can be said of the outlook for Sweden in the 1980s? On the energy front, a major government bill is scheduled to be presented in January 1981 with proposals for reducing the country's heavy dependence on oil. Meanwhile an agreement has been reached with Denmark for the purchase of natural gas with effect from 1985 and negotiations are in progress with Norway to the same end. The development of new sources of energy at home – solar, peat, wood and so on – is under consideration in expert commissions of enquiry, but this is bound to be a slow and often costly process beset by technical problems (e.g. the effect of peat extraction upon hydrology). A special loan fund, however, is foreshadowed for promoting investments in research and development in this area. The ecology lobby has been strongly resisting the harnessing of four northern rivers for hydro power: these, it has been calculated, would increase energy resources from this source by roughly 50 per cent. In the longer term, the pressures against the phasing out of nuclear power would appear likely to increase rather than to diminish, despite the formulation of all three alternatives in the referendum of March 1980.

More immediately, the problems of heavy budget deficits, an adverse trade balance and inflationary pressures indicate a restrictive demand policy, a strenuous effort to expand market shares and possibly a further devaluation of the currency. On the credit side, there has been an increase in the willingness to invest; on the debit side, one result of the 1980 wage round and its attendant conflict has been to complicate the problem of maintaining market shares. Labour-market policy has also had its concealed costs, among them being labour hoarding and a tendency to under-emphasise progressive sectors. Thus a governmental commission report of March 1978 singled out communications technology, micro-electronics and bio-technology as three areas worth special study as possible targets for state assistance on the research and development front. Meanwhile non-socialist governments in particular face the difficult problem of attempting to set a limit to the growth of the public sector, with its locking effect upon labour mobility and ultimately upon Sweden's competitiveness in international markets.

These more imminent problems and difficulties appear likely to sharpen the debate between the proponents and opponents of greater collectivisation and centralisation within production. Those in favour of this trend would appear to have the current running with them at the moment; those who essentially put their trust in free-market mechanisms seem likely to counterbid with an appeal in favour of schemes, e.g. for employee shareholdings on an individual basis, in the hope that the prospect of individual profit will prove a more attractive inducement than the prospect of collective power. These wider issues will of course crystallise out when the funds question comes to the forefront in the 1982 electoral campaign.

POSTSCRIPT

Meanwhile, briefly to update this summary of trends and events up till August 1981, Swedish economic difficulties have intensified in the past year and with them the strains on the non-socialist administration – to the point at which the tripartite Fälldin II coalition burst asunder in May 1981. A docks strike following immediately after the costly labour market conflict in Spring 1980 both signified an unusual refusal to settle within the generally agreed norms and further dammed up exports awaiting shipment in the wake of the earlier conflict. This did nothing to improve the already sharply increasing adverse balance of payments deficit and, with foreign indebtedness beginning to approach the Danish level and a steep increase since 1979 in the budgetary deficit, the government called an extraordinary session of Parliament late in August 1980. It was the first time in four decades that such a step had been felt necessary. Here credit squeeze measures were combined with stiff increases in indirect taxation, VAT for example being pushed up by 1.9 per cent to 19 per cent. This naturally gave the inflationary pressures a further impetus, estimated in total to be in the region of 2.7 per cent. In September the Social Democrats moved the first ever vote of no-confidence in the Swedish government – the procedure had been introduced as part of the new Constitution in 1975. Predictably the result followed strict party lines and the government survived on a vote of 175 to 174, but the episode served as a demonstration. In the following month the government put through the first of what promised to be a series of annual retrenchment exercises. It involved, *inter alia*, cuts in food subsidies and schools grant, increases in rail fares (it had not been long since the railways had boosted their traffic by halving passenger fares), and the removal of fuel prices from the cost of living index used in connection with fixing the levels both of taxes and of social security benefits.

All this provided a dark background to the wages round early in 1981 but, despite initial noises from the union side to the effect that compensation would be sought for the fall that was taking place in living standards, the main settlement was reached in February speedily and at a modest level: a 7.1 per cent increase over a two-year period, with provision for compensation if the rate of inflation exceeded agreed levels in either of the two years. Superficially the climate on the labour market front appeared to be once more what it had been in 1977–8, but the hard economic times gave the government less room for manoeuvre in the provision of sweeteners for the necessary pills. However, in an effort to solve one of the knottier long-term problems, a bill was laid before Parliament in February seeking to reduce oil dependence from 70 per cent of fuel consumption to 40 per cent by 1990. This provided for a major switch to the use of coal, peat and forest products and, to a lesser extent, of solar power. It also authorised for the first time the extraction of uranium from domestic sources. On this last point the Centre and Communist Left parties lost out, but they were reconciled to the package by a declaration that the phasing out of nuclear power stations in accordance with the referendum decision would begin in the late 1990s, and that strict environmental and worker protection would prevail in connection with uranium mining. The argument on the other side was that the phasing out process would be eased by the substitution programme and by a substantial three-year project (costing 1.4 milliard Swedish crowns) for energy research. Provision was also made for a new State Fuel and Power Board, to begin operation in July 1982. Eventually the bill received general support after some amendments of detail, e.g. the tightening of the restrictions on sulphurous pollution from coal-fired plant.

The Fälldin administration disintegrated in May 1981 on the issue of a longer-term tax reform. Agreement was reached within the coalition early in the year on a three-year plan to cut the marginal rate of taxation, starting in 1982: the method of financing the reform was left open for discussion. Talks were promised with both sides of the labour market, but the union side expressed its hostility. In April the Centre and Liberal components of the coalition opened negotiations with the Social Democrats directly on the issue, and within a day agreement was reached. The indexation arrangements which had been brought in at the end of the 1970s were to go, thereby removing a source of friction with the unions; other means of providing a hedge against inflation were to be explored; marginal taxes were to be cut, but starting in 1983 – a year later than the original plan; the shortfall was to be financed by a levy on employers and/or a production factor tax (a Social Democratic electoral plank from the 1970s). Shortly after this agreement was reached, the Conservatives withdrew from the coalition amid recriminations with their former partners and disagreement about the precise nature of the original coalition tax-reform scheme. However, they did not press for fresh elections. The opinion polls had long been showing a majority for the combined parties of the Left. Accordingly, a minority Fälldin III coalition of the Centre and Liberal parties (10 Centre Ministers, 7 Liberals) was formed with every prospect of lasting out until the elections of September 1982.

Opinion polls conducted immediately after this crisis showed marked gains for the Social Democrats, to a point at which they would have been able to form a majority government; continued losses for the Centre and Liberals, to a point at which the Liberals were sinking uncomfortably close to the 4 per cent barrier on parliamentary representation; and a modest gain for the Conservatives, to approximately a quarter of the total electorate.

We come back in conclusion to the issue of worker funds. The official enquiry on this matter wound up in disagreement in May 1981, leaving the decision to be taken by the parties. The Centre and Liberals had reached agreement in the latter half of 1980 on the basis of accepting the principles of compulsory savings, individual shareholding and a variety of decentralised schemes. The Conservatives stick by voluntary savings schemes to be promoted by adjustments in the tax system. They thus wish, for example, to abolish the tax on shareholders' profits after 1–2 years' holding. The Social Democrats and the union movement agreed on a draft early in 1981 envisaging on increase in worker influence through shareholdings *faster* than in the original Meidner plan. They propose the formation of 24 funds at provincial level, to be financed partly by a 1 per cent increase in supplementary pensions charges and partly by a 20 per cent levy on *all* profits over 15–20 per cent. Clearly the battle-lines are being drawn up for a major confrontation on the issue in the September 1982 elections. On present evidence they appear likely to follow bloc lines, badly dented on the non-socialist side by the question of tax reform.

NOTES AND REFERENCES

1. Membership figures quoted in this paragraph are based on Elvander (1969) pp. 47–9.
2. Assar Lindbeck, *Swedish Economic Policy* (London: Macmillan, 1975) pp. 1–2, is the source of these figures and also of those immediately following.
3. This phase is explored at greater length in G. Ohlin, 'Sweden', in R. Vernon (ed.), *Big Business and the State* (Cambridge, Mass.: Harvard University Press, 1974).
4. OECD, *Economic Report* (1977) pp. 11–12.
5. N. Elvander, 'Organisationerna och staten på arbetsmarknaden i Sverige', *Tidskrift utgiven av Juridiska Föreningen i Finland*, vol. 5 (1978) p. 448.
6. Figures also from Elvander, ibid., p. 448.
7. OECD, *Economic Report* (April 1980) pp. 37–8, 40.
8. The course of events is exhaustively analysed in Vedung (1979); a somewhat less cursory account than that in the text of this present chapter will be found in Elder (1979).
9. O. Petersson (1977) pp. 214–31.

SELECT BIBLIOGRAPHY

Cerny, K. H. (ed.), *Scandinavia at the Polls* (Washington, D.C.: American Enterprise Institute, 1977).

Elder, N. C. M., 'Bipolarity or Indeterminacy in a Multi-Party System?', *Hull Papers in Politics*, no. 14 (University of Hull, 1979).

Elvander, N., *Intresseorganisationerna i dagens Sverige* (Lund: Gleerup, 1969).

Elvander, N., 'Organisationerna och staten på arbetsmarknaden i Sverige', *Tidskrift utgiven av Juridiska Föreningen i Finland*, vol. 5 (1978).

Elvander, N. *et al.*, *Sju Socialdemokrater om Löntagarfonderna* (Tiden, 1979).

Elvander, N., *Scandinavian Social Democracy: Its Strengths and Weaknesses* (Stockholm: Almqvist & Wiksell, 1979).

Korpi, W., *The Working Class in Welfare Capitalism: Work, Unions and Politics in Sweden* (London: Routledge & Kegan Paul, 1978).

Lindbeck, A., *Swedish Economic Policy* (London: Macmillan, 1975).

Lindbeck, A., *Fondfrågan* (Stockholm: Albaidé, 1979).

Meyerson, P. M., *Swedish Economy at the Crossroads* (Stockholm: Federation of Swedish Industries, 1979).

OECD, *Economic Reports: Sweden* (Paris: OECD, 1977, 1980).

Ohlin, G., 'Sweden', in R. Vernon (ed.), *Big Business and the State* (Cambridge, Mass.: Harvard University Press, 1974).

Petersson, O., *Valundersökningar, Rapport 2. Väljarna och valet 1976* (Stockholm: Statistiska Centralbyrån, 1977).
Ruin, O., 'Participatory Democracy and Corporativism: the Case of Sweden', *Scandinavian Political Studies 1974*, vol. 9, pp. 171–84.
Vedung, E., *Kärnkraften och regeringen Fälldins fall* (Stockholm: Raben and Sjögren, 1979).

4 The Netherlands: a Permissive Response

BRAM PEPER

INTRODUCTION

In all highly industrialised European countries prospects for economic growth in the 1980s are slight. The continuous increase of oil prices has created pessimism and uncertainty, reducing willingness to take any initiatives which contain risks. Apathy and anxiety for the future are prevalent.

The seventies have brought confusion on many fronts to the Netherlands.[1] There is the fear of becoming one of the swelling army of unemployed and the number of people who have become unemployable on the grounds of illness, unsuitability for work or for other reasons has grown enormously. The burden which this group is placing on the shoulders of the active professional population is starting to become unbearable. As a result the social security system – the heart of the Dutch welfare state – is threatened with erosion.

Organised interest groups moreover are unwilling to accept a voluntary incomes policy. Professional bodies, trade unions and other interest groups are therefore in conflict over the distribution of the national income. Employers and employed are increasingly in opposition to each other and a polarisation of attitudes is evident. Employers blame workers for refusing to moderate their wage demands, so that profits (which are so necessary for investment) are at an extremely low level. Workers accuse employers of seeking higher profits only to reduce further the size of the labour force and of failing to allow workers participation in investment decisions. The population as a whole is suffering the increasing burden of higher taxation which reduces their real disposable income. As a result, a 'black economy', with people avoiding taxation whenever they can, has developed. This large, informal 'black economy' is estimated to be worth tens of millions of guilders. Unfortunately the government has not been able to involve interest groups in a national policy for economic recovery. The only available solution, therefore, has been to reduce public expenditure.

While a similar situation can be observed in most other European countries, the Dutch case has its own peculiar problems. It is in the nature of things that all European countries are being hit by the decline in world trade, increases in oil prices, monetary crises and the uncertainty which characterises international politics. But individual circumstances differ greatly. For instance, the Netherlands is a very rich country while Britain, Denmark and Belgium are experiencing a relative national impoverishment. In the previous ten years the real national income in the Netherlands rose by 30 per cent, and while this was less than in the 1960s, it has been a remarkable record. Between 1970 and 1980 private consumption rose in volume by 40 per cent, real exports by 75 per cent. Additional economic indicators confirm this image of continuous prosperity (see Table 4.1). Yet a depression persists which is similar in essence to that of other European countries.

One can therefore ask whether the unmistakably international character of the recession leaves much freedom of manoeuvre for specially national political, social and economic structures? Are 'national' answers (within certain limits) possible and what can European countries learn from each other? Many academics and politicians see solutions through international collaboration but this writer is sceptical, because such an approach gives insufficient weight to the specific national character of the economic and political structures of any one country.

To describe the Dutch political and economical structure adequately or even to 'get the feel of it' is not possible within the confines of this paper. But I will try to give a brief insight into some of the major political and economic problems with which Dutch society is struggling, and alternative solutions under discussion. First, the influence of the recession on economic activities and economic structure will be examined. The recession has exposed a number of only partially perceived trends and economic weaknesses in the Dutch economy, which can perhaps form the starting point for a new economic policy. Secondly, since economic policies depend not only on broad economic trends but also on the perception of and reactions to these by the major political and social interest groups, their response will be discussed. Thirdly, the way in which the government has reacted to the often opposing demands and ideas which have accompanied economic stagnation will be discussed. On the whole the independent influence of the government on the conduct of social-economical factors has not been large. The government is dependent for policy on the tacit or voluntary agreement of all sorts of social groups, and although it does have some scope for a

TABLE 4.1 Some Historical Indicators (annual averages, percentage changes unless otherwise specified)

	1966–71	*1972–8*	*1972–3*	*1974–5*	*1976–7*	*1978*[a]
Total economy						
GDP	5.3	2.9	4.6	1.3	3.4	2.5
Current balance (£ billion)	−0.1	1.3	1.8	2.0	1.5	−1½
Employment	0.9	0.2	0.1	0.6	0.0	0.0
Unemployment (% labour force)	1.7	4.3	2.9	4.2	5.3	5.2
Consumer prices	5.0	8.3	8.7	10.0	8.1	4.1
Enterprise sector[b]						
Output	5.9	3.3	5.3	1.4	3.7	2.5
Employment	0.5	−0.6	−0.8	−0.7	−0.4	−0.3
Productivity per head	5.2	3.9	6.0	2.0	4.3	2.7
Unit labour costs[c]	5.9	7.7	7.5	12.1	5.0	4½
Wage share[d]	63.3	66.9	65.4	68.3	67.1	66.5
Manufacturing industry						
Output	6.4	2.1	5.3	−2.2	3.9	1½
Employment	−0.6	−2.7	−2.5	−1.9	−3.3	−2½
Productivity	7.0	5.0	8.0	−0.4	7.7	4.0
Compensation per employee	11.6	12.1	15.0	13.9	9.9	7.5
Unit labour costs[c]	4.3	6.8	6.5	14.4	2.1	3½
Relative unit labour costs[e]	0.0	1.9	3.8	0.5	1.0	3.0
Market share[f]	5.0	5.5	5.7	5.9	5.2	4.9
Trade balance, excluding gas[g]	—	−2.6	0.6	−1.7	−3.8	−8.4
Gross fixed investment[h]	6.2	−2.5	−8.1	−6.3	4.6	5.0
Investment share[hi]	21.8	16.9	17.8	17.2	15.6	17.0
Wage share	69.8	77.5	71.5	77.7	81.3	81½
Memorandum:						
Natural gas production	—	—	64,627	87,289	97,100	90,000

a Estimates.
b Whole economy, excluding government sector.
c Wages and salaries plus employers' social security contributions per unit of output.
d Wages, salaries and employers' social security contributions as a percentage of national income originating in the sector.
e Increase in £ unit labour costs in excess of trade-weighted average of the increase in £ unit labour costs in major trading partners.
f Share of Dutch exports of manufactures in imports of six most important trading partners.
g £ billion.
h Total industry.
i Percentage of national income originating in total industry.
j Million cubic metres.

SOURCE Central Planning Bureau, Central Economisch Plan 1978, Nationale Rekeningen 1977, and OECD, Paris, Secretariat estimates

policy of its own, its willingness to take unpopular – if necessary – steps is limited by the need to face the judgment of voters at general elections. Fourthly, some attention will be focused on whether or not there are any new policies or ideas in the Netherlands which offer a prospect for the solution of the economic problems specified. It is argued that each individual country is capable of contributing to its own recovery. Finally, it is contended that it may well be that conventional solutions – recovery of economic growth and an end to unemployment – are illusory and that totally different social relationships and solutions are necessary.

THE INFLUENCE OF THE RECESSION ON THE ECONOMY[2]

In analysing the economic problems and possibilities facing the Netherlands in the 1970s and 1980s one has to realise that the Netherlands is a comparatively young industrial nation. Although there were already large industrial, internationally orientated firms working in the Netherlands before the Second World War (Royal Dutch, Philips, Unilever), industrialisation in the Netherlands has really only taken off since the last War. Until that time the Netherlands concentrated on traditional trading and industrial activities, supported by an extensive colonial empire (Indonesia). Further more, agriculture and the export of agricultural products were a major element is the economy. The expansion of the Dutch economy after the War (growth of industry and decline of employment in the agrarian sector)[3] can be associated with a number of factors, such as:

(a) a favourable geographical location at the mouth of the Rhine, with Germany as the most important hinterland

(b) the existence of a good commercial infra-structure with an international orientation

(c) the existence of peaceful social relationships especially between employers and employees, as a result of which a controlled development of wages at a low level was possible

(d) the development of an educational and research capacity which made it possible to compete internationally.

This summary is certainly not exhaustive. If one were to characterise the structure of the Dutch economy, then the following images prevail

- a highly developed industrial sector, electro-techniques, electrical engineering, metallurgical industry (foundries), chemical works, which are overly directed towards exports;
- a highly developed commercial sector, which has traditional, historic links with Empire and also with the enormous international trade in and around Rotterdam – the largest sea-port in the world – and Amsterdam;
- a highly developed and export-orientated agricultural, foods and allied-products industry.

With hindsight, one can argue that the fact that wage levels in the Netherlands were lower than those in comparative industrial countries until about 1964 was an important brake to the further diversification and specialisation of the structure of Dutch production. As a result development in the economy took the form of expansion in existing industries rather than through investment in new industries. In a recent publication of the Scientific Council for Government Policy post-war industrialisation – in terms of specialisation pattern and capitalisation – has been characterised as follows

- large scale in contrast with small scale;
- one-sided specialisation in contrast with pluriform;
- volume in contrast with differentially refined;
- intermediary in contrast with capital goods;
- process skill in contrast with 'engineering' skill.

When the Netherlands had adjusted its wage levels to those of surrounding countries at the end of the 1960s, the discovery of enormous supplies of natural gas gave a new momentum to economic growth. There were however, as early as this, the first symptoms of a decline in trade. Some sectors of industry were not able to stand up to international competition and a number of large firms went bankrupt and there were mass redundancies. One reason for this was that the national enrichment brought about by natural gas led, in retrospect, to a slackening in the field of industrial innovations: Dutch exports did not really change in composition, although natural gas did become a stimulant for the energy-intensive branches of industry.

It is therefore understandable that the 1973 oil crisis was seen as a major problem in the Netherlands. Many production processes are dependant on oil as a raw material, while the advantages of natural gas for energy using industries began to diminish due to the failure to index the price of natural gas to the price of oil immediately. The Netherlands could only hope to earn back an important part of the deficit caused by the increase in oil prices by charging a higher price in the export market for natural gas.

Not only an increased oil bill but a number of unfavourable economic indicators reveal how the Dutch economy has developed in the period from 1970–80. There has been a general decline in *economic growth*. Economic growth at the beginning of the 1970s was still at about 4–5 per cent. After 1973 the growth rate declined, recording at its lowest point a negative growth (–0.5 per cent) in 1975 rising to level of 2–3 per cent, declining again to an estimated annual rate of 0.5–1 per cent for 1980. This decline in growth has not been without consequences for *work opportunities*. Unemployment has risen from 1.4 per cent in 1970 to over 6 per cent in 1980. When we add to these figures unemployment which lies hidden in the application of the General Disablement Benefit Act and the National

Assistance Act, then actual unemployment could be as high as 10 per cent. Furthermore, unemployment is higher among certain categories of the population, such as youngsters, women and foreign employees. It is also higher in certain regions in the north, east and south of the country; and the unemployment in the big cities (Rotterdam, Amsterdam) is higher than the country's average, due to the concentration of one or more of the population groups just mentioned. Employment opportunities have declined especially in the industrial sector, while the opportunities in the public (government) sector and the non-commercial sectors chiefly financed by the government (such as health and welfare services) have grown strongly. *Inflation* in the 1970s began with a rate that was high for the Netherlands of about 8 per cent, rising in the middle of that period to 10 per cent afterwards declining to about 6 per cent through the application of anti-inflation policies. Owing to the second increase in oil prices in 1979 the expectation is that inflation will go up to 7 per cent in 1980.

Underlying these unfavourable indicators are a number of fundamental economic causes. First of all, in relation to *expenditure*, private consumption has been growing strongly throughout the whole period. This can be ascribed to increases in wages and in real income; to the levelling in income differentials; to the growth of incomes transfers; and to the increased credit facilities available through the banks. Secondly, although industrial investment has witnessed considerable fluctuation, overall it is still at 1970 levels, while production has risen by 30 per cent. This means, therefore, that capital formation has lagged behind. The rise in the *cost of wages* has been considerable in the 1970s. The level of the wage costs has risen more in the Netherlands – with the exception of Belgium – than in the other countries of the Common Market. The cost of wage rises was however insufficiently compensated for by a rise in labour productivity, so that the development in the cost of wages per unit product also deteriorated with regard to other EC countries. This has contributed to an overall decline in *profitability of industries* with all the consequences thereof to investment capacity.

Another pointer to the weakening wealth structure of firms is the ratio between loan and reinvested capital. Of the limited companies registered on the Stock Exchange loan capital increased from 56 to 64 per cent of total capital. Another factor which has attacked the competitive capacity of Dutch firms is the continuing *appreciation of the guilder*. Until the end of the 1970 and the beginning of the 1980s the Netherlands experienced considerable surplusses on the current account of the balance of payments. In 1970 the deficiency on the current account was 1.6 per cent of the national income, between 1972 and 1976 surplusses were at 3–4 per cent, while in 1978 and 1979 deficiencies of 0.5–1 per cent were recorded. The cost advantages resulting from cheaper imports have not however offset the competitive disadvantages to exports experienced from the dearer guilder. As a result the competitive power of trade and industry has declined globally by 10–20 per cent in the 1970s. *Increases in taxation and social security contributions* have also become a burden for industry, increasing the size of the so-called collective sector from 41 per cent of national income in 1970 to 54 per cent in 1979. Furthermore, the fact that wage increases are nearly totally indexed to the price level has put into motion a wage and price spiral, which has affected the profits position of firms. Finally, the State budget has also come under pressure, experiencing a financing shortage (or public sector borrowing requirement) of nearly 6 per cent.

The best summary of the state of affairs can be seen in the previously mentioned report of the Scientific Council for Government policy. The conclusions are as follows

(a) Work opportunity has not kept pace with the development of labour supply. Unemployment rose from 1.4 per cent in 1970 to over 6 per cent in 1980. With hidden unemployment (social security) the actual figure is around 10 per cent. The only sectors showing growth in work opportunity were the State, the non-commercial services and the local services – the so-called *quaternary sector*.

(b) The specialisation pattern of the Dutch economy has not really changed. The trade branches, agriculture, foods and allied products industry and the intermediary sector remain the dominant export industries. However problems have arisen inside the last sector (i.e. base metals and petroleum) such as a drop in production volume, under-staffing and falling investment quotas. There is talk of *de-industrialisation* in the Netherlands, due to a declining share of industry in the volume of production.

(c) The competitive power of Dutch trade and industry has declined. This can be attributed to the developments in wage rates, including social charges (rates and taxes), and to the continuing increase in the value of the guilder.

(d) Wage costs in industry have risen more quickly in the Netherlands in comparison with other European countries.

(e) One can speak of an increasing market penetration in the Netherlands. All industrial branches are being confronted with a falling domestic market share. That applies very strongly to the textile, clothing and shoe industries, while the electro-technical industry is also experiencing a decline in its share of the domestic market. Import penetration is also very strong in consumption commodities.

(f) In the second half of the 1970s Dutch exports also declined. The heavy concentration of Dutch exports in European markets resulted in a decline in foreign sales due to the decline in economic growth in these countries.

Insufficient compensation has been found in other foreign markets.
(g) The worsening profitability position of firms, and also the slow growth of production has negatively influenced the development of investments. The investment volume of factory buildings went down in the period 1970–6 by 21 per cent, while investment in equipment (plant) only rose again above the level of 1970 in 1977. Investments were becoming more and more for replacement rather than innovation and expansion.
(h) The financial position of trade and industry has weakened. Several branches of industry have a labour income's quota of above 100 per cent.

THE REACTION OF IMPORTANT POLITICAL AND SOCIAL MOVEMENTS TO THE RECESSION

Politics: in general

The Netherlands experienced an exceptional stable political climate until the middle of the 1960s. The political system was based on the existence of three large ideological groups: Catholics, Protestants and Socialists, of which the followers respectively totalled over 30 per cent, almost 30 per cent and around 25 per cent of the electorate. Because a large part of other social activities also took place *within* these different circles – known as columnisation – the political-social climate could be considered *rigid*.[4]

Since 1966 a process of decolumnisation began in Dutch society. In other words: it became less a matter of fact that a Catholic voted for the Catholic Party, a Protestant for a Protestant Party. The reasons for this decolumnisation were varied. No doubt the process of industrialisation with accompanying urbanisation has played an important role. Young people especially were less sensitive to the ties imposed from the factions, and the authority of the older generation began to wane (for example see the Provo-movement). Another factor was the expansion of prosperity and communication which made people socially and geographically more mobile, so that they could withdraw from traditional social ties. Similarly, the movement towards democratisation which swept over Europe around 1968–9 has not been without consequences for the social-political climate in the Netherlands. One can speak of an intensification of political activity, especially on the left. As a result, activities outside parliament have increased in importance, with many thousands of *community and action groups* coming into existence.

The Netherlands therefore entered the 1970s in a climate of heightened political activitism. Because the younger generation is more politically active, a greater sensitivity has been generated for new economic problems. Increasingly, environmental and pollution questions are seen as threatening the quality of life, especially in the western part of the Netherlands, where the density of population and political activism is highest. A widening of interest in and discussion of the costs of the economic growth (Mishan) has also developed. The report of the Club of Rome probably had its greatest influence, except for Japan, in the Netherlands and the need for a more frugal lifestyle has been proselytised by different political and social groups (amongst them the churches), especially on behalf of the developing countries. The problems of the Third World have become of intense interest, and this is the reason why the Netherlands still has, percentage-wise, the highest amount of foreign aid in its budget. Indeed, when the 1973 oil crisis hit the Netherlands – due to strong support for Israel – many Dutch people were mentally prepared for it, as indicated by the relative cheerfulness with which petrol rationing and 'carless' Sundays were accepted.

Politics: specifically

The major political parties however reacted rather differently to the discussion about the disadvantages of economic growth and to the stagnation which actually came to the fore after 1973.

The progressive parties

In 1966 a new political movement came into existence – Democrats '66 (D66) – which advocated a new political order, detached from the traditional basis for party formation in the Netherlands. This movement quickly obtained about 5 per cent of the electorate. D66 wanted a radical democratisation of society, political emancipation for the population and new economic development to be concerned foremost with issues of environmental quality. In 1968 radicals left the Catholic People's Party (KVP) to form the Radical People's Party (PPR), which advocated an even more radical approach to the environment, economic growth and Third World problems. The PPR claimed about 3–4 per cent of the electorate and even progressive protestants were able to join what was now a non-sectarian political party. These two new parties, together with the large Labour Party (PvdA), formed the core of a progressive alliance, which stood at the 1972 elections on a platform in which the environment question, the problems of the developing countries and the decline in economic growth were pre-eminent. A special committee created by the three parties – which comprised prominent politicians, such as Pronk (Minister of Development Co-operation, 1973–7), Den Uyl (Prime Minister, 1973–7) and Mansholt (ex-chairman of the European Commission) – published a report in 1972 in which many of these new ideas were outlined. The influence of the Club of Rome was clearly evident in this report.

The PvdA, the largest party in the coalition cabinet led by Den Uyl, also committed itself to a course of selective growth because it had accepted by 1975 the consequences of lower growth after 1973 more quickly than the other major parties. At the end of the Den Uyl cabinet's period in office in 1977 there was a clear commitment to a policy of income restraint and erosion of income differentials in order to maintain the size of the public sector, and move towards an equalisation of incomes between the employed and unemployed in the population. In a recently prepared draft election programme for the period 1981–5, priority is to be given to the fight against unemployment (through the use of part-time jobs and reduced working hours), secondly to the maintenance of the public sector and only finally to the maintenance of the purchasing power of the 'average worker', and if the latter – due to low growth – cannot be maintained, then assistance is to be given to those who are dependent on a minimum wage or upon social security.

The Christian parties

These parties – consisting of the large Catholic People's Party (KVP) and the smaller, though almost as large, orthodox Protestant Anti-Revolutionary Party (ARP) and liberal-protestant Christian-Historical Union (CHU) – were somewhat dilatory in their acceptance of the problems associated with lower economic growth when compared with the progressive parties. Eventually however – due in part to the influence of church interests – the need to embrace the concepts of selective growth, austerity and additional aid for the Third World was accepted. In practice however, because their electorate is pluriform (consisting of employers, employees, farmers and middle-class shopkeepers and tradespeople) they were less prepared to support the egalitarian policy consequences which flowed from these concepts, unlike the progressive parties.

The Conservative Party

The Conservative Party, the People's Party for Freedom and Democracy (VVD) experienced solid growth in the 1970s and has opted for a policy of continued economic growth. The basic policy goal of the VVD is to ensure control of wage costs so that profits can expand, allowing re-investment to reduce unemployment eventually and end the recession.

Electoral developments

The economic and social changes which have taken place in Dutch society since the middle of the 1960s have also resulted in shifts in support for the political parties. In general interest in politics has increased; the rescinding of the obligation to vote has not reduced political participation. Indeed by the end of the 1960s, and the beginning of the 1970s an intensification of political conflict has been apparent. The progressive parties have conducted a policy of political non-cooperation with the political centre, which represented mainly by the Christian Parties over the last decades has dominated politics and has held power. The progressive parties have refused for some time to work with the conservatives, and since 1958 the conservatives have refused to form a government with the Labour Party (PvdA). However, the dismemberment of the Christian parties through the erosion of traditional factions and the radicalisation of the social and political environment has greatly assisted the progressive parties. Furthermore many right-wing christians have left their traditional party to join the Conservative Party. As a result there has been a growth of the left and right in the 1970s and a polarisation in Dutch politics.

In 1967 the three Christian parties still held 69 (i.e. 44.5 per cent) of the 150 seats in Parliament; in 1971 that number had shrunk to 58 (36.8 per cent); in the 1972 elections they gained only 48 seats (31.3 per cent); and in an electoral system based on proportional representation. The Labour Party has developed from 37 seats (23.5 per cent) in 1967, through 39 (24.7 per cent) in 1971 to 43 seats (27.3 per cent) in 1972. Adding these Labour seats to those of the two new, smaller progressive parties – D66 and PPR – the progressive parties gained a total of 56 seats in 1972. The conservatives lost one seat between 1967 and 1971 (from 17 to 16) but in the polarised climate at the beginning of the 1970s they have now won 22 seats.

In 1973 a Cabinet was formed which had a progressive majority for the first time but it had a weak parliamentary basis – due to the polarisation of politics in the Netherlands. Only two of the three Christian parties – KVP and ARP had ministers in the Cabinet and the support from Parliament was not therefore wholehearted for the new government. Despite this the Labour Party which had not been in office since 1958 – apart from a short interlude of a year and a half (1965–6) – was keen to push through a progressive reform programme under pressure from a radical rank and file.

The progressive Cabinet was in office for almost four years and the subsequent elections of 1977 led to large gains for the Labour Party: it increased its seats in Parliament from 43 to 53 – the greatest election victory ever achieved in Dutch political history. D66 gained 8 seats (after having been in electoral decline) and the PPR managed to retain only 3 seats. As a result however the progressives increased their total number of seats from 56 in 1972 to 64 in 1977. The Christian parties tried with some success to halt their decline by entering into co-operation with one another, which led ultimately to the creation in 1980 of one Christian-Democrat Party (CDA). In 1977 they gained 49 seats compared with 48 seats in 1972. Finally, the smaller parties on the left and on the right were totally ignored by the electorate.

Despite the gains made by the progressives, however, they did not maintain control of the cabinet and, at the end of 1977, a Conservative–Christian-Democratic alliance formed a cabinet under Van Agt. This new government had the support of 77 of the 150 members of Parliament. Political tensions have therefore not abated because while the cabinet may have a majority in Parliament it lacks the support of the working class which is essential if it is to tackle the social-economic problems facing the Netherlands.

Society: in general

Growing political tensions in the Netherlands are a reflection of deeper social divisions. In many fields between the end of the sixties and the beginning of the seventies there was growing confusion: the universities were experiencing radicalisations; innumerable environmental action groups were created; and there were similar radical developments in housing, abortion and women's liberation. The chuches were also increasingly active in social issues. Nuclear energy became a contentious issue despite a growing shortage of oil, and citizens have become more and more concerned with government policymaking. Various groups that were normally politically quiescent have undertaken militant forms of civil disobedience, such as blockades (i.e. inland waterworkers, farmers, filling-station managers and truck drivers). These groups – which if not right-wing certainly have anti-progressive leanings – were especially active during Den Uyl's period in office.

Direct political activism has not slackened however in recent years. Increasing tensions in society – the result of the growing discrepancy between aspirations, vested interests and reduced economic possibilities – are leading to an intensification of the political struggle between various socio-economic groups and interests. The growing housing shortage – exacerbated by the existence of a large number of unoccupied houses – has generated a squatters' movement which is totally illegal. The threat of atomic energy and the neutron bomb has created a mass movement in which all sorts of church groups (which have connections with the Christian-Democratic Party) actively participate. Similarly, the implementation of voluntary and statutory incomes policies – which have tended to erode income differentials – has led to permanent conflict between the government and many groups of professional people (doctors, specialists, notaries, and so on).

In order to indicate fully the problems facing the Netherlands in the 1970s we must now concentrate on the relationships between the two most important actors in the social-economic field: the employers and workers. These two groups play a decisive role, at the national level, in the various possible 'responses' to the recession and also in the possibilities of their successful implementation.

Society: specifically[5]

Trade unions

At the end of the 1960s the historically quiescent, centrally directed, trade-union federations became more politically active. Worker discontent increased, not only due to wage demands, but also because of the threat of unemployment through mass redundancy. Similarly there was a general trend towards democratisation of union structures in line with rank-and-file attitudes. This fuelled opposition to the 1970 Wages Formation Act, which limited the recently acquired freedom to negotiate wage rates, if the government decided that restraint was in the national economic interest.

In 1970 wild-cat strikes broke out in the port of Rotterdam and in the shipbuilding industry. The strikes were so massive that they could hardly be contained by the trade unions and this indicated that a division had developed between the leadership and members of the trade unions. Increasingly a faction of paid union leaders has grown up and is critical of society. As a result industries where trade unions were never firmly established (unlike in England, Germany, France and Scandinavia) are now seeing the development of groups of active union members, and the trade union movement as a whole is becoming steadily more active, as indicated by the large and successful strikes in 1971 in the building and metallurgical industries. These new antagonisms led in 1973 to a steel strike; the major issue revolved around the erosion of pay differentials as between salaried employees and wage labourers, but the strike largely failed.

Because the Den Uyl government was basically well disposed towards the trade unions, the incidence of strikes fell between 1973 and 1977. The government was prepared to offer the trade unions many of the policies that they desired (including policies for capital profit sharing and proposals to enlarge the role of works councils). It was not until 1977 that worker organisations found themselves once more in conflict with employers; this time over the attempt by employers to abolish the automatic indexation of pay to prices introduced in 1969–70, by which the workers protected their standards of living against inflation. The massive strikes which flowed from this resulted in a victory for the workers. The outcome was very different in 1978, when strikes were called to support the demand that job protection should be written into collective contracts. Employers refused to give this guarantee and in the end the workers had to call off their strikes. The workers did not fare much better in 1979 when they attempted, through strikes, to shorten the working week as one solution to the problem of mounting unemployment. The trade unions' idea was to begin a process of reducing working hours so that by 1984 the 36-hour working week would be a reality. In some cases the issue revolved around whether the shift system should be changed from four to five and result therefore in a 34-hour working week. Only on a few occasions was this goal successfully achieved.

Underlying these broad trends was the fact however that the Catholic and Socialist Trade Unions (which together have more than one million members) were becoming increasingly co-operative, while the Protestant-orientated Trade Union (which has roughly 300,000 members) was increasingly isolated. This co-operation, which is remarkable in Dutch trade-union relationships, is expected in the future to result in the complete merger of these two organisations into one body known as the Dutch Trade Unions Federation (FNV). This body, with the Protestant Trade Union (CNV), organises about 32 per cent of the total labour force in the Netherlands. Despite increased militant action by the largest trade union – FNV – this did not however lead to a total lack of awareness of the problems facing the national economy. Although the government had to concede a number of policies to the trades unions, all of these unions remained prepared to accept a certain responsibility for the prosperous development of the Dutch economy. Four times in 1971, 1974 and twice in 1976 the government imposed wages and incomes restraint and this was accepted, if under protest.

The trade unions however have always made their acceptance of moderation in wage claims dependent on the willingness of the government and employers to give the workers more participation in both workers' councils and investment decisions, and a commitment on job protection. Trade unions have also called for profit-sharing for the community in those companies seen as making excessive profits – the basic goal being the creation of a state-controlled fund to improve pensions. Dutch trade unions however are still, despite these goals, very sensitive to macro-economic arguments and since 1975 they have contributed to the fight against inflation by attuning their initial wage demands to what is economically possible. Despite this there are different opinions about whether or not this moderation in pay claims has been sufficient. According to employers and many economists the trade unions have not shown sufficient moderation. Furthermore it is argued that the decentralisation and democratisation of the decision-making structure for pay makes it difficult to agree on one national rate for pay increases. As a result, due in part to the difference in profitability of different sectors of industry, a total lack of national co-ordination arises, with national wage levels following the highest wage rates set in the most profitable sectors.

Over the last decade, then, although Dutch trade unions have become more militant in their bargaining with employers and have acquired increasing influence with management, they are ultimately responsible and willing to give careful consideration to national economic interests. Despite this, the willingness of the largest trade unions to accept moderation in policy goals has led to a certain fragmentation amongst the institutions representing workers. The Christian Trade Union (CNV) is willing to pursue even more moderate policies and a 'white-collar union' (which grew from 30,000 members in 1973 to 140,000 members in 1980) has developed in response to the impact on the middle-class of erosion of pay differentials induced by the policies of the largest unions. Notwithstanding this fragmentation Dutch trade unions have certainly accepted in the 1970s that economic decline must lead to a limitation in wage demands. They have therefore increasingly fought for non-material goals, such as the quality of working, workers participation, guarantees of job security, a shortening of the working week and participation in investment decisions. The difficulty however is that the employers in general do not support these demands, and the current centre-right Cabinet shares this antipathy. As a result the possibility of a social contract covering these goals in return for further wage restraint appears illusory.

Employers' organisations

Traditionally employers' organisations have been less monolithic than the trade unions, due to the fact that employers' interests and positions are rather different to those of workers. Businessmen can be in all types of markets and in competition with one another so that solidarity amongst employers has traditionally been weak. This image was however only valid until 1970, before which workers activities, or the threat of them – although rare – soon led to the appearance of divisions in the stance of the employers.

Since 1970 employers' organisations have gradually developed a more offensive attitude in response to worker militancy associated with the wave of strikes at the beginning of the 1970s. The move by employers from a defensive to an offensive stance was expressed in a number of ways:

- a firm attachment to their own bargaining stance, even when this resulted in strikes;
- a move to a more directive role in negotiations, on top of the normal process of consultations;
- a professionalisation of administration, administrative machinery and publicity;
- the creation of a defensive fund to help members hit by strikes;
- a willingness to use civil judges in resolving conflicts.

Furthermore at the end of the 1960s two large central unions, the Christian employers union (NCW) and a neutral union (VNO) were formed through the merger of smaller employers' organisations. These unions have worked together in a number of spheres, but especially in the co-ordination of a policy for conditions of work and pay, which has led to the development of a harder line being taken against workers.

This tougher bargaining stance has been generated due to increased demands by workers: now, on top of increased wage demands, workers' organisations are in pursuit of policies which are seen to affect the freedom of management within the firm. Thus, added to material conflicts are internal organisational and decision-making conflicts which have increased the cohesion and resilience of employers' which have increased the cohesion and resilience of employers' organisations. The fierce resistance to the reform of the Industrial Council (a consultative body), national sharing of profits, guarantees of job security and the shortening of the working week are examples of this new-found offensive attitude and ideological conflict with workers. Unfortunately this has not made the task of finding solutions to pressing social-economic problems any easier. Particularly because employers' organisations see the restoration of profits as the only means to restore prosperity and job prospects.

In conclusion it can be argued that employers' organisations have gained in power in the last ten years by rallying their forces. Organisation structures have been strengthened, internal cohesion of policy has been increased and the commitment by members to overall policy has grown. Publicly therefore employers have taken on an offensive role.

The relationships between employers and workers

At the national level for the first twenty-five years since the war there were intensive contacts between employers and workers. Co-operation has been seen by many commentators as a decisive factor in post-war economic growth. This co-operation has been embedded in many types of bipartite organs and incorporative consultative structures, of which the Social Economic Council (with its many committees) is the most important. Through these bodies policy formulation by co-operation between social partners has been possible and a role in policy implementation by the government afforded. These consultative relationships between employers, workers and the government promoted a useful compromise over national-economic goals through discussion of sectional interests.

The deterioration of relations between employers and employees which occurred around 1970 also had serious consequences for this institutionalised co-operation. Before this however – especially after 1968 when employers and workers were freed from their shared responsibility for wages policy with the government under the *free wage policy* – a more detached, businesslike relationship had already begun to develop. The conflicts which occurred after 1970 strengthened this growing militant attitude on the part of the social partners, as co-operation and consultation was replaced with detachment and strikes. This trend was mirrored in the Social-Economic Council, with fewer unanimous policy recommendations forthcoming after 1970.

Nevertheless the inherent centralism within Dutch social-economic policymaking forces the social partners to arrive at *central agreements* in wages almost every year. But there has not been one single year recently in which these discussions have resulted in clear guidelines for the unions or for the employers involved. At first sight this might appear strange because it might be thought that the economic problems of the recession would lead everyone to agree on the need for a common, central policy. But now that economic growth is stagnant *problems of income distribution* between different groups have become more problematical. The growth of ideological and militant tendencies in Dutch society had added a political dimension to the struggle between workers and employers, which before 1970 was not evident. Ironically therefore as the necessity to co-operate and to make central agreements becomes 'objectively' more pressing, the growing polarisation of interests in the Netherlands undermines this reality.

Despite this, there still exists an extensive network of corporatist consultative bodies, where the social partners are able to discuss problems of common interest and attempt to formulate long-term policies. Thus, though the national consultative machinery has been affected by this polarisation it still continues to operate, especially in the settlement of wages policy. Furthermore it was recently decided not to alter the structure of the Social-Economic Council – the symbol of consultation and corporatism – with regard to its tasks, composition and procedures. The tradition of, and the necessity for, national-economic consultation is still accorded a significant place in the Netherlands.

GOVERNMENT POLICY

By the beginning of the 1970s there was a realisation of the declining economic situation and poor prospects as inflation rose and some branches of industry went into deficit. As a consequence the central-right coalition of Christian-Democrats and Conservatives under Biesheuvel (1971–2) used the 1970 Bill for Wage Negotiations to impose statutory wage restraint, which brought the government into conflict with the trade unions. Unfortunately once incomes restraint was rescinded wage rates increased dramatically with two detrimental effects: inflation continued to rise and the trade unions developed a grudge against the government because in the past in the Netherlands corporate and pseudo-corporate relationships between the government and interest groups were instituted only to be undermined by the one-sided statutory action by the government on wage levels, with other interests avoiding government intervention.

The centre-left cabinet under Den Uyl which was formed in 1973 as a partial reaction to this was however soon confronted with the oil crisis. Because of this the cabinet introduced an Enabling Act which imposed restraint on all incomes (wages, interests, rents, dividends and tariffs), but which received wide public support due to the exceptional circumstances being experienced. When the initial oil crisis was quickly resolved this statutory policy was repealed and in fact it only operated in 1974. But it became apparent that the growth of the public sector, which, through the extension of the social-security system, had grown to 55 per cent of national income and which would rise above 60 per cent if there was no change in policy, would have to be restrained. Thus 1975 saw the beginning of a policy aimed at *lower growth* in the public sector (known as the 1 per cent policy). Similarly, a restrictive stance on wages was adopted and when negotiations between employers and workers broke down in 1976, through fear that negotiations at branch level would result in excessive wage demands, the progressive government twice intervened. This intervention was not confined to wages but extended to incomes generally: a nominal rise in incomes was allowed for everybody on top of the normal indexation of wages to inflation, so that there was a levelling effect on income differentials.

Little was achieved in the U-turn of policy for the public sector before the Den Uyl cabinet lost office in March 1977. This political defeat led to a long delay in the formation of a cabinet after the elections in May 1977, eventually, in December 1977, a centre-right cabinet under Van Agt was formed. In June 1980 this more restrictive cabinet published a plan for the government's period in office until 1981, with the aim of further reducing the size of the public sector in favour of higher profits for trade and industry. It was hoped that this policy would reduce the expected unemployment rate of 275–300,000 in 1981 to 150,000 (at the time of writing – Winter 1980 – the effective rate was 320,000). Of the ten million guilders which were to be pruned from anticipated public expenditure plans, one-third was to be raised through curbing government expenditures directly and two-thirds through a reduction in transfers and redistribution through the social security system. Similar measures had been introduced in this field under the former government: cuts in the anticipated growth of some government-expenditure plans; a cut in the growth of civil-servants' salaries which had been index-linked to the average wage rises in trade and industry; and small adjustments in social-security payments.

The deflationary policy has had to suffer opposition from within Dutch society, in particular from progressive voters and the trade unions, and the difficulties facing the government – of whatever ideological persuasion – are immense. In particular, because social-welfare payments have been linked to the *statutory minimum wage*, the government's budget faces permanent upward pressure due to negotiations in trade and industry. When, at the end of 1979, the government could not reach agreement with employers and workers about a moderate increase in wages of 0.5–1 per cent, it was decided to impose a statutory incomes policy which gave only a nominal increase to everyone. Unfortunately the policy has not proven successful due to the large increase in oil prices in 1979. As a result, government expenditure has hardly been reduced at all, many interests groups are preparing to defend their existing roles and unemployment has continued at an unacceptably high level.

It is therefore true that, irrespective of the ideology of the goverment, the public sector has continued to grow constantly throughout the 1970s, as a percentage of national income. Even the conservatives, who also announced their intention in 1977 of reducing government expenditure substantially, have not succeeded in this task. Furthermore, throughout the period the government has continually rescued industries and branches of industry whenever they have collapsed (for example in textiles, steel and shipbuilding). Individual grants for tax relief have also risen in recent years to millions of guilders, but the present government wishes to end this indiscriminate subsidy to declining industries by creating corporations at a central level and in certain threatened regions to reorganise the economy – although with little success to date. This goal has been supported by the fact that the recession has revealed that the regional economic policy pursued since the war has been a failure: the declining regions have continued to decline with little prospect of growth. As a result since the government's 1976 memorandum on *Selective Growth*[6] investment options have become less indiscriminate and more centrally directed to national goals. The Investments Accounts Bill (WIR) for example has given an extra investment premium for depressed regions to stimulate labour-intensive developments and small businesses. Furthermore the memorandum on selective growth seeks to stimulate export industries. But the Selective Investments Account (SIR: a combination of taxation and grants), aimed at counteracting the heavy concentration of industry in the West of the Netherlands, has been scrapped due to increasing unemployment levels in the large cities here. It is now felt to be more important to encourage a moderate growth of industry in this region than to encourage even higher unemployment.

In conclusion while lack of economic growth has generated social and economic problems there has also been a lack of willingness by governments to tackle these issues vigorously. The intertwining of the government with different interest groups in corporatist bodies has not made it easy for governments to adopt radical measures, because such measures would not receive wide social support. To put it schematically: on the one hand conservatives can frustrate progressive policies, on the other hand, the progressives can frustrate conservative policies, even though in practice the positions of the two factions are not diametrically opposed. As a result the possibility of any government conducting an independent radical policy is unlikely. The firmly institutionalised consultation between government and all types of interest groups clearly hinders speedy and radical action, even though there is little doubt that the Netherlands has lived beyond its means, with public expenditure remaining at a constantly high level and the government's ability to run deficits and borrow to finance those deficits having reached its limit. The only reason that the Netherlands has been able to continue this relatively financially insolvent practice has been due to natural-gas receipts – although reserves are dwindling! With the finance from natural gas it has been possible to continue with levels of public expenditure even though the productive potential which is necessary to sustain this in the future has been in decline. The problems that this poses for the Netherlands in the future will be outlined in the next section.

PROBLEMS AND PERSPECTIVES

The problems posed by the 1980s are unprecedented and while we are aware of many potential developments it is debatable whether the Netherlands will be able to solve these problems. A number of questions are important such as the nature of the base from which the Netherlands must face the economic recession and whether or not the Netherlands will be able to maintain the high level of social welfare and security which has been the basis for social cohesion.

The Dutch economy is vulnerable in a number of ways. First of all, about 50 per cent of the national income is earned through exports. Secondly the productive sector in the Netherlands is rather one-sided, and existing industrial structures and orientations are in need of fundamental renovation because many sectors can no longer compete with Japan and the newly industrialised countries like Korea, Taiwan, Singapore and others. Thirdly, declining reserves of and receipts from natural gas will pose problems in the future. Fourthly, since there is such strong interdependence between the public and private sectors of the economy only two roads are open: either a strengthening of corporatist co-operation and consultation – old Dutch virtues – between the most important social and economic partners and the government; or a rather ruthless fight between interest groups over the distribution of a stagnating or perhaps shrinking national income.

As intimated earlier the Netherlands retains an extensive network of corporatist or pseudo-corporatist consultative structures. The strength of this system is that all types of social groups are allocated a role in policy formulation and implementation. The system is based on negotiation, bargaining and discussion, with detailed consultation leading to government decision-making. This system's strength is that due to participation many groups and individuals are prepared to accept the consequences of decisions taken. The weakness of that system is that it is not a suitable vehicle for radical, innovatory policies which question existing constraints, because the system pursues the line of least resistance and is threatened when really drastic decisions have to be taken. Because the government and Parliament in the past have left many economic-policy decisions to interest groups, with whom it keeps close connections, Parliament is not in a powerful enough position to force through difficult decisions which question group interests. At the present time therefore Parliament lacks the power to intervene effectively even if it had the courage and will to do so.

Neverthless, due to the existence of extensive interdependence and cohesion between the public and private sectors – added to the institutionalised consultative processes – there is the possibility of and framework for a bold stabilisation policy. Cohesion in Dutch society derives from the fact that all of the political parties in Parliament and all of the major interest groups outside are involved in policy formulation. This point can be illustrated most effectively in the socio-economic field. Employers and workers agreed ten years ago to introduce a system to index wages automatically to inflation, although in recent years a number of reforms have limited the passing on to wages of increases in energy prices and increased taxation. Several years ago Parliament agreed to the introduction of a national statutory minimum wage and a statutory minimum wage for young people, which has contributed to the continuous increase in wage levels. Furthermore, six years ago the trade unions and Parliament decided to link minimum social-welfare payments to the statutory minimum wage. Finally, salaries of civil servants – or at least increases thereof – are directly linked to wage developments in trade and industry, and the government has become the largest single employer.

From this summary it becomes clear how closely the private and public sectors (including the social-security system) are linked together in the Netherlands. Since they are interdependent, when employers and workers pursue their own sectional self-interest, then the government is forced to make extensive cuts into its own direct expenditure and into the social-security system. This is inevitable, but, given the tradition of responsibility for the general management of the economy, employers and workers' organisations – if for different reasons – are likely to co-operate in the future to discuss long-term policy possibilities. This is particularly true because employers' and workers' organisations have always been interested in more matters than merely wage rates – especially the trade unions because of their concern to liberalise and reform society.

Unfortunately these future corporatist discussions will be difficult because the topics on the agenda are likely to require drastic policy changes. It is not just the question of how to tackle the economic recession but of what concessions the social partners are prepared to make to resolve this dilemma which is at issue. Any compromise is likely to necessitate fundamental changes in social and economic structures. The trade unions – including the most radical iron and steel union in a recently published memorandum – are quite prepared to moderate wage demands and even to accept a reduction in their purchasing power, but only if they are granted more participation in investment decisions and extensive guarantees of job security.

Although it is difficult to predict the future, it would seem that in principal the institutional structures and the willingness to solve the problems of the 1980s are present in the Netherlands. It is alien to Dutch traditions to allow the alternative scenario of an unrestrained conflict between sectional interest groups to take its course. As a consequence there are a number of indications that there is a realisation of the need for radical policies dawning amongst a majority of the Dutch population. Within the Dutch corporatist tradition it is likely that the quasi-corporate consultative bodies will be created to resolve these problems, where policy formulation in a co-operative atmosphere will be possible. In this sense then the 1980s are unlikely to represent a major break with the past.

CONCLUSIONS

(a) The Netherlands has resigned itself to the consequences of having to deal with a worldwide economic recession.
(b) The decline of Dutch growth rate has however only recently resulted in some reduction of wage and price levels.
(c) The Dutch economy is in a weak position because it is heavily reliant on a few products.
(d) In the initial stages of the recession the possession of large natural-gas reserves allowed the impact of declining growth to be hidden. But this tendency for the Dutch to live beyond their long-term economic means has created an additional problem for the country as it tries to deal with the problems of the recession in the 1980s.
(e) Declining economic growth has exacerbated tensions in Dutch society and enhanced the polarisation between various interest groups. Conflicts increasingly focus on the problem of income distribution.
(f) The inter-connection between the private and public sectors of the economy is so firmly established through corporatist institutions that it is likely that in the future the problems of economic recession will be tackled by even closer co-operation and consultation between employers, unions and the government.
(g) The cultural and historical consensus within Dutch society and the strongly rooted principles of social justice and equality are still so firmly

entrenched that a laissez-faire/monetarist solution (Thatcherism) does not seem a probable scenario for the Netherlands in the 1980s. Moreover, the power of Parliament in the economic sphere is relatively weak and social co-operation is firmly accepted as the only legitimate system of policy formulation by the majority of Dutch people.

I would like to thank Mr Ivo Blom (Head of the Cabinet of the Lord Mayor of Rotterdam) for translating this article and Dr Andrew Cox for his editorial advice.

NOTES AND REFERENCES

1. J. Pen, 'Conflicting Aims' in L.v.d. Geest (ed.), *The Blocked Society* (Amsterdam: 1980) p. 84.
2. The data and views mentioned in this paragraph I have mainly quoted from Pen, pp. 82–100; *The Nature and Future of Dutch Industry*, Report of the Scientific Council for Governments policy (The Hague: 1980) pp. 7–60; *The Netherlands Bank: Report for the year 1979* (Deventer: 1980); *Central Economic Plan* (The Hague: 1980).
3. In 1965 people working in agriculture, industry and services (including government) represented 8.6 per cent, 41.9 per cent and 49.5 per cent of the employed population respectively. In 1978 the figures were 6.1 per cent, 31.8 per cent and 62.1 per cent respectively. See Pen, *The Nature and Future*, p. 21.
4. On the structure of the Dutch political and social system, one can refer to – amongst others – A. Lyphart, *The Politics of Accommodation* (Berkeley: 1968); and Hans Daalder, 'The Netherlands: Opposition in a Divided Society', in Robert A. Dahl *et al.*, *Political Oppositions in Western Democracies* (New Haven and London: 1966) pp. 188–236.
5. I have presented an introduction to Dutch labour relationships in 'The Netherlands: From an Ordered Harmonic to a Bargaining Relationship', in Solomon Barkin *et al.* (eds), *Worker Militancy and its Consequences, 1965–75* (New York: 1975) pp. 118–53; on the phenomena of the 'trade offs' which have taken place frequently in the 1970s between government employers and workers, see my article 'Trade-Offs and Politicisation', in *Collective Bargaining and Government Policies* (Paris: OECD, 1979) pp. 139–49.
6. On regional policy and the different instruments to stimulate investments by the Government see Lotty Boersma, 'Regional Incentives in The Netherlands', in Douglas Yuill, Kevin Allen and Chris Hull *et al.*, *Regional Policy in the European Community* (London: 1980).

5 France: the Strategic Management of Impending Collective Impoverishment

JACK HAYWARD

While the National Plan ceased until 1981 to be the framework within which the French government fits both its own medium-term policy decisions and attempts to co-ordinate in a comprehensive way the activities of the public and private sectors, it nevertheless still offers the best source from which one may discover how the government of the day perceives the current economic situation and the prospects facing the country. Consequently, if we wish to understand the state of mind of the official decision-makers, confronted by the post-recession problems of the 1970s, an indispensable starting point and permanent point of reference is the 1978 *Report on the Adaptation of the Seventh Plan*. Published in September 1978, just halfway through the duration of the Seventh Plan (1976–80), it helps us to understand the considered response of the tandem of President Giscard d'Estaing and Prime Minister Barre, drastically modifying the over-optimistic Seventh Plan's presuppositions of 1975–6 and preparing the way for the Eighth Plan's stoic summons to batten down the hatches for a stormy long haul. Though the Planning Commissariat (CGP) documents pay some passing attention to the views of other economic actors, we shall have to go beyond their increasingly governmentalised confines to consider how these other political and economic actors responded both to the 1970s' recession and to the French government's own attempts to cope with its consequences.

The opening chapter of the 1978 Adaptation Report wryly recalled that in 1976, when the Seventh Plan was officially approved, the widely held view was that

> France was emerging from the crisis and that it would soon return to conditions of growth similar to those that had prevailed prior to 1974. We

> have to admit today that at the time all the consequences of the crisis were not appreciated, especially with respect to the growth, changes and disequilibria of the world economy, of which the oil crisis and the recession of 1974–5 were only a *révélateur*.[1]

The increasing exposure of France to the constraints of international developments that were beyond its control dated from the late 1950s, once its traditional protectionism was replaced by an acceptance of the competitive consequences of membership of the EEC. As its own industrial expansion gathered pace in the 1960s and as the volume of its international trade expanded, the domestic impact of fluctuations in its external environment became ever more imperative in their effects. The Government, whatever its desire to assert its own independent strategy – such a will was undoubted in the period 1958–69, when General de Gaulle was at the helm – found itself increasingly compelled to adapt to foreign forces that it could not compel, cajole or induce to conform with the schemes devised in Paris. Even when the inflationary pressures were in the first instance domestic – as in 1963, with the Stabilisation Plan following the coal-miners' strike, or in 1969, with the devaluation of the franc by Pompidou after de Gaulle had refused to do so in the wake of the massive 1968 wage concessions to buy off the extended general strike – it was the inability to sustain their balance of payments and international monetary consequences that led to the corrective action taken.

Because France had managed to sustain a steady, high rate of growth for most of the 1950s and 1960s, its citizens and leaders had become accustomed to the idea that this cumulation of wealth would continue indefinitely. They were not prepared for the increase in inflation following the escalation in oil prices (after twenty years in which the real cost of oil had been halved) to be accompanied by a dumbfounding descent into deflation throughout the industrially developed world, from which there was no separate escape for France. Though less prone to stagflation than most other countries, France shared the overcapacity in basic steel, chemicals and shipbuilding that afflicted her major competitors and like them was ill-equipped to face competition from the newly industrialised countries of the Third World. Just as the so-called developing countries were being dramatically differentiated into two categories: those condemned to grinding poverty and those who had managed to make the breakthrough into certain areas of industrial specialisation where they could supersede the old industrialised countries, a similar dualism was developing amongst the latter. Some, like Federal Germany – thanks to their technical and commercial mastery in particular industries due to the innovative drive and efficiency of their national champion firms – would enjoy a secure balance of payments and a strong currency, aided by a financially orthodox monetary policy. Others, like Britain, would sink into an industrial decline rendered all the more spectacular by its former dominance; a decline which its oil revenues would cushion but not of themselves correct. France was seen as not firmly among the front-runners, even if she had left the laggards well behind her. The salient ambition of French planning since Jean Monnet had been to steer France into a position in which it could triumphantly sustain the pressures of European and then international competition. In the grim circumstances of the late 1970s and early 1980s, without its own national oil resources, France would have to redeploy its industry to take on the challenge of conquering foreign markets and defending its home market.[2]

GOODBYE TO FULL EMPLOYMENT

While in 1976 it was still possible to harbour the illusion that a rapid return to full employment was attainable, by 1978 it was possible openly and officially to assert that for the foreseeable future mass unemployment would endure in France, particularly because of the 'external constraint' on which we have dwelt. The choice offered to the French people was between general impoverishment and the reinforcement of the competitive capacity of French firms. 'Thus employment is linked to growth. Growth is linked to the balance of payments, which in turn is linked to the adaptation of our industry.'[3] This chain of reasoning, subsequently reiterated *ad nauseam*, was intended to compel those who believed that it was a prime duty of the state to ensure conditions conducive to full employment that this could only be achieved indirectly – through and subsequent to the prior concentration upon combating inflation and promoting industrial redeployment. By 1980, the Employment Commission of the Eighth Plan could regret that the concentration upon competitiveness had made the fight against unemployment a secondary concern. This was true not only of employers (whose pursuit of profitability required them to reduce manpower costs) but also of state economic policymakers. Though the trade unions were a conspicuous exception,

> There seems to be a sort of general acceptance of unemployment within French society. Consequently, when the main economic, social and political forces attach greater importance (sometimes unconsciously) to other objectives, the growth of unemployment becomes, after inflation, a way of regulating an economy confronted by serious problems of structural adaptation.[4]

It is important, if one is to see the employment problems caused by the mid-1970s recession in perspective, to be aware of the fact that in France the number of people unsuccessfully seeking employment had already doubled in the preceding decade (1965–74), despite the rapid rate of economic growth. This domestic increase in unutilised labour was due to three main factors, only the first of which had a particularly marked incidence in France. The post-Second World War population boom meant that there was a rapid increase in the active population in the 1960s and 1970s, the high birth rate coinciding with a low death rate among the cohort of survivors from the First World War. Thus the average annual rate of active population growth increased from 20,000 in the years 1954–62 to 132,000 in 1962–8, 170,000 in 1968–75 and an estimated 200,000 in 1975–80. Secondly, the regular growth in the number of women seeking employment has meant that the average annual increase has risen from 18,000 in 1954–8 to 90,000 since 1974. Thirdly, there has been a marked change in the role of immigrant labour in the workforce; from a probably underestimated annual net inflow of 70,000 in 1968–73, there appears to have been a significant net outflow, estimated at a total of about 160,000 for the years 1973–6.[5] Unlike the first two factors, the outflow of foreign labour can be directly attributed to the economic recession, coupled with a change in government policy.

The period since 1974 has been characterised by two other changes that have an important bearing upon unemployment. Firstly, there has been a marked decline in the average annual increase in productivity: from 5.1 per cent in 1969–74 to 3.6 per cent in 1974–9 (and even 3.3 per cent in 1977–9). Such a decline has been evident in all the OECD countries – smaller in Federal Germany, greater in Britain. The reduction in working hours – which became a prominent controversial issue in the debate on remedies for unemployment and so merits more extended treatment – has had a more specifically French evolution. Because of the chronic shortage of labour and low hourly wages in the period up to the 1960s, working hours *increased* slightly – on average 1 hour over the whole period 1945–60. Then, until the 1968 'events', working hours were stable, thereafter commencing an average annual decline of 1 per cent, thanks to legislation and collective bargaining, which has continued since 1974, though at the slower rate of 0.7 per cent from 1977–9. As an increasing number of people reach the forty-hour work-week (48 per cent in 1979 as against 18 per cent in 1974 for manual workers; and 69 per cent in 1979, compared with 47 per cent in 1974 for white-collar employees) there has been a tendency to cut back on overtime working. Prior to the 1974 recession, the reduction of the work-week was most marked in the large firms in the most dynamic industries, with high rates of productivity and wages; whereas since the recession the reduction has occurred mainly in small firms in the declining industries, with low productivity and pay, as a way of adjusting to falling demand.[6]

This difference in behaviour as between the expanding and declining sectors leads us to a pre-recession cause of unemployment that has since been accentuated: the restructuring of production under the influence of technical change and the pressure of foreign competition. Agriculture, which had been characterised by a rapid reduction in its workforce in the decade 1963–73 (annual fall of 128,000, mainly among farmers rather than farm labourers) has since experienced a slowdown to 72,000 per annum (even lower since 1975 at 60,000 to under *half* the pre-1974 rate) playing its traditional role as a rural refuge from the full impact of industrial slump. Whereas industrial employment had been increasing annually by 64,000 in the period 1968–73, from 1973–9 it was falling by an average of 68,000 each year, the fall first being registered in the last quarter of 1976. Over half the jobs lost in the period from 1973–8 were in industries – notably textiles, iron and steel – that had been declining even before the recession. However, the mainstay of industrial employment, the expanding motor-car industry, itself went into recession in 1980.[7]

Before turning to the regional dimension and to the rapid growth in service-sector employment (the principal source of new jobs both before and since the recession), the building and public-works sector merits special mention. This is because its decline, which pre-dated 1973 but which was severely accentuated thereafter – owing to a fall in industrial investment and to the decline in house building–had a very widespread impact, notably in areas with almost no other secondary sources of employment. Prior to 1974, industrial expansion had helped somewhat to reduce the disparities in employment opportunities between regions but the 1.5 per cent annual fall in the number of industrial wage-earners had levelled downwards, hitting hardest those regions that had expanded fastest in the period 1968–74, though they continue to have the least unfavourable rates of growth in industrial employment. Services (which like building have helped correct regional employment imbalance) expanded the number of jobs by an annual average of 170,000 in 1962–8, 240,000 in 1968–73 and 223,000 in 1973–9. However, this overall growth conceals a change in the type of tertiary employment, from an emphasis on trade prior to 1968, to public-service employment since then, especially health services in the most recent period. Since 1977, there has been a rapid expansion in non-food retail shops, stimulated in part by the same 'refuge' factors that account for the slowdown in migration from farming. Finally, there has been steady growth in the number of white-collar employees, managers and members of the liberal professions, which is consistent with the expansion in the service sector despite the dire predictions for the future arising from foreseeable technological advance, notably in electronics.[8]

Quite apart from the incalculable human costs of unemployment, the probability of becoming unemployed, which in 1970 was less than 5 per cent and exceeded 12 per cent ten years later, has had important financial implications, it being estimated in 1977 that for each 100,000 people unemployed the cost to the community was 4 billion francs (shared equally between transfer payments made and social-security contributions not received). Despite the official 'smokescreen' spread about the diversity of types of unemployment, it was calculated in 1978 that unemployment in the singular had nearly doubled between 1974 and 1978, rising from 2.7 per cent to 5.2 per cent.[9] The staccato stress upon the competitiveness of French firms as a precondition of permanent employment should not distract us from the fact that since 1974 employers have taken advantage of this stronger bargaining position to reverse the 1960s' trend towards unified and stable conditions of employment. This has been done notably by multiplying the number of special types of fixed term and temporary contracts to increase managerial capacity to reduce manpower costs and facilitate management's freedom of action. While only 2.5 per cent of the wage-earners were in 1980 covered by such precarious forms of employment, this number has rapidly increased since the recession. While the end of fixed-term contracts accounted for 25 per cent of those registering as seeking employment in 1976, the number had risen to over 35 per cent in 1980, the under-25 year olds, women and white-collar employees being particularly affected by this increasing job insecurity. The number of full-time, permanent jobs offered through the National Employment Agency (at a time when it was receiving priority budgetary funds to extend and improve its services) fell from 1.4 million in 1974 to just under 800,000 in 1979. This decline coincided with an increase in the number of part-time jobs *offered* through the agency from 24 per cent of all jobs in 1974 to 33 per cent in 1977, while those *seeking* full-time jobs increased from 75 per cent in 1974 to 87 per cent in 1977. The underground economy generally and 'moonlighting' in particular also appear to have increased notably since the recession, and have softened the impact of short-time working and unemployment.

The duration of unemployment has continued to increase – from an average of 8.9 months in March 1976 to 11.1 months in March 1979 – but the number of those registered as unemployed for over a year nearly doubled from 145,000 in the same three-year period to 270,000, of which 47 per cent were under forty years of age. However, those worst affected seem to be people who combine at least two of three characteristics: being over fifty years old, suffering from illness, being unskilled. While the probability of becoming unemployed falls with age, the young have predictably found it easier to find a job; once the older become unemployed, they are more inclined to retire from the labour market. The recession seems to have especially affected male manual workers; the rate of unemployment among men rising from under half to over half the rate of jobless women: 3.1 per cent as against 6.7 per cent in March 1976, compared with 4.1 per cent and 7.9 per cent in March 1979, while the number of jobless manual workers rose from 4.7 per cent to 6.4 per cent over these three years. Regionally, the rate of unemployment (those seeking employment as a percentage of wage-earners) seems to continue to be highest in South-east France (11–12 per cent in 1978 compared with 4.7 per cent in 1973), followed by the South-west, Nord – Pas de Calais and Brittany – all approximating 9.5 per cent in 1978 as against 3–4 per cent in 1973 – with Alsace continuing to be best placed with 4.3 per cent compared with 1 per cent. The Paris region was somewhat better off than the national average with 2.6 per cent compared with 2.7 per cent in 1973 and 5.8 per cent as against 7.6 per cent for France as a whole in 1978.[10] Lorraine – severely affected by closures in the steel industry – did not do much worse than triple its rate of unemployment by 1978, which was broadly in line with the national figures.[11] Since 1978, the lugubrious process of running down the steel industry has continued in Lorraine and the Nord.

The high and sustained French rate of economic growth – the pride and joy of its governments under the Fifth Republic – took a very sharp knock in 1975. Table 5.1 shows that after a good recovery in 1976, thanks to expansionist policies at home and abroad, it fell back to a modest rate of about 3 per cent in 1977–8. France did better than most of its EC competitor countries but whereas it had managed to sustain a favourable margin over them of 1.5 per cent in its gross domestic product in the period 1960–74, this gap has now been halved to 0.7 per cent, in line with the fall in GDP. One of the French government's objectives is to open up the gap at least to 1 per cent but it is concerned to stress that with its dependence upon international trade

TABLE 5.1 Comparative Increase in Gross Domestic Product, 1974–8 (%)

	1974	*1975*	*1976*	*1977*	*1978*
France	+2.8	+0.3	+4.6	+2.9	+3.2
EC	+1.7	−1.6	+4.7	+2.2	+2.5
OECD	+0.3	−0.6	+5.2	+3.4	+3.5

SOURCE *Rapport sur les principales options du Huitième Plan*, p. 31

and the state of the world economy, 'growth cannot be decreed'.[12] In particular, it is aware of the need to curb the inflationary pressures that pre-dated the oil crisis. These go back to the 1960s' cost-push to prices, due particularly to the increasingly capital-intensive nature of production (investment necessary to improve productivity to overcome international competition) and the rise in real wages at the expense of profits. However, since the mid-70s recession, the major preoccupation has been the rapid growth in public expenditure, due especially to the sharp rise in disbursements and fall in revenue consequent upon the rapid increase in unemployment.

The French record in the matter of developing its public services without recourse either to substantial increases in taxation or to budget deficits was an enviable one, prior to the oil crisis. Table 5.2 makes clear that from 1965–73 the French share of the Gross Domestic Product taken in national and local taxation and social security contributions, while high, remained virtually unchanged, whereas they increased rapidly in Sweden and the Netherlands, somewhat more moderately in Federal Germany and only

TABLE 5.2 Tax and Social Security Charges as a % of GDP

	1965	*1973*	*1976*
Sweden	35.6	43.0	50.9
Netherlands	35.5	43.7	46.2
France	35.0	35.5	39.5
United Kingdom	31.0	32.6	36.7
Federal Germany	31.6	36.3	36.7
Italy	29.2	28.6	35.8
All OECD	28.0	32.0	36.0

SOURCE OECD, reprinted in *Rapport sur les principales options du Huitième Plan*, p. 38

slightly faster in the United Kingdom. However, by 1976, while Federal Germany was able to hold its charges almost steady, France and the UK both increased theirs by 4 per cent, while the Italian increase amounted to 7.2 per cent and the Swedish to 7.9 per cent! As far as the government's borrowing requirement is concerned, Table 5.3 indicates that France has kept its public finance under control far more effectively than its major EC partners, even if the days of the balanced budget, dear to Giscard d'Estaing when he was de Gaulle's Finance Minister, are now merely a memory.

However, the French government is especially conscious of the fact that from 1974–8 public and social-security expenditure had grown annually 1 per cent faster than revenues and 3 per cent faster than the Gross Domestic

TABLE 5.3 Government Borrowing Requirement as % of Gross National Product

	1975	*1976*	*1977*	*1978*
Italy	14.6	9.9	9.8	12.6
United Kingdom	4.8	5.0	3.2	4.0
Federal Germany	5.7	3.6	2.5	3.0
France	2.2	0.4	1.3	1.9

SOURCE OECD, reprinted in *Rapport sur les principales options du Huitième Plan*, p. 31

Product. Table 5.4 reveals that because social transfer payments have been growing annually at 7.9 per cent on average, compared with all other public expenditure, by 1978 they accounted for over half of the total. (It is worth noting that despite talk of government 'disengagement' and although 'economic transfers' were only one-seventh the size of 'social transfers', they expanded almost as fast – 7.6 per cent – from 1971–8, owing to the

TABLE 5.4 French Public Expenditure, 1971–8

	Billions of francs (current)		*1978*	*Rate of average annual growth (%)*
	1971	*1978*	*%*	*(Constant francs)*
Wages	61.6	169.8	18.8	5.8
Consumption	41.1	95.3	10.5	3.2
Investment	29.2	65.8	7.3	2.8
Social transfers	145.6	460.5	50.8	7.9
Economic transfers	21.6	67.2	7.4	7.6
Other public expenditure	19.7	47.4	5.2	3.7
Total public expenditure	318.8	906.0	100.0	6.2

SOURCE French National Accounts, reprinted in *Rapport sur les principales options du Huitième Plan*, p. 39

recession.) The government's anxiety is that by the mid-1980s taxation and social-security charges would need to rise towards 50 per cent of GDP, so the Eighth Plan suggested that they should not be allowed to expand, on pain of 'discouraging initiative and leading to inertia and irresponsibility'.[13] This liberal-conservative language should not surprise us and we shall have occasion to explore more fully the theory and practice of the French government that expounded it.

Turning to the changes that occurred in the constituent elements of final demand – consumption, investment and exports – Table 5.5 provides us

TABLE 5.5 Average Annual Growth Rates in French Final Demand, 1960–79 (%)

Constant Prices	*1960–9*	*1964–74*	*1974–9*
Consumption:	4.6	3.8	3.8
Households	4.9	4.2	3.7
Public Administration	5.2	3.2	3.9
Gross Investment:	6.9	4.2	0.4
Firms	7.8	5.2	0.7
Public Administration	–	1.0	0.4
Households	9.8	7.5	0
Exports	7.5	9.6	5.7

SOURCE INSEE, reprinted in *Commission de l'Emploi, Huitième Plan*, op. cit., p. 30

with a comprehensive view of the trends in the French economy on the demand side over the 1960s and 1970s, showing that investment has borne the brunt of the halving in the pre-1974 rate of economic growth.

We have already discussed the fall in housebuilding, which helps explain the collapse in investment by households, so we shall concentrate upon the effects of the recession upon investment by firms. Table 5.6 shows the impact of the slump upon competitive private-sector investment, which did

TABLE 5.6 Investment and Self-Financing by Non-Nationalised Firms, 1972–8

	1972	*1973*	*1974*	*1975*	*1976*	*1977*	*1978*
Investment (1970 = 100)	118.7	124.1	120.8	108.3	117.9	115.4	118.6
Rate of Self-Financing	74.5	69.0	57.7	62.3	64.0	61.6	78.4

SOURCE INSEE, reprinted Commissariat Général du Plan (CGP) Service Economique, 28 February 1979, p. 17

not recover to the 1972 figure until 1978, while the rate of self-financing also made a comeback in 1978 and again in 1979. Further explanatory factors account for the sharp decline in investment by firms, which fell as a percentage of sales from 4.9 in 1972 to 3.5 in 1976. Between 1972–6, their long-term debt increased by 79 per cent and short-term bank loans by 96 per cent, while profits suffered from the growth of wages and consumption.[14] Fortunately, the nationalised industries increased their investments by 75 per cent in volume between 1973–8 and by an annual rate of 10.4 per cent in volume over the period of the Seventh Plan (1976–80) though by 1979 investment was down to 9 per cent. This generally good record was due particularly to two major public-investment programmes: the modernisation and doubling in capacity of the telephone system (which alone accounted for over half the 200 billion francs set aside for the Seventh Plan Priority Action Programmes) and the controversial electro-nuclear programme of *Electricité de France*, which is the largest effort by any nation in the world to substitute nuclear power for other sources of energy.[15] The Barre Government refused to continue boosting public enterprise investment to avoid threatening the private sector's place within the mixed economy.

The government's desire to promote investment in the competitive sector has been frustrated on the cost side by the increase in real wages in the early 1970s and by the increasing share of the wage bill represented by employers' social-security contributions – 22.7 per cent in 1972 and 25.6 per cent in 1978 – which encourage the substitution of capital for labour. Consumption was sustained by the rapid growth in social transfer payments already noted and by the increase in the minimum wage, which grew in real terms by 7 per cent in 1970–5 and by 3.5 per cent in 1975–8. This increase in the minimum wage represented a modest reduction in differentials between wage-earners, which also occurred as between the less and more skilled.[16] Table 5.7 shows the slowdown in the increase in the purchasing power of wages from 1974, though it was not until 1979–80 that this fell to zero and then to an actual fall in workers' purchasing power. Though Prime Minister Barre continued to assert in 1979–80 that the purchasing power of wages would be

TABLE 5.7 Annual Growth of Prices, Real Wages and Social Security Receipts, 1972–8 (%)

Annual Growth Rate	*1972*	*1973*	*1974*	*1975*	*1976*	*1977*	*1978*
Household consumption prices	6.0	6.8	13.3	11.6	9.8	9.1	9.4
Purchasing power of the per capita wage	4.1	5.5	2.6	3.7	3.4	2.3	2.3
Purchasing power of households' social security receipts	7.2	8.1	4.8	13.8	6.0	6.4	7.2

SOURCE INSEE, reprinted CGP, Service Economique, 28 February 1979, p. 17

maintained – itself a regression – this claim rapidly lost credibility but a context of growing unemployment and a politically and industrially divided Left until 1981 meant that the trade-union capacity to resist was more vociferous than effective. However, the French government could point to the fact that wage-earners in other EC countries had suffered a fall in real wages even earlier. By 1978 the French government had become sufficiently confident in the political and industrial weakness of the Left to dismantle most of the price controls that had provided an instrument of indirect wage control since its failure to secure an agreed incomes policy in 1964.

The oil crisis of 1973–4 marked the end of a period, going back twenty years, when the falling real cost of raw materials and energy ensured very favourable terms of trade for the industrially developed countries, whose manufactured goods were increasing in price. 'On the basis of the French minimum hourly wage, it cost eight hours work in 1950 to pay for 100 litres of unrefined petrol but only 2.25 hours work in 1970.'[17] To meet the balance of payments deficit of 28 billion francs in 1974 and 22 billion francs in 1976 (after a year in balance thanks to negligible economic growth in 1975) there was a spectacular growth of exports (6.6 per cent in volume in the difficult world market of 1977) while invisible exports doubled in 1977 their 5 billion francs surplus of 1976. In 1978 there was a balance-of-payments surplus of 6 billion francs but the renewed increases in oil prices from mid-1979 put France back into increasing deficit in 1980. On capital account, France continues to have one of the lowest debt burdens in the world calculated as a percentage of Gross National Product.[18] So, despite the intractable choices France had to face in the late 1970s, they posed less insuperable problems to its political and economic elites than some of its European competitors faced.

CONFLICTING POLICY PRESCRIPTIONS

French public opinion has not been favourably impressed by the French government's attempts to cope with the consequences of the oil crisis and there can be little doubt that had the various national electoral confrontations between Left and Right been exclusively socio-economic issues the Left would have won power before 1981. In a poll conducted at the end of August 1979, only 25 per cent thought that the government's policy would deal successfully with the country's difficulties, whilst 63 per cent thought that the government was improvising without any sense of direction.[19] In April 1980, when asked about the success of the President of the Republic's policies over a wide range of issues, the public's response was very negative on all economic issues (see Table 5.8). This was true even of President Giscard's own partisans, between 61–76 per cent of UDF voters admitting that his policies to deal with unemployment and price increases had been failures.

Though the President and (especially) the Prime Minister's popularity sagged markedly between elections, at the decisive moments of choice – in the 1974 Presidential Election and the 1978 General Election – the fact that the French public were presented with a *choix de société* rather than a choice of economic policies to deal with the international crisis meant that

TABLE 5.8 Public assessment of Giscard d'Estaing's record in the previous six years (%)

Issue	*Success*	*Failure*	*Difference*	*No opinion*
Energy policy	31	41	−10	18
Strengthening French industry	25	42	−17	33
Reduction of differentials in standards of living	20	65	−45	15
Struggle against unemployment	12	78	−66	10
Struggle against price increases	5	88	−83	7

SOURCE *L'Express* (10 May 1980) p. 113 (Louis Harris – France Poll)

discontented voters swung over to the Right because they were not willing to face what was presented to them as a dramatic and possibly irreversible change in the character of France's socio-economic system. The effects of the economic recession upon the popularity of President Giscard were reflected in the collapse in public satisfaction with him, from a peak of 59 per cent in May 1975, to 57 per cent in January, down to 39 per cent in December 1976. This was the lowest level to which a President had sunk since the inception of the Fifth Republic. 1976–7 was also a time when the Union of the Left was winning sweeping local electoral victories but it is significant that Presidential popularity began its steady recovery in May 1977 – before the open split – overtaking the number of discontented in June. However, it was not until the September 1977 break between the Communists and Socialists that a 9-point excess of the satisfied over the discontented opened up, growing to an 18-point gap just before the March 1978 General Election (56 per cent as against 38 per cent). In the wake of the victory of his supporters, Giscard's popularity returned briefly to its peak of 59 per cent in April as against 30 per cent discontented but the gap closed over the next seventeen months and by September 1979 the number of discontented (44 per cent) again exceeded those satisfied (40 per cent).[20]

The much greater and semi-permanent unpopularity of Prime Minister Barre (1976–81) – in which he positively revelled, regarding it as a measure of public incomprehension of his severe commitment to the austerities of classical economic orthodoxy or at least their desire to protest at the sacrifices they realised had to be made – is much more directly related to the public's perception of the government's handling of the world recession. Chosen by Giscard as France's best economist (whereas he only merited the title of the author of France's most widely used elementary economics textbook) specifically to exert a grip upon an economic situation that his predecessor Jacques Chirac had failed to master, the President deliberately utilised the formal, institutional duality of the French political executive to shift on to the broad and willing shoulders of the anti-populist Prime Minister the burden of hostility which his own policies provoked. Though at the beginning of 1977 – shortly after Barre took office – his rating was close to that of Giscard, the number of the discontented quickly exceeded the satisfied by margins far in excess of the President's rating. Thus in May 1977, Barre's 'deficit' was 16 per cent as against Giscard's 6 per cent and the dissatisfied consistently exceeded the contented right up to the 1978 General Election (3 per cent in February), falling briefly below the contented in April, only to recommence the ascent to new heights of unpopularity. In September 1978 and June 1979 Barre's 'deficit' was 29 per cent, whereas Giscard had a 'surplus' of 12 per cent and 4 per cent. By the time the President had plummeted to a 4 per cent 'deficit' in September 1979, dissatisfaction with the Prime Minister had reached the record deficit for the Fifth Republic of 31 per cent (57 per cent dissatisfied as against 26 per cent satisfied)! If one takes the average quarterly figures, the popularity gap between President and Prime Minister significantly widened. In 1977 they were 4, 5, 7 and 11 per cent; in 1978 they increased to 11, 15, 19 and 16; modestly continuing this late 1978 reversal in early 1979 with percentages of 15 and 14.[21] This seems to confirm the earlier poll data that indicated that Barre's government was held directly responsible for increasing inflation and unemployment, even though the voters were not prepared to dislodge his political master from presidential office until 1981.

When Prime Minister Barre introduced his 'Stabilisation Plan' in September 1976 (recalling the similar 1963 Plan which de Gaulle claimed he 'imposed' upon his Prime Minister Pompidou and Finance Minister Giscard d'Estaing) he had to face not merely the intra and extra-Parliamentary opposition of the Left but also the constant sniping of more than half his parliamentary majority, the RPR deputies, led by his disgruntled predecessor Jacques Chirac. The initial reaction to the crisis had been to concentrate upon fighting inflation, reducing energy consumption and developing exports. The anti-inflationary measures consisted of a combination of tight money, increased interest rates and balanced budgets with the accentuation of price control, especially from October 1974. However, the initial concentration on controlling industrial prices was not consistent with the Seventh Plan's priority for industrial development. Following a period of hesitancy over the future of planning, the preparation of the Seventh Plan in 1975–6 was characterised by an ephemeral revival of optimism in the possibilities of returning to the pre-crisis expansion and a growth rate of 5.5 per cent (7.2 per cent for industry) was envisaged, based notably on a high rate of investment.[22] This return to 'go' after 'stop' quickly caused France to run into balance-of-payments deficit and Raymond Barre was called upon to carry out a more consistently deflationary policy in August 1976, following a conflict between President Giscard and Prime Minister Chirac that was broader and more political than their differences over how to tackle the economic recession.

Despite the temptation to follow a more 'soft-sell' policy with a view to the 1978 General Election which, it was generally assumed, would be won by the then United Left, Barre's 'Stabilisation Plan' – which made nonsense of the Seventh Plan and foreshadowed its mid-term 'adaptation' after the 1978 Election – sought not merely to improvise a short-term anti-inflationary set of measures but to prepare the way for a switch towards a less *dirigiste* policy which we shall consider later. Whether the German social-market model was appropriate to France is a central issue. The spectacular start in 1978 to the reversal of decades of price control was accompanied by the claim that because Federal Germany had successfully curbed inflation without price control, it could be abandoned with equanimity; whereas it is arguable that it was *because* Federal Germany had mastered inflation that 'medieval price control'[23] was unnecessary. The Seventh Plan's commitment to full employment was tacitly abandoned and the stability of the currency was presented as a pre-condition of containing the growth in unemployment. Membership of the European Monetary System had the virtue of making the parity of the franc a matter of international commitment, restraining domestic propensities to laxness. Those on the Left and in the RPR who took a different view were peremptorily dismissed as economic illiterates. The *Guidelines Report of the Eighth Plan* (in whose redrafting Barre and his staff took a direct hand) made a virtue of 'rejecting the mirages of a "general expansion" that would certainly reduce unemployment temporarily but would make inflation and the balance of payments deficit and consequently, in the longer term, unemployment, worse'.[24] Not content with dismissing as unrealistic Chirac's view that public investment should be rapidly expanded and the threatened social-security deficit painlessly avoided thanks to a fall in unemployment, Barre disingenuously engaged in his own brand of provocative unrealism when he declared: 'Why should the unemployed not solve their difficulties by setting up as artisans or creating a small industrial or commercial firm; not only for their own sake but for the community, which will profit from their success and will not have to carry the burden of providing them with benefits?'[25] This Guizot-like summons to social-through-self-enrichment carried the implication that it was not just the fortunate and bustling few that had the entrepreneurial equivalent of a field-marshall's baton in the private's knapsack but that creating one's own small business was a solution to mass unemployment, not simply a private refuge from recession, with many aspirants rapidly joining the swelling ranks of the bankrupt. The public outcry at his reiteration of this Panglossian precept indicated that Barre could not get away entirely unscathed as a politician with sentiments that can usually be proffered by a professor of economics to his students with impunity. 9,200 firms were established in 1979 and 6,200 in the first half of 1980 by the unemployed, helped by some modest public financial assistance.

The divided French Left sought to fight the 1978 General Election on the basis of its pre-crisis 1972 Common Programme and thereby provided an easy target for criticisms of its economic unrealism. Attempts by those in the Socialist Party, such as Michel Rocard, to adopt a more realistic stance were attacked by the Communists and a section of his own party as defecting to the enemy and veering towards the defeatism attributed unilaterally to advocates of Social Democracy. Barre scored an early victory in a pre-electoral debate with François Mitterrand because whatever the future President's talents as a politician, he is most definitely an economic semi-literate. So, armed with a programme lacking economic credibility, advertising their mutual suspicions and inability to govern together so that they also lacked political credibility, the Left contrived to snatch defeat from the jaws of victory. The all-or-nothing line of argument – 'nothing will change unless everything changes' – embodied in the view that the electors were really (rather than rhetorically) faced by a 'choice of society', meant in practice that even modest improvements were not made; rather, things changed for the worse! One of Barre's electoral arguments had been that if the Left won office the purchasing power of the workers would fall because of the resurgence of inflation, whilst if the Right were returned to power they would preserve the worker's living standards. As we have seen, though this was true for about a year afterwards, the French workers had followed in the wake of workers in adjacent countries by the end of the decade. This was not easy medicine to swallow in a country where living standards had tripled in the preceding thirty years.

Many planners and senior officials in the ministries, who had looked forward with enthusiasm to a change of government and policy (some, out of idealism or *arrivisme*, had even rallied to the rejuvenated Socialist Party and become active members) were very disgruntled at the retention, in an exacerbated form, of the previous men and measures. The overt scepticism towards forecasting and hostility towards planning of Giscard and Barre naturally led the practitioners of these arts to regret the Gaullist past and the provisionally lost Socialist future. However, the more ambitious and cynical sought to swim with the international-market-economy tide, which brought with it not merely the need to restructure French industry to face the intensified competitive pressure but also the need to protect electorally important small business from the full impact of the recession. The Chirac government had created in November 1974 the *Comité Interministériel pour l'Aménagement des Structures Industrielles* (CIASI) but it quickly lost its initial function of pump-priming the provision of funds for purposes of restructuring industry and instead became a small business and job-preserving operation, under the pressure of circumstances. CIASI came under the control of the *Direction Général de l'Industrie* (DGI was established in July 1974) to enable the Ministry of Industrial Development to change from being a clientele-dominated, sectoralised ministry, left to look after small firms, into one dedicated to restructuring French firms into large multisectoral groups that wanted more than the public financial assistance obtainable through the Finance Ministry, e.g. the negotiation of large export contracts. As the instrument *par excellence* of the government's industrial policy, DGI could carry out the selective approach of deciding which industries – such as machine tools and micro-processors – should receive priority help and which firms would be favoured, especially important in the placing of large public contracts such as those in the electro-nuclear field.[25]

The intra-bureaucratic implications of the recession can be seen to advantage in two aspects of the increased exposure to international pressures in the 1970s. The fragile nature of France's trade surplus in the years immediately preceding the oil crisis – the favourable balance in car sales exceeded that of French industry as a whole – meant that the Ministries of Industrial Development and (especially) Foreign Trade became commercial travellers for French goods. Financial assistance for exports were stepped up at a time when credit was being restricted and the Finance Ministry's Foreign Relations Division wanted to make all financial assistance to firms conditional upon their increasing exports. This division has played an increasing role in industrial decision-making since 1974, including decisions on French overseas investment, having a vested interest in policies that will reinforce its place within the industrial policymaking process.

On the sensitive issue of the inflow of foreign investment – it was estimated by the Industry Ministry in 1971 that one-fifth of French industrial jobs and one-quarter of sales were due to foreign firms, which were concentrated in large firms, especially in the oil, electrical and electrical engineering, chemicals and motorcar industries – there continued to be policy confusion because of the different priorities of the various public agencies. The Ministry of Finance (which was reconstituted with the 1981 Mauroy Government) through the Treasury Division, that is generally unfavourable to overseas investment by French firms because this involves a drain on the balance of payments and involves expensive guarantees, is primarily concerned with the short-term balance of payments advantages of foreign investment in France. The Regional Planning Agency (DATAR) is always favourable to investment inflows because of its desire to create jobs in areas that are under-industrialised or suffering from recession. On the other hand, the Ministries of Industrial Development and of Defence usually champion 'national solutions' so that foreign firms may be amazed at their inconsistent treatment – invited in by DATAR yet repulsed by the Ministry of Industrial Development – though the Treasury Division will have the last word[27] if the issue does not escalate to prime ministerial or presidential level. So national policy can become the plaything of intra-bureaucratic battles between various parts of the state apparatus, subject to the superimposition of a decision at the highest levels in the light of political considerations.

The attitudes towards public economic policy of business interests present a sharp contrast with that of the major trade unions. Big business never felt closer to the Government under the Fifth Republic until 1981 – witness the harmony between François Ceyrac, President of the CNPF peak business organisation with first Jacques Chirac and then Raymond Barre. (This identification with the Right did not only occur when the Left threatened, if elected, to implement an extensive nationalisation programme.) The unions, the Communist-dominated CGT and the Socialist-aligned CFDT, effectively represented two-thirds of the workers. The intransigent opposition to private business and their political allies of these two unions, not just on matters of short- or medium-term economic policy but on the very existence of the capitalist system of production as such, can be contrasted with the reformist-to-quietist unions – FO, CGC and CFTC – that are usually willing to accept the modest concessions offered by business organisations and government both during collective bargaining over wages and working conditions, as well as in the forums for consultation on general economic-policy matters: the Economic and Social Council and the Commissions connected with planning at the national level, as well as the Economic and Social Committees at the regional level. Despite their intense distrust of the Right-wing governments of the Fifth Republic, even the CGT and CFDT were inclined to accept the official view that 'The role of the State is essential if negotiations between employers and employed are to take place satisfactorily';[28] an acknowledgement that they were too weak to rely upon collective bargaining alone to achieve their objectives. The 1970s recession has increased this weakness by reducing the demand for labour and – rather than the fiasco of the 'United Left' in 1977/8 – led to a serious fall in trade-union membership. Desperately seeking for a way out of their predicament, the unions have sought to mobilise their remaining strength to pressure the government into persuading the employers to reduce working hours which, in addition to helping to deal with unemployment, would restore workers support for their unions.

France has shared with Britain in the post-war period the position of having the longest working hours, despite the nominal achievement of the forty-hour work-week in 1936, thanks to the Popular Front electoral victory and subsequent general strike. We discussed earlier the steady movement towards an effective forty-hour work-week in the 1970s commencing before the onset of the recession and leading on average to a reduction of five hours over ten years or half an hour annually. This was achieved thanks to a combination of collective bargaining and the reduction of the maximum legal work-week. However, the resistance of employers increased at a time of falling profits, when they were particularly reluctant to accept any increase in labour costs and any reduction in the utilisation of capital equipment. The Plan's Employment Commission had in 1978 circumspectly considered the issue of 'work sharing' prior to the report adapting the Seventh Plan but made clear that the official view was hostile to a general reduction of the work-week with full wage compensation, as demanded by the trade unions, on the grounds that it would lead to an *increase* in unemployment. In its Eighth Plan report, the Employment Commission stressed that unemployment would only be significantly reduced if wage increases were moderate and if businessmen considered it worthwhile to invest. This meant that the reduction had to be gradual, diversified and negotiated to fit special circumstances; 'the gradual fall in working hours would only be the result of a variety of reductions carried out in the firms'.[29]

This was very much the line taken by the business organisations and prompted sharp criticism from the trade unions who looked to the reduction of the work-week to 35 hours by 1985 as an indispensable element in their struggle to return to full employment. While the Employment Commission did envisage an average annual reduction of a half to one hour over the period of the Eighth Plan (1981–5) it left the government-appointed conciliator, Pierre Giraudet, to make precise proposals. Giraudet, who had been at work from January 1980, following the breakdown in the prolonged government-prompted negotiations between the CNPF and the trade unions, made his proposals in April of the same year. They failed to secure acceptance because there was an insistence by employers that in return for reduced working hours, there should be greater flexibility. While this was agreeable to some workers, the trade unions were bitterly opposed to what they saw as a loss of control over a standard work-week. The unions – particularly the CFDT – had belatedly managed to persuade the Planning Commissariat to calculate in detail the effects of a substantial reduction in the work-week, thereby placing increasing employment at the centre of policy rather than treating it – as Barre certainly conceived it – as a mere by-product of competitive business. In the spring of 1980, 27 scenarios – involving 90 economic variables and essentially comparing the effects of concentrating upon protecting the balance of payments (A), upon a high rate of investment (B) and upon a reduction to a 35½ hour work-week (C) – were presented by the Planning Commissariat, showing that genuine alternative priorities to those of the Government existed. However, they came too late and the Government was too firmly committed to its policies for these alternatives to provide more than debating points in the arguments in the press, planning commissions, Economic and Social Council and in Parliament. Though the CFDT and CGT did not boycott the final phase of the preparation of the Eighth Plan – as they had done in the case of the Seventh Plan – they vehemently made clear their general rejection of the policies envisaged in a thoroughly governmentalised Plan.[30]

The Government – despite frequent protestations of its wish to seek concerted views with all interested parties – made clear in practice that its real 'partners' were the heads of big businesses and the CNPF. This is clear not merely from its policy statements but from its behaviour over issues like ending price controls, tax concessions for investment in shares and the reduction of the work-week. In the latter case, it was not prepared to go further than encourage firms to pursue their own interests, which were envisaged as broadly synonymous with the national interest. As a Ministry of the Economy report on 'Public Aid to Industry' put it

> Out of 40,000 industrial firms, only 1,500 employ more than 500 people. Many of them are financially linked, which further reduces the number of wholly independent entities. These 1,500 firms make 80 per cent of the investments, account for 90 per cent of all exports and employ almost all the research staff. So it is not abnormal that actions aimed at strengthening the complete freedom of our economy should, at least in the first instance, concentrate upon this 'hard core' of French industry.[31]

It conceded – in the wake of the leaked Hannoun Report – that 56 per cent of all public financial aid to industry in 1976 (3.3 per cent of industrial added value compared with 3.2 per cent in 1972) went to nine firms: 31 per cent to public corporations or agencies dealing with Aerospace, Coal and Atomic Energy; 7 per cent to a Franco-American computer firm, CII-Honeywell-Bull with a minority public holding and 18 per cent to five private firms – Dassault (aircraft), CGE (electrical engineering), Thomson-Brandt (electronics, etc.), Creusot-Loire (nuclear reactors, etc.) and Alsthom-

Atlantique (turbines, etc.). These nine firms received 80 per cent of aid to dynamic industries and 70 per cent of aid to industries undergoing rapid change but only 43 per cent of export aid. The three headings accounted for 83 per cent of public aid, so the fact that the 'big nine' received little aid towards restructuring (11 per cent of the total) and for employment and regional development (6 per cent of the total) is not significant. Despite assertions that there would be closer public supervision of the extent to which assisted firms invested and exported, the whole atmosphere of the post-1978 period was suffused with the desire to restore the confidence of businessmen and was irradiated by the confidence of an entrepreneur-minister like René Monory (Minister of Industry from 1977–78 and Minister of the Economy thereafter) and of Raymond Barre in the profit-making businessman, until the advent of the Mitterrand Presidency.

THE THEORY AND PRACTICE OF POST-RECESSION PUBLIC ECONOMIC INTERVENTION

The liberal-conservatism, which was enunciated and implemented after the Right wing electoral triumph of March 1978, by the team of Giscard–Barre–Monory (with Giraud, Monory's successor at Industry, adding a more *étatiste* touch as a possible fourth member) was not new and the recession made it harder rather than easier to carry into effect. In contrast to the Pinary–Poujade style of the Fourth Republic, which despite the pursuit of economic planning and creation of the EC – both at the instigation of Jean Monnet – placed the protection of small firms and declining industries and trades as the top priority to preserve the socio-political status quo, the modernising Fifth Republic had from the start regarded the potential or actual internationally competitive French firms as the spearhead of national economic activity. Two key reports, those by the Committee on the Financial Situation in December 1958, headed by the liberal economist Jacques Rueff and the 1960 report on 'Obstacles to Economic Expansion', headed by the public-sector technocrat Louis Armand and Rueff, heralded the subsequent onslaught upon protectionism, the stress upon competitiveness and the restraint upon public expenditure. Though many of their detailed proposals were not applied, they gradually became the accepted philosophy of much of both the administrative and business elites over the next decade. Operationally, it

> consisted in making of the industrial firm the economy's essential decision-making centre and of profit the driving force of growth. It did not

> signify 'disengagement' by the State but the introduction of new forms of state intervention based upon supporting private business rather than defining objectives and direct intervention.[32]

Although Gaullism placed a particular emphasis upon military and space projects and actively promoted a national champions policy, it did not succeed in establishing an autonomous French industry, independent of international capitalism. Nevertheless, it remained *dirigiste* in the sense that the government was the senior and directive partner in the collaboration with big business, which was still lacking in self-confidence and habitually looked to the State for support.

However, in the second half of the late 1960s – even before de Gaulle was replaced by Pompidou, during the latter's premiership and under the aegis of his protégé the Planning Commissioner René Montjoie – the new doctrine took another decisive step forward, notably with the belated publication of the Montjoie Report on Industrial Development in 1968, though the Nora Committee Report on Public Enterprise – with its stress on promoting competitiveness in the public sector – was an indispensable adjunct. The Montjoie Report analysed French industrial backwardness as due to a small industrial base, arising from the transfer of resources away from the sectors exposed to foreign competition to the non-industrial sectors and those that were 'administered' or sheltered from foreign competition. The result was low profitability and low investment. If France was successfully to face foreign competition it was essential that 'The general policy of the State should become industrial policy.' The interlocking directorate of graduates of the National School of Administration (especially Finance Inspectors) and Polytechnicians (especially Mining engineers) – who largely made up the membership of the Montjoie Committee – that ran much of the French state and through *pantouflage* big business, should be left to run affairs in a businesslike rather than in a bureaucratic way. (To run affairs democratically was regarded as wholly utopian.) Where the market failed to allocate resources correctly, it was accepted that selective state intervention was necessary.[33] So the new doctrine is not to be confused with a simple-minded adoption of laissez-faire but rather as a sophisticated form of neo-corporatism.

Ironically, at the very time that these new doctrines were becoming dominant in official circles, the French government played a major role in the 1966 constitution of a duopoly in basic steel and worked out a long-term investment strategy that was to create the over-capacity and lack of competitiveness that forced a government rescue operation in September 1978 that virtually nationalised the bankrupt industry. It is even more ironic that in the same month, in the preface to the section on 'The New Industrial Imperative' in the report on the adaptation of the Seventh Plan, appeared a ritual denunciation of help for lame ducks:

> the old ghost of *dirigisme* is once again haunting France; many want the state prodigally to assist firms in distress, providing them with a sort of social security that would guarantee them against foreign competitors, helping them financially to preserve jobs. Such a policy of public aid to firms would anaesthetise their natural antibodies and atrophy their vitality. It is the way to decadence.[34]

France is by no means the only country where general anathemas on this subject evaporate in the face of acute particular problems. As far as the frequency of state intervention is concerned, 'There is no evidence . . . that the scale of State intervention (measured by the number of *dossiers* handled or the volume of public funding) has diminished under Barre.'[35]

The abandonment of price control in 1978–9, first in manufacturing industry and more prudently in the service sector, was the most spectacular example of the switch from *dirigisme* to the reliance upon macro-economic monetary and fiscal instruments for combating inflation. This change not only restored the firms' cash flow but – Barre argued – also 'acted upon the real domestic causes of price increases. As for the external causes of price increases, we can do nothing except protect our economy from them by the strength of our currency.'[36] The monetarism of the French government was not as doctrinaire as either that of Milton Friedman or Margaret Thatcher. As the Development and Finance Planning Commissions put it in 1978

> The increase in the money supply should be . . . adequate to accommodate the expected change in the gross domestic product in volume and price increases compatible with the improvement of competitiveness. . . . The policy of controlled increase in the money supply should be continued. . . . The gradually and prudently but continuously decelerating increase in the money supply is a fundamental element in the fight against inflation, [together with a] high and stable rate of exchange for the French franc.[37]

In 1977 the Government decided to fix quantitative targets for the growth in money supply related to the expected increase in gross domestic product, the 1978 target being 12 per cent. Though the increase in the money supply fell from 16 per cent in 1975 to 13.9 per cent in 1978 – its lowest level since

1970 – and interest rates were high by traditional French standards, the Government was not able to deflate to the extent that it had intended.

National planning continued to have the traditional early warning function of trying to secure a medium-term, socio-economic consensus by revealing the foreign and domestic constraints upon political decision-makers but even the Economic and Social Council – dominated by a majority of businessmen, farmers and government nominees – could not conceal its anxiety at the very partial character of public policy. Faced with the projected rise in unemployment to two million, it advocated the abandonment of a wait-and-see employment policy because 'realism risks simply becoming resignation'.[38] The Employment Planning Commission was quite clear that specific policies such as the National Pact for Employment launched in 1977 and extended in a modified form in 1978–9, *following discussions with business but not trade-union organisations*, were no more than panaceas that blurred the distinction between training, employment and unemployment; while the implementation of the 1967 recommendations of the Ortoli-Delors Report on 'The social consequences of the evolution of the economy's structures', such as the creation of a National Employment Agency and the development of industrial training, were not on a sufficient scale to cope with the manpower problems created by the 1970s recession. A more aggressive policy of 'industrial redeployment', conceived as a life-and-death international struggle, meant that the nation's private savings and public funds had to be mobilised in the service of industry because it was 'the central lever of growth, of employment equilibrium and the preservation of our independence'.[39] The tendentious assertion was even made that 'among all institutions, the firm is one of those that has retained greatest strength and contributes most to the integration of our society'.[40] The feeble attempts at pursuing the Gaullist policy of reconciling capital and labour in the firm have made little headway owing to opposition from the businessmen, who have succeeded in getting their political friends in Parliament to amend out of existence the modest reforms proposed by the government.

To galvanise a people disheartened by policies that demanded sacrifices and effort without offering any attractively ambitious hopes for the future, the Eighth Plan emphasised the fear that France would dwindle into an insignificant and dominated country within an increasingly threatening international context unless it made Herculean efforts.

> It is the very reverse of the truth to describe as a crisis the sequence of events that has occurred since the beginning of the 1970s; these events represent long-term tendencies. In truth, we are not living through a crisis

> but its opposite: it is not a sudden or brief change but as we have seen the beginning of a structural and fundamental change in the economic geography of the world. Not a gap that can be quickly bridged but a break (with the past) that leads to entirely new perspectives.[41]

To meet this challenge, the authors of the Eighth Plan considered that an increase in the French birth-rate – which has fallen below replacement since 1974, the year in which abortion was legalised – and the development of its electro-nuclear programme would be the tests by which the France of the early 1980s would be judged. Compared with these long-term human and energy factors, all other issues receded into the status of the subsidiary. Of the two, significantly increasing the French birth-rate – the subject of much exhortation by Michel Debré – is the objective that will be hardest to attain.

POSTSCRIPT

The Socialist electoral victories of May–June 1981 not merely changed the political leadership in France; they also resulted in a drastic change of direction in terms of the order of priority between the economic objectives pursued and the way in which they were to be attained. The election of a Left-winger, François Mitterrand, as President of the Republic, followed by the dissolution of the National Assembly and the election of an absolute majority for the Socialist Party, were unprecedented under the Fifth Republic. They led to the formation of a Socialist-dominated coalition, headed by Pierre Mauroy as Prime Minister, four Communists entering the government but 'on their knees'. An early casualty was the Eighth Plan. 1981 will be the first year since 1947 in which France will have no plan. The new Minister of National and Regional Planning, Michel Rocard, has replaced the previous Planning Commissioner with Hubert Prévot, a Finance Ministry senior official who from 1974 to 1981 had been on detachment to the CFDT trade union! He will be responsible for preparing a two-year Interim Plan (1982–3), prior to the reversion to medium-term planning to cover the years 1984–8, the last five years of President Mitterrand's term of office. The latter plan will take a while to prepare as it intends to give regional planning a much larger role than ever before, as part of the Socialist decentralisation programme aimed at what Rocard has called 'institutional decolonisation'. However, the Interim Plan – approved by Parliament in autumn 1981 – was to meet the immediate emergency. Its six priorities were: rapidly increase employment; develop social security; help firms meet their current difficulties; substantially increase funds for research; make improvements in the people's daily work and leisure; follow-up the results of collective bargaining (notably in the matter of reduced working hours) and structural reforms (particularly the nationalisation programme discussed below). Unemployment having increased to 1.8 million and by 25 per cent between June 1980 and June 1981, this economic strategy promotes full employment to top priority, with the fight against inflation and the defence of the franc being demoted to a subsidiary role, although both in terms of the people carrying out the policy and the policy itself, the intention is to act with a rigour worthy of Pierre Mendès France.

The attempt to return to full employment was to be achieved by a modest Keynesian expansion of demand (thanks especially to an increase in the minimum wage), the hiring of 210,000 people in the public sector (to improve educational, hospital, postal and local public services), the promotion of public investment and the reduction of weekly working hours to 35. An important step towards this last objective was made with the July 1981 agreement between the CNPF and all the unions other than the CGT, ending three years of fruitless negotiation, thanks to the new political context. Though relatively modest in terms of the initial reduction of the maximum average legal workweek from 40 to 39 hours (the maximum in any one week being reduced to 48 hours from 50 and over any 12 consecutive weeks from 48 to 46 hours) there were other important provisions. Annual holidays with pay were to be increased from four to five weeks for the 50 per cent of the French workforce that did not currently enjoy them. By the end of September 1981, negotiations were to start in 90 or so different industries to adapt the general agreement to their special circumstances, particularly to reduce costs by allowing full utilisation of the plant through the workers accepting more flexible hours of work to suit employers. In those industries where no agreement was reached on the upper limit upon overtime not requiring authorisation by the factory inspector, this total would be fixed at 130 hours annually. A procedure was, furthermore, established to monitor how the agreement was working and to prepare the way for further reductions in the workweek. This was to take the form of indicative annual programming of the workweek, particular attention being paid to the incidence of the cuts on employment and on costs. Difficulties can be anticipated when it comes to the implementation of this agreement by the mass of small- and medium-sized firms. Furthermore, the scope for promoting employment in the private sector by further reducing working hours is limited by the reluctance of France's competitors to follow her lead, the constraint of competition being used by the employers as an argument against proceeding quickly or far in France alone. Employers and unions have agreed that legislation should follow to formalise the results of collective bargaining, a combination of voluntary and statutory action that hopes to achieve the benefits of both while correcting the weaknesses of each.

Another Keynesian instrument for promoting fuller employment is an increase in productive investment, which had fallen heavily in the private sector since 1974. With public sector investment being envisaged as the driving force, there was a further practical incentive – over and above the traditional Socialist ideological motivation – to extend public ownership. It would enable the planners to reckon in a more secure way upon the support of an enlarged public sector in the implementation of the government's economic policy guidelines. In addition to nationalising the merchant and deposit banks that had escaped de Gaulle's grasp at the Liberation (though their industrial holdings would be sold off except when they formed part of firms that would themselves be taken into public ownership) nine major industrial groups were nationalised, whilst negotiations were conducted with a further three which had a major foreign shareholding. The nine consisted of the military aircraft firm of Dassault and the military part of MATRA; the basic steel duopoly of SACILOR and USINOR (already largely publicly owned); the electrical and electronic giants Compagnie Générale d'Electricité and Thomson-Brandt; Péchiney-Ugine-Kuhlmann (aluminium and chemicals) and Rhône-Poulenc (chemicals and pharmaceuticals); lastly, Saint-Gobain Pont à Mousson, the largest, highly-diversified group of them all (glass, building materials, etc.). The three firms with which negotiations, aimed at their nationalisation while preserving technological, industrial and commercial links with their foreign 'partners', were started in July 1981 are: CII-Honeywell Bull (computers), ITT-France (telecommunications) and Roussel-Uclaf (pharmaceuticals), the last two having majority foreign control. Collectively, these twelve firms represent about 28 per cent of French industrial turnover and 16 per cent of the workforce. The state as a result will control all French aluminium production and half that of glass and computers, large portions of the chemical, shipbuilding, electrical and electronic, as well as a significant part of pharmaceuticals, building and public works industries. The Mauroy Government has a junior minister attached to the Prime Minister specifically responsible for the extension of the public sector. However, President Mitterrand and his Prime Minister have reiterated that only those firms put before the electorate would be nationalised, 'no more and no less', so no further extension of public ownership is planned for the early 1980s. These will be the national(ised) champions on which the Socialists particularly count to defend the home market, win new export markets and develop the investment that will keep France at the forefront of industrial innovation as well as generating new employment opportunities.[42]

France has broken away in spectacular fashion from the orthodox deflationist–monetarist mainstream and has – with an impressive combination of boldness and prudence – struck out in a direction that offers rosier prospects for the young people whose procreation Mitterrand's predecessors had encouraged without having jobs for them to do when they completed their education. While many predict fiasco, it is in the resilient tradition of a country that refuses to resign itself to despair – 'the worst is not inevitable' – that it should attempt heroically to revive something of the expansion of the fifties and sixties, not revert to the depression of the thirties.

NOTES AND REFERENCES

1. *Rapport sur l'adaptation du 7e Plan* (Paris: La Documentation Française, 1978) p. 13.
2. Ibid., pp. 8, 15, 18–20, 34; cf. J. Pelletier and H. Guillaume, *Rapport de la Commission du Développement: Options du 8e Plan* (Paris: Commissariat Général du Plan, 1979) paras. 212 and 521.
3. *Rapport sur l'adaptation du 7e Plan*, p. 9; cf. p. 79.
4. Introduction to *Rapport de la Commission de l'Emploi et des Relations du Travail, 8e Plan* (Paris: La Documentation Française, 1980) p. 15; cf. pp. 14, 234.
5. Ibid., pp. 24–8; cf. *Rapport sur l'adaptation du 7e Plan*, pp. 81–3.
6. *Commission de l'Emploi, 8e Plan*, pp. 31–3, 37–8, 41–2.
7. Ibid., pp. 46–50. On motor cars, see Christian Stoffaës, *La grande menace industrielle* (Paris: Calmann-Lévy, 2nd ed., 1978) pp. 135 ff.
8. *Commission de l'Emploi*, pp. 47, 52–7.
9. *Rapport sur les principales options du 8e Plan* (Paris: La Documentation Française, April 1979) pp. 26–30; cf. Pelletier and Guillaume, op. cit., p. 36. For an analysis of the structural causes of French unemployment in the 1970s, see an INSEE study in *Economie et Statistique*, no. 123 (July 1980).
10. *Commission de l'Emploi, 8e Plan*, pp. 68–74, 83 and *Révision du 7e Plan: Synthèse des Travaux des Commissions et Comités Consultés pour la révision* (Paris: Commissariat Général du Plan, 1978) pp. 16–17.
11. *Commission de l'Emploi, 8e Plan*, pp. 74–82; and *Révision du 7e Plan*, pp. 17–18, 72–3.
12. *Rapport sur les principales options du 8e Plan*, op.cit., p. 33; cf. *Rapport sur l'adaptation du 7e Plan*, pp. 39–40.
13. *Rapport sur les principales options du 8e Plan*, p. 40.
14. *Révision du 7e Plan*, pp. 42–3. See also *8e Plan de développement économique et social, 1981–5* (Paris: Journal Official, 1980) pp. 84–5.
15. *Rapport sur les principales options du 8e Plan*, pp. 34–5. On the Priority Action Programmes, see J. Hayward 'From planning the French economy to planning the French State', in Vincent Wright (ed.), *Giscard, the Giscardiens and Giscardisme* (London: Allen & Unwin, forthcoming). On the context of

the electro-nuclear programme, see N. J. D. Lucas, *Energy in France: Planning, Politics and Policy* (London: Europa Publications, 1979).

16. *Commission de l'Emploi, 8e Plan*, pp. 64–5; *Révision du 7e Plan*, pp. 55–7
17. *Rapport sur les principales options du 8e Plan*, p. 8; cf. p. 9.
18. *Révision du 7e Plan*, pp. 62–4.
19. SOFRES poll in *Le Nouvel Observateur*, no. 773 (3 September 1979) p. 23; cf. pp. 21–4.
20. Jean-Luc Parodi, 'L' échec des gauches', *Revue Politique et Parlementaire*, no. 873 (1978) pp. 5–6, and Jean-Luc Parodi, 'Profil de l'année, Septembre 1978–Août 1979', *Pouvoirs*, no. 11 (1979) pp. 174–5.
21. Parodi in *Revue Politique et Parlementaire*, no. 873, pp. 5–6, and Parodi, *Pouvoirs*, no. 11, pp. 174–6. See also Jean-Dominique Lafay, 'Les conséquences électorales de la conjoncture économique: essai de précision chiffrée pour mars 1978', *Vie et Sciences Economiques* (October 1977).
22. *Rapport de la Commission Industrie, 7e Plan* (Paris: La Documentation Française, 1976) pp. 9–10, 49–51.
23. *Rapport sur l'adaptation du 7e Plan*, pp. 64–5. The Barre quotation is from an interview in *Le Progrès de Lyon* (15 April 1980).
24. *Rapport sur les principales options du 8e Plan*, p. 33.
25. *Le Progrès de Lyon* (15 April 1980) and *Le Monde* (16 April 1980).
26. Liliane Sardais, *L'Etat et l'Internationalisation du Capital: Un essai sur la politique industrielle en France*, Doctoral thesis (University of Paris X, Nanterre, 1977) pp. 387–91; cf. p. 380 ff.
27. Ibid., pp. 444–9; cf. pp. 350, 359–72. See also 'Les implantations étrangers en France au 1 Janvier, 1971', *Développement industriel et scientifique*, no. 17 (December 1973); and 'Les participations étrangèrs dans l'industrie française en 1971', *Economie et Statistique*, no. 52 (January 1974).
28. *Rapport sur les principales options du 8e Plan*, p. 73. On the impact of the recession on CFDT membership, see Françoise Lozier, 'La CFDT en chiffres' in the special issue of *Esprit* on 'La CFDT et la crise du Syndicalisme' (April 1980) pp. 16–17. See also J. Bunel, 'L'action syndicale, crise et recentrage', *Economie et Humanisme*, no. 245 (January–February, 1979).
29. *Commission de l'Emploi, 8e Plan*, p. 176; cf. pp. 175–81, 207–12, 227. See also *Révision du 7e Plan*, pp. 28–30; *Rapport sur l'adaptation du 7e Plan*, pp. 84–5; *Rapport sur les principales options du 8e Plan*, pp. 70–2. On the issue in the mid-1960s, see Jack Hayward, 'The Reduction of Working Hours and France's Fifth Plan', *British Journal of Industrial Relations*, VIII (March 1969) pp. 84–112. See also the book by Jacques Delors, *Exchange et Projets club: La Révolution du temps choisi* (Paris: Editions Albin Michel, 1980). *Le Monde, dossiers et documents* devoted a special issue to 'La Durée du Travail', no. 70 (April 1980).
30. See the declaration by the CGT and CFDT representatives appended to the Economic and Social Council's *Avis* on the *Adaptation du 7e Plan* (October 1978) pp. 44–6 and on the *Principales Options du 8e Plan* (May 1979) pp. 39–41. See also their views appended to *Commission de l'Emploi, 8e Plan*, pp. 231–7; and the extended summary in *Le Monde* (14 June 1980) p. 41, of the 27 scenarios for the Eighth Plan. For the earlier background, see Jean-Pierre Oppenheim, *La CFDT et la Planification* (Paris: TEMA-Editions, 1973).

31. Ministère de l'Economie, *Rapport sur les aides publiques à l'industrie* (1979) summarised in *Le Monde* (25 December 1979) p. 22.
32. Sardais, op.cit., p. 601; cf. pp. 215–27, 252, 582.
33. Ibid., pp. 42–8, 255–76, 288–94, 342, 400; cf. Lionel Stoleru, *L'Impératif Industriel* (Paris: Seuil, 1969). *Pantouflage* in this context is the practice by which many large industrial, banking and insurance firms recruit their senior management from the ranks of the senior civil service.
34. *Rapport sur l'adaptation du 7ᵉ Plan*, p. 55. On government-business collaboration in this industry, see my chapter on 'Steel' in Raymond Veron (ed.), *Big Business and the State in Western Europe* (Cambridge, Mass.: Harvard University Press, 1974) pp. 265–9.
35. Diana Green, 'Economic Policy and the Governing Coalition', in Philip Cerny and Martin Schain (eds), *French Politics and Public Policy* (London: F. Pinter, 1980) p. 167; cf. Plan's Finance Committee views in *Révision du 7ᵉ Plan*, p. 46. On what he called 'the contradictions between liberal doctrine and interventionist practices' in the Government's petroleum policy, as reflected in its treatment of its chosen instrument ELF-ERAP, involving a 'hesitation waltz between liberalism and interventionism', see Bruno Dethomas, 'Retour au libéral-dirigisme', *Le Monde* (18 July 1980); cf. his 'La réorganisation du groupe ELF-ERAP', *Le Monde* (1 August 1980).
36. Interview published in *Sud-Ouest* (6 March 1980). See also *8ᵉ Plan de développement*, op.cit., pp. 61, 70.
37. *Révision du 7ᵉ Plan*, pp. 7, 41–2; cf. Economic and Social Council's *Avis* on the *Adaptation du 7ᵉ Plan*, p. 14.
38. Economic and Social Council's *Avis* on the *Principales Options du 7ᵉ Plan*, p. 28; cf. p. 4.
39. *Rapport sur l'adaptation du 7ᵉ Plan*, p. 57; cf. 56ff and *Révision du 7ᵉ Plan*, pp. 11, 20–3, 44–50, 121. See also Sardais, op. cit., pp. 2–9, 331–9, and Alain Boublil, 'Stratégies et Financement de l'Industrie Française' (14 December 1979).
40. *Rapport sur l'adaptation du 7ᵉ Plan*, p. 67.
41. *Rapport sur les principales options du 8ᵉ Plan*, p. 11; cf. p. 16. On the view that 1965 rather than 1974 marks the decisive break in French post-war development, see Henri Mendras (ed.), *La Sagesse et le Désordre: France 1980* (Paris: Gallimard, 1980), notably the introductory chapter by Mendras, pp. 18–24 and Gérard Pavy, 'Le retournement de l'année 1965', p. 63ff.
42. On the Socialist conception of nationalisation and its pre-electoral programme, see *Socialisme et Industrie* (Paris: Club Socialiste du Livres, 1981). See also Alain Boublil (on the staff of President Mitterrand), *Le Socialisme Industriel* (Paris: Presses Universitaires de France, 1977) especially part II, and *L'Agression: L'Etat – Giscard contre le Secteur Public* (Paris: Club Socialiste du Livre, 1980).

6 Britain in the 1970s: Economic Crisis and the Resurgence of Radicalism

DAVID COATES

BRITAIN'S ECONOMIC PROBLEM

The world recession of the 1970s did not qualitatively alter the character of British political life. Instead, it threw into sharper relief issues and processes that have long been of central concern to British politicians and their electorates. For most of this century politics in Britain have been dominated by the problems of an ailing economy, and at least since the war electorates have come to measure their governments primarily against the benchmark of economic performance. Indeed, both governments and party support have been persistent casualities of that measuring exercise. No government since 1959 has managed to win the general election with which its first full five-year term of office closed, and neither of the major political parties has managed to reverse permanently the long-term loss of electoral support. In 1951 the Conservative and Labour Parties together captured 96.6 per cent of all the votes cast. By October 1974 they could only manage to capture 75 per cent[1]; and at the heart of that loss has been the growing alienation of voters from politicians who have repeatedly failed to deliver that economic regeneration which they had so regularly promised in their pursuit of government office.

To understand the full impact of the world recession on British politics in the 1970s it is necessary to recognise the character of this long-term economic malaise. The twenty-five years of sustained growth in the capitalist world after 1948 had not been able to prevent the dwindling competitiveness of the British economy from emerging as a major political issue from the late 1950s. Through the years of the long boom the performance of British capitalism, relative to that of its major competitors, weakened significantly. Over the period as a whole the British economy grew at a rate that was significantly slower than that achieved by any other major industrial power in the West[2], and the percentage of that slowly growing domestic product finding its way into the provision of new manufacturing plant and equipment was persistently lower than elsewhere[3]. As a result the productivity of labour in British manufacturing industry rose less sharply than in other OECD countries[4], and the share of world trade captured by commodities manufactured in the United Kingdom steadily fell[5]. Even before the world recession intensified international competition in the 1970s, the degree of penetration of the United Kingdom home market by foreign imports was rising rapidly; and this was enough to give British politics a particular agenda throughout the 1960s. From 1957 economic expansion was repeatedly blocked, by balance-of-payments crises that brought with them periods of deliberate deflation, reluctantly adopted devaluations of sterling and occasional recourse to foreign loans and to internationally organised support for the pound. All this had already educated British politicians and their electorate in the political limits that economic crises could bring, long before these lessons were generalised throughout the OECD area by the world recession.

The quadrupling of oil prices after the Yom Kippur war brought to an end, in the United Kingdom as elsewhere, the short-lived boom of the early 1970s, during which even the British economy had grown at an annual rate of 5 per cent, with the usual heavy cost to the balance of payments. As Harold Wilson later said, his government inherited in 1974 what 'was already the grimmest (balance of payments) on record before a single oil producer had raised his price or turned off his tap'[6]. The oil crisis then turned this deficit (of 3 per cent of GNP) into one of 5 per cent by the end of 1974, forced the new Labour government into its first set of massive foreign loans, and weakened sterling significantly. As world trade fell sharply in the first half of 1975 the British economy went into a sustained slump. The index of industrial production, which had risen to 110.7 (January 1970 levels equalling 100) by the third quarter of 1973, fell back to 100 by September 1975, and by early 1978 had still not regained its 1973 levels. Industrial production did revive briefly in 1978 and 1979 (the new oil-inflated index reached 117.7 by June 1979–1975 levels now equalling 100) but it was falling again by 1980.

This industrial stagnation was accompanied, and indeed compounded, by a weak currency and a high rate of domestic inflation. Before the arrival of North Sea oil, the pound steadily, and often dramatically, lost value against other major currencies, including the weakening dollar. Sterling lost 29 per cent of its value against the dollar between December 1971 and June 1975;

and then, in six hectic months of currency speculation, fell from 2.0 dollars in March to 1.60 dollars in October to precipitate a political crisis that effectively destroyed the Labour government's social programme. In fact, as we shall see, that social programme had by then already been jeopardised by the Labour Cabinet's relentless pursuit of price stability in the face of persistently high rates of domestic inflation. The inflation rate in the United Kingdom, at 6.4 per cent in 1970, reached 15 per cent by March 1974 and 30 per cent briefly in June 1975. It was still only just below 10 per cent by the general election of 1979 and had returned to 20 per cent by the end of the decade. It was this mixture of industrial stagnation, a weak currency and persistent inflation which dominated British politics in the 1970s, and which brought with it high and growing levels of unemployment. In 1970 the officially registered level of unemployment in Great Britain was 523,000, and though this reached 1,000,000 in January 1972 it fell back to 545,000 by March 1974. Under the Labour government unemployment then rose steadily to reach 1,370,000 by September 1977, and remained at much that level through to 1979, before rising again (to over 2,500,000) by the middle of 1981. And those national figures, high as they were, masked even worse regional experiences that gave unemployment percentages for 1980 of 11.6 per cent for Northern Ireland and 9 per cent for Scotland and the English North-east.

Moreover, as British politicians struggled with these problems in the 1970s they found that their freedom of manoeuvre was seriously restricted by three other features of the economy's competitive weakness which the world recession then accentuated. They found first that market forces were already 'deindustrialising' Britain at a rate faster than elsewhere in the OECD area – were leaving them, that is, with a manufacturing sector capable of employing fewer and fewer people. Between 1961 and 1975 the number of people employed in the manufacturing sector of British industry fell from 8,600,000 to 7,400,000 as the labour force in total grew by at least 500,000. This meant that even with the modest rise in labour productivity characteristic of the British manufacturing sector, politicians in the late 1970s needed to organise the creation of an extra 1,300,000 jobs merely to achieve a relatively modest reduction in unemployment (to 800,000); and this in its turn required the achievement of a 5 per cent rate of growth in the economy as a whole between 1978 and 1981 that was literally beyond the capacities of governments of either party.

In addition, politicians found themselves increasingly trapped by the way in which earlier British governments had systematically expanded public-sector employment and activity to absorb the discarded labour of a shrinking private manufacturing sector and to meet the rising social expectations of their electorate. Between 1961 and 1978 the number of people employed in national and local government, education and health services in Great Britain grew from 2,900,000 to 4,700,000, and throughout the 1970s just about half of the entire Gross Domestic Product passed at some stage through the hands of the state. Indeed one reason that was often given for the economy's disproportionately high rate of price inflation was this expansion of public-sector employment and spending, and this meant that, from the middle 1970s at least, governments came under very heavy pressure from the rising tide of monetarist opinion to cut their expenditure and to reduce the public sector's claim on real resources and investment funds.

Yet in doing so these same politicians found themselves faced with opposition to just these policies from that third feature of the British crisis in the 1970s that had few parallels elsewhere in the OECD area, namely from the existence of a growing, well-organised, relatively disciplined and at times industrially militant trade-union movement. For the story of British politics in the 1970s is really one of a struggle between those forces released on and through successive governments by the deepening recession of world capitalism and those hesitant but at times very real forces of resistance that emerged from within the labour movement. In fact it is impossible to understand the full complexity of recent British politics without recognising that there were such contradictory pressures operating on the British State, and without seeing that those pressures arose directly out of the class relationships of a capitalist system in recession. It is with the full impact of these on the freedom of manoeuvre and effectiveness of successive British governments that the rest of this chapter has necessarily to be concerned.

THE RISE OF THE RADICALS

The persistence of the competitive weakness of British capitalism, and its accentuation during the world recession, had at least one important and direct political consequence in the 1970s. It altered the weight of factional support within each major political party, strengthening within each party that faction which wished to make a sharp break with the form into which government economic policy had settled in the 1960s. It strengthened, that is, those who wished to replace the 1960s legacy of indicative planning, indirect State aid to industry and periodic periods of incomes restraint with policies that were closer to their parties' very different and quite particular political philosophies.

This is as true for the Conservative Party as it was for the Labour Party. On two separate occasions in the 1970s Conservative governments were returned to power arguing for a neo-liberal solution to Britain's economic problems and offering as a result less government activity and more market competition as the key to economic recovery. Edward Heath's successful election campaign in 1970 was built on the promise of 'a quiet revolution' that involved new laws to curb trade-union power and less government intervention in the private sector. Though his government (unlike its Thatcherite successor) still expected a Conservative cabinet to accept direct and immediate responsibility for the levels of inflation and employment – and was in that sense still Keynesian in its general outlook – the whole thrust of Edward Heath's 'Selsdon Park'[7] strategy was to pull government back from detailed intervention in economic activity, to expose firms to greater competition with fewer state subsidies, and to leave private employers free to settle wages and conditions with their employees within limits set only by the play of market forces. Under the initial Conservative policies (those ruling in 1970 and 1971) these market forces were to be strengthened primarily by entry into the Common Market, but they were also to be consolidated by the removal of regional investment grants, and by the curtailment of public subsidies to 'lame duck' private firms. In addition, they were to be underwritten by the removal of interventionist agencies inherited from the Labour government – most noticeably here the National Board for Prices and Incomes and the Industrial Reorganisation Corporation – and they were to be accompanied by a new Industrial Relations Act that would restrict the trade unions' legal right to organise, to picket and to strike.

When Margaret Thatcher led the Conservatives back to power in 1979 her 'revolution' was similar in trajectory but much less 'quiet', in that by then the party leaderships' commitment to such a neo-liberal economic strategy was far more developed. In part this was because her cabinet was staffed by the very men who had helped to design the Selsdon Park policies, and who had felt most betrayed by their abandonment in 1972. But it also reflected the more general rise of a monetarist orthodoxy among right-wing economists in the 1970s, as the recession destroyed the credibility of the Keynesian alternative on which more conventional tri-partite government strategies had rested in the post-war period. In any event, and for whatever reason, the Conservative Party returned to office in 1979 committed to large-scale reductions in government spending and taxation that would redistribute resources from the provision of social welfare towards the coercive apparatus of a more authoritarian state, and to reducing significantly the scale of public subsidies to private firms. That government entered office too promising new laws to restrict trade-union rights, and arguing again that the regeneration of British industry required its exposure to the forces of world competition within a taxation system that facilitated the accumulation of private wealth and under a government that had the political will to control the money supply (and if need be, to cut, at least temporarily, the real living standards of the poor, the sick and the unemployed as it did so).

In the years between these two Conservative administrations the Labour government of 1974–9 also began life dominated by its very different brand of radicalism. Labour Party policy in opposition moved sharply to the left between 1970 and 1974, under the impact of a trade-union movement drawn into the centre of the political arena by the struggles against the Conservatives' Industrial Relations Act. As a result the Wilson government entered office committed to the renegotiation of the terms of entry into the EC, and to British withdrawal if those terms were not publicly supported by a referendum. Moreover, it entered office committed to greater public control of the very market forces which the Conservatives wished to unleash – greater control that was to come through the extension of public ownership into the profitable sections of manufacturing industry and through the negotiation of planning agreements with the large firms left in private hands. Far from wishing to reduce trade-union power or to alter the taxation system in favour of the holders of private capital, the Labour government entered office committed to new labour laws that would increase the rights of unionists and workers alike; and to wealth taxes, more government expenditure on social services and an extension of industrial democracy which would in total achieve 'a fundamental and irreversible shift in the balance of power and wealth in favour of working people and their families'[8].

Though these radical solutions differed qualitatively from one another in the substance of their proposals, they at least shared certain features that it is important to draw out. Radicals in both parties agreed that there was something profoundly wrong with the distribution of class forces in British society which it was the job of the State to redress as the key to economic recovery, and this meant that the Conservative neo-Liberals and the Labour Left held a common specification of what the important questions of economic and social policy ought properly to be. As a result governments in Britain entered office in the 1970s holding principled views on whether industrial regeneration would be helped or hindered by the encouragement or control of market forces, by curtailing or extending state aid to industry, by reducing or increasing public expenditure, by expanding or compressing inequalities in income, wealth and industrial power, and by reducing or adding to the guaranteed legal rights of trade unionists and workers. And though the parliamentary debate on these issues was periodically scarred by the ferocity of the radicals' own disagreements, the intensity of this set of public exchanges should not be allowed to obscure the underlying consensus that bound them together. The radicals in each party clearly felt, and did so in opposition to more moderate views regularly expressed inside their own parties, that the middle position on each of these aspects of economic and social policy needed to be abandoned, and that the State either had to go beyond (or to retreat from) the playing of a simple brokerage role of the 1960s type. It was, in their view, not enough for politicians to restrict themselves to the co-ordination of the activities of leading business and labour spokesmen – a co-ordination which left intact the respective degrees of social power which those spokesmen (and their private constituencies) enjoyed. On the contrary, it was just this alteration in the balance of power which preoccupied the radicals in both parties through the decade.

And of course there is one other sense in which the radical position in each party had more in common than their adherents would probably care to admit, for in the 1970s they shared not only a common set of preoccupations but also a common fate. The Thatcherite radicals apart (at least to date), the Conservative neo-Liberals and the Labour Left in the 1970s experienced not only a common predominance whenever their party was in opposition. They also found, in spite of that predominance, that their policy proposals were all abandoned within the lifetime of the first Parliament elected to oversee their implementation. They found too that they were abandoned in favour of that very middle ground (of indicative planning, generous public aid to a loosely controlled private sector, and incomes policies) that they were supposed to replace. It is this 'retreat from radicalism' and the reassertion of the centre in British politics, which provides the underlying continuity to an otherwise disparate sequence of domestic political events in the 1970s, and which now has to be documented and explained.

THE DEFEAT OF THE RADICALS

This defeat of radicalism was a direct consequence of the entrenched defensive strength of the main economically based pressure groups faced by politicians, and of the particular pattern of class forces to which those groups gave expression. The particular group in the forefront of the confrontation varied with the government and the time, but over the decade as a whole politicians of both parties failed to alter in any fundamental way the defensive strengths of either labour or capital, and in that sense failed to break the impasse between them. The first evidence of this defensive strength was shown by the trade-union movement after 1969, when union opposition effectively prevented the full implementation of a new body of labour law by first a Labour and then a Conservative administration. The

Labour government of 1966–70 did not even manage to legislate. The publication of its White Paper (*In Place of Strife*) was enough to inspire a concerted trade-union campaign and to precipitate a rare but completely successful revolt by backbench Labour MPs against it[9]. That discredited Labour cabinet then saw the last vestiges of its incomes policies destroyed by union militancy in the public sector, and lost the 1970 election to a Conservative Party committed to even more rigorous industrial relations legislation, which this time became law in 1971 as the Industrial Relations Act.

That Act, explicitly presented to the electorate as a mechanism for reducing 'irresponsible' trade-union power, restricted legal protection against civil damages to those unions willing to register with a new Registrar, and to make their internal rules comply with his specifications. The Act enabled collective agreements to be made legally binding even where the trade unions were opposed, and created a new court structure (the National Industrial Relations Court) to enforce those agreements and to punish unions whose members refused to respect their terms. Indeed the Act, and its associated codes, specified a set of widely used trade-union tactics (the sympathy strike, the blacking of goods, unconstitutional strike action and striking for a closed shop) as beyond the protection of the law, and gave to government ministers new powers to order 'cooling-off periods' and compulsory strike ballots. In these ways the Act tipped the balance of legal (and hence social and economic) rights against the unions. It left unregistered unions liable to additional taxation and to claims for civil damages. It created a situation in which breaches of the code of industrial relations practices by individual trade unionists could leave their union liable to fines and to levies for compensation (imposed by the NIRC) and leave themselves open to civil damages; and it meant that unions or members ignoring or refusing to comply with the orders of the NIRC were liable to be held in contempt of court, with its attendant fines and imprisonments.

No post-war government had taken such powers to itself, nor shed them so quickly. Within twelve months of the Act's implementation it was effectively abandoned by the Cabinet which had initiated it, as a direct result of sustained and mounting opposition from within the trade-union movement. As the Industrial Relations Bill passed through its parliamentary stages, the TUC staged a series of demonstrations and marches that brought 160,000 trade unionists to London in February 1971 in the largest show of political opposition from the official union movement since the General Strike of 1926; and when that failed to stop the Bill becoming law the General Council instructed unions not to register, and expelled unions that did. Moreover, when that official campaign looked in danger of wilting under the first set of fines handed down by the NIRC, it was bolstered again by the militancy of the miners, by the railwaymen's massive vote for strike action in the spring of 1972, and by the intransigence of dockers in Liverpool and London which took five of them to jail and the country to the edge of another General Strike.

The sharp 'U turn' which the Heath government made in its economic strategy after July 1972 was partly a reaction to all this. For by then, in any case Conservative ministers were beginning to discover that the free play of market forces was more likely to encourage speculative investment in property than it was to bring about investment in manufacturing plant and equipment; and that discovery was already sapping cabinet confidence in the Selsdon Park strategy for reasons that were quite unconnected to this rising tide of working-class resistance. What the militancy of the dockers then added was the clear indication that, in the relatively favourable market conditions of the early 1970s at least, that strategy was likely to be counter-productive in the area of labour relations as well. In a very short space of time Conservative ministers found that they could not force a new body of labour law (and an associated set of more moderate trade-union industrial practices) on well-organised, self-confident and industrially militant groups of workers without escalating the level of industrial unrest that their new labour law was supposed to bring down. Nor were they able to withdraw their subsidies to private firms without driving unemployment up to what were then thought to be politically unacceptable levels, without inspiring workers to take possession of closed industrial plants (as at Upper Clyde Shipbuilders in the summer of 1971) and without alienating significant sections of industrial capital who looked to the State for aid in their own restructuring. The legal rigidities of the NIRC, and its dramatic effect on levels of industrial militancy, only antagonised that section of capital still further (the CBI, no less than the TUC, came to believe that the Industrial Relations Act was unworkable in its existing form); and this left the Heath government by the middle of 1972 effectively isolated not only from the labour movement but also from significant sections of its own business constituency. It was this isolation that prompted the Heath government to return to a more conventional search for tripartite agreement between unions, management and the State from the summer of 1972, and which led it back to economic policies that concentrated on prices and wages controls, and on the provision of extensive state aid to industry.

Instead of altering the balance of class forces in favour of capital by a direct assault on trade-union legal rights, and by exposing British industry to stronger market forces, the Heath government's policies precipitated the greatest explosion of industrial militancy since the early 1920s, and encouraged the unions to negotiate with the then Labour opposition its most radical political programme for at least forty years. The number of days lost in industrial disputes in 1972 was the highest for any year since the General Strike, and included groups of workers who had never previously been involved in industrial action. As a result the immediate legacy of the Heath years was not a docile labour movement but rather, a situation in which wage settlements began to rise to record heights (they touched 30 per cent in the early summer of 1975) and in which a Labour government was returned committed to the rapid implementation of a vast range of trade-union economic and political demands. These included, as we have seen, the repeal of the Industrial Relations Act and the Housing Finance Act, the renegotiation of Britain's terms of entry into the EC, extensive public ownership, tight government control of large private firms, greater social expenditure, and a redistribution of wealth and industrial power away from the rich. Never before had trade-union political influence so shaped the agenda of British politics; so that when Paul Johnson wrote in May 1975 that the unions 'in recent years . . . have exhausted or beaten down any opposition, and have finally succeeded in making themselves the arbiters of the British economy'[10], there was no shortage of evidence to sustain his case.

In fact, Paul Johnson's strictures were misplaced, as subsequent events were to show, because he (and the Labour Left of which he was so critical) continued to under-estimate the defensive strength of industrial and financial capital in the face of rising trade-union power. Between 1975 and 1980 trade union political leverage waned, and union control of the agenda of British politics vanished, as the unions' ability to prevent cuts in real wages, social expenditure and employment levels was eroded by the deepening recession, and by organised capital's refusal to co-operate with Labour government radicalism. It must be said, however, that between the two elections of 1974, and immediately afterwards, this was not obvious, and trade unionism did enjoy a rare moment of political dominance. Price controls were tightened, as promised. Basic foods were subsidised, and rents frozen. The incomes policy of the Heath government was abandoned, a new trade union act was introduced, pensions and other social-security payments were raised and index-linked, a wealth tax was proposed and the extension of industrial democracy was promised. And in addition the National Enterprise Board was created to extend public ownership, British Leyland was nationalised, and planning agreements were foreshadowed in Tony Benn's controversial White Paper, *The Regeneration of British Industry*.

But in spite of (or more properly, in reaction to) this heady start, the Labour government's radicalism was eventually blocked by the stubborn resistance of industry and finance. The new labour law and indexed pensions survived (to be the targets of the Thatcher government), evidence of 'the trade unions' residual political power under Labour. But the wealth tax was quietly abandoned. Large companies simply refused to negotiate planning agreements (Chrysler apart)[11], and the Labour government declined to force them, for fear of alienating investment and hence economic growth and employment. The promise of industrial democracy was repeatedly delayed in the face of the CBI's defense of managerial prerogatives, and price controls were systematically eased (until rising trade-union militancy forced their temporary tightening again in the winter of 1978–9) to facilitate profit-making and private capital accumulation. Moreover, the strength of the labour movement in the early days of the Labour government, and the continuing competitive weakness of British capitalism, combined to leave sterling weak, and a series of financial crises prior to the arrival of North Sea oil precipitated a new series of incomes policies after July 1975 and, via an IMF loan, brought cuts in social expenditure after December 1976.

It is worth stressing here that the CBI itself played only a modest role in the organisation of this Conservative reaction to Labour radicalism, and that national industrial capital in general was less potent a pressure on Labour ministers than were the institutions of the City and the international financial community. The Labour government had consistently to operate within the 'political space' allowed to it by speculative movements of foreign currency in and out of the City; and was literally driven to the IMF by the systematic refusal of foreign holders of sterling (mainly oil-producing governments and large multinational corporations) to leave their short-term funds in London while inflation was so high, output so low and government social spending so ambitious. Nor could the Labour government impose its policies on recalcitrant multinational corporations, and instead – to take one important example of a general feature of political life between 1974 and 1979 – was forced eventually and with considerable loss of face to abandon its 'blacking' of companies that broke its pay code because of the Ford Motor Company's refusal to abide by those pay restraints. Trade-union pressure and multinational corporate power acted in collusion here, as an eleven-week strike forced Ford's hand, and made the company call the government's bluff. Desperate to attract new motor factories to Wales, Labour ministers could not bring themselves to withdraw a large subsidy as a penalty for Ford's 'generosity' to its workers; and in abandoning its stance in this way the Labour government's weakness in the face of multinational industrial capital prepared the ground for its later confrontation with sections of its own employees – a confrontation that brought it to electoral defeat in 1979 after the 'winter of discontent' that followed the Ford settlement.

CBI pressure in all this was marginal if persistent, and throughout the

1974–9 Labour government the CBI ranked a poor third to the City and to international firms as an effective blockage on Labour radicalism. For Labour ministers normally controlled enough political resources to be able to cope with industrial firms operating primarily within the national market (the blacklist, for example, was highly effective as a way of disciplining small and medium-size firms in industry and transport, for all that the CBI opposed the manner of its use); and for this reason ministers could afford largely to ignore a CBI which spoke mainly for the nationally-based concerns. What leverage the CBI did enjoy – on industrial democracy and on price controls – accrued to it because even Labour ministers had to pay some heed to its small and medium-size industrial firms whose investment performance they needed to bolster. But what the Labour government could not handle in so cavalier a way was internationally based capital, both industrial and financial. That kind of capital had a capacity to move away from the United Kingdom with potentially disastrous local consequences, and it was its international mobility that left Labour ministers so dependent on its voluntary co-operation, and so supine as a result in the face of its terms.

So, like the Heath government before it, the Labour government after 1974 was forced to 'U turn'. It was forced back into a centrally organised incomes policy which it then sustained only at the cost of growing union opposition; and it moved away from a detailed control of large companies into a new industrial strategy which allowed it to channel large amounts of public money into private firms without those firms being in any way subject to the majority of the controls, or to the scale and character of public ownership, that had been envisaged in Opposition. And the result, as with the Heath government, was that the Labour government ended its days isolated from its natural constituency – in this case, the trade-union movement – as its industrial strategy failed to work and as its income policy was broken by prolonged and at times bitter industrial disputes.

The Conservative and Labour governments were pulled to similar positions from different starting points. For the Heath government, a dependence on the free play of market forces and an attack on trade-union legal rights were abandoned in favour of a strategy which sought to win union support for incomes restraint in return for a more interventionist role in industry that extended as far as price controls and generous state funding. For the Labour governments of Harold Wilson and then James Callaghan, an attempt to win voluntary wage restraint by a radical change in the distribution of income and tight government control over all aspects of industrial production was quickly abandoned in favour of a looser relationship with private capital that sought to facilitate private capital accumulation by leaving the distribution of national income unaltered and the freedom of trade-union bargainers subordinated to centrally specified wage norms. The two parties remained as governments distinguishable only by the residues of their very different starting points. The Labour government remained to the end more keenly interventionist in industry than the Conservatives, more committed to consulting trade unionist and to strengthening the legal rights of union members and other workers, and more prone to present the long-term equalisation of income as essential to industrial recovery and social peace. But increasingly, even under a Labour government, these distinctions were more verbal than real, and in practice what is striking about the policies of British governments prior to 1979 is how the world recession drew from them a broadly similar set of reactions and responses.

THE IMPERATIVES ON THE STATE

This experience of frustrated radicalism, of both the Left and the Right, tells us something of importance about the character of the modern State, about its role, and about the limits which exist on its power. Politicians, for all their rhetoric, do not constitute a major social force in their own right. Rather they periodically preside over a state bureaucracy which has itself to be galvanised into action[12], and they face a multiplicity of centres of private power that have to be won over to voluntary co-operation by the harnessing of their private self interests to the policies of the State. It is true of course that the State has an enormous battery of powers and sanctions against the recalcitrant, and that it enjoys a legitimacy which gives it considerable leverage in the perpetual struggle for support. But politicians in the 1970s found, as they have found repeatedly down the years, that it is literally impossible to coerce and control all the groups they seek to mobilise – or at least that it is impossible to do that without dismantling the democratic rights and constitutional structures of the modern liberal state – and that as a result democratic politicians have to govern in the face of very powerful counter-sanctions over which they enjoy no direct control.

The experience of British governments between 1970 and 1979 also tells us something of importance about the particular imperatives operating on the British State in the context of a world recession. The worsening competitive position of British capitalism left politicians with very little freedom of manoeuvre. Governments of each party found it vital (for their own electoral survival, to finance their own expenditure plans, and to achieve economic growth) to strengthen private capital accumulation, and to create the market and production conditions that would encourage that. In the process of doing this, they found that State spending was just too vital a part of the markets and investment sources of significant sections of private manufacturing capital to be removable without immediately affecting profit levels and employment (not least because the profit levels of many major British-based companies throughout the 1970s were just too low to produce that investment and those jobs without extensive state funding). And if that were not serious enough, successive governments found too that the working class was so well organised industrially that workers and their representatives could not be easily and persistently ignored in the planning and implementation of that restructuring investment programme. Indeed it was the coming together of these features of British industrial life in the 1970s that pulled successive governments to a kind of corporatist industrial strategy in which cabinet after cabinet initiated national tripartite discussions in order to build a common alliance between industrial capital and labour under the leadership of an interventionist State.

But politicians also found that their situation was full of contradictions and pitfalls. Throughout the 1970s that corporatist strategy struggled for effectiveness against the tide of world-market forces. Because of the economy's competitive weakness, private capital showed a persistent tendency to move abroad, seeking more profitable outlets at the cost of de-industrialising the home base; and so politicians were obliged to seek a national industrial consensus that ran counter to the new international division of labour that market forces were calling into being, and which the world recession was intensifying. And the tensions which that released then helped to make clear that the interests of industrial capital and labour which the politicians sought to harmonise were not so much similar as incompatible. It was true, of course, that both management and workers shared a common concern with the achievement of a healthy competitive economy and it was on this that the politicians perpetually dwelled; but it was also true that in practice the restructuring of British capitalism which that required could take place only at the cost of jobs and established work practices which the trade-union movement had in some sense to resist, and which governments and managements had therefore either to buy out or to seize. Because of this, politicians would have found it difficult to win organised labour's support for extensive industrial restructuring even in a period of sustained economic growth, and in a recession that support was even harder to produce and to sustain. For the recession made the degree of restructuring that was necessary all the more severe, rapid and far-reaching; and the nature of the 1970s recession, combining as it did inflation with stagnation, prevented governments from absorbing some of the resulting unemployment in an expanded public sector, since to do so would be to fuel the very inflation which made the lack of competitiveness so evident in the first place. Politics in Britain in the 1970s was, in a genuine sense, the politics of Catch 22: as politicians found that they could neither strengthen British capitalism without attacking the labour movement nor attack the labour movement without heavy industrial disruption and electoral unpopularity. The dilemma of British politics in the 1970s was that the defensive strength of the class forces faced by politicians drove governments to the centre, but the incompatibility of interests that divided those class forces meant that, except for those brief periods in which politicians managed to beat the drum of national crisis, the centre would not hold.

THE ATTACK ON THE UNIONS

For beneath the oscillation in policy lay two other features of British politics in the 1970s that have yet to be fully noted and explained. The first is the ineffectiveness of government initiatives, the persistence of inflation and unemployment through the decade in spite of the activities of the politicians. The second is the persistent propensity of each government's strategy to culminate (even when, as with a Labour government, it had not begun with that intention) in a confrontation with sections of the trade-union movement. These two phenomena are, of course, closely related. The first is a consequence of the particular severity of British capitalism's competitive weakness. The second is a result of the way in which that weakness could, in capitalist terms, only be resolved by increasing the rate of exploitation of labour (to which union power stood as the major obstacle).

We have seen already that the growing competitive weakness of British capitalism was of long standing, that the British economy entered the 1970s with lower rates of economic growth, industrial investment and labour productivity than its major competitors, and that in consequence (and even before the world recession) it was more than averagely vulnerable to balance-of-payments difficulties and rates of domestic inflation that left its currency weak and business confidence low. What the recession then taught British politicians after 1973 was not that economic problems have a habit of being intractable – they had discovered that in the 1960s – but rather that, in a world recession of this severity, weak capitalisms have a distinct tendency to stay weak, locked into their positions of relative subordination by a series of self-sustaining disabilities.

Certainly successive British governments in the 1970s found themselves confronted by a series of self-defeating and mutually reinforcing set of constraints. The economy that they inherited was competitively weak (and in balance-of-payments difficulties) because its investment record was poor and its inflation rate correspondingly high. Yet to cope with the balance-of-payments problem and to help to stabilise the currency governments were obliged to hold interest rate up, and levels of internal demand down, at the cost of making investment even less attractive. The weakness of sterling fuelled the inflationary process still further, and yet by its very weakness encouraged speculation and currency movements that left sterling weaker still; so that, ironically, when North Sea oil arrived to strengthen sterling, it proved to be less a source of salvation than the final blow, eroding still further the competitive strength of a by-now extremely under-capitalised and demoralised industrial sector. Nor could governments in Britain in the 1970s look to an expansion in world trade to soften the domestic impact of this steady loss of competitiveness, as had been the case in the long boom (when British exporters had hung on to a growing volume of trade as their percentage of world business had steadily diminished). For after 1973 the British economy faced foreign markets that were themselves stagnating under government-induced retrenchments across the entire OECD area, and in which growth after 1975 was only sluggish and modest. Moreover it was in these very markets that competition was intensifying dramatically, as each government sought to solve its own domestic difficulties by a mixture of export-led growth and protectionism. Undercut by stronger competitors at home and abroad, the British economy in the 1970s fell victim to what one economist has called 'a cumulative and circular chain of causation' which left it perpetually and necessarily weaker. As A. Singh has written,

> the most important point to note here is that if the economy happens to be in disequilibrium (e.g. in a weak competitive position with balance of payments difficulties) all these effects *may* work together . . . to perpetuate the disequilibrium. Such a country . . . will tend to have a lower rate of increase of effective demand, and hence a lower rate of investment, and a lower rate of technical progress and growth in productivity. It will thus be in an even weaker competitive position than before, especially as the same forces will be working in the opposite direction to improve the position of its more successful rivals . . . such an economy, if it continues to participate in international economic relations on the same terms as before, will suffer a continual contraction[13].

Not surprisingly in the face of that, certain sections of industry and the broad mass of the labour movement turned increasingly to protectionism to ease the immediate impact of this dwindling competitiveness. But so far at least successive governments have refused to adopt that strategy out of a fear of retaliation, and because of their recognition that, protected or not, the long-term competitive strength of British capitalism could be guaranteed only by lower levels of inflation and higher rates of labour productivity to which import controls alone could make no direct contribution. They came to recognise that the lowering of inflation required a reduction in government spending in areas (such as social expenditure) that were unproductive of capital and which only served to strengthen the labour movement; and that a higher rate of labour productivity required a major reorganisation of capital that was incompatible with existing levels of working-class control over jobs and work practices. Far from the regulation of British industry requiring a strengthening of the labour movement, as the Labour Left argued consistently through the decade, governments came to recognise that the economy's competitive strength could be enhanced only by the erosion of existing levels of wages, employment and social expenditure, and only by redistribution of national income back to profits and industrial power back to capital. Politicians continued to disagree on whether this could be best achieved by the voluntary incorporation of the trade-union hierarchy into a neo-corporatist planning structure or by relying instead on a greater exposure of industry and workers to the full force of market competition, but few of them (the Tribunite wing of the Labour Party aside) when in power could avoid the inevitable confrontation that each strategy necessarily entailed with the workers and their families who had to pay the price of British capitalism's attempt to restructure itself out of crisis.

British politics in the early 1980s is dominated by the Thatcher government's determination to hold to the strategy that Edward Heath abandoned in 1972. The whole thrust of the government's economic policy since its election in May 1979 has been to weaken the power of the trade-union movement by a twin strategy of new tough labour laws and deliberately created unemployment. Conservative ministers have repeatedly asserted their belief that the dwindling competitiveness of British capitalism cannot be resolved by government subsidies and intervention, but only by a drastic fall in inflation and sharp changes in work practices – and that those in their turn will be forthcoming only if the government forces employers and workers to experience the full impact of market pressure by restricting the growth rate of the money supply, no matter what the short-term cost may be in terms of unemployment and bankruptcies. Neither organised labour nor small- and medium-size industrial capital have relished that learning process, but even so the TUC and CBI have both been unable so far to persuade ministers to moderate their policies, and in particular to ease the high interest rates and strong pound sterling which monetarist orthodoxy and North Sea oil have combined to produce. Like the Heath government before it, the Thatcher cabinet seems to be isolating itself from national industrial capital as well as from the trade-union movement. But unlike Edward Heath, Mrs Thatcher has not yet shown any signs of wishing to break that isolation by a reversal of policy. On the contrary, ministers seem ever more determined to hold to a monetarist-induced deflationary path until wage settlements ease, job practices change and inflation and interest rates fall. But that has not happened on any scale yet, and instead the government-induced recession has deepened severely. By the autumn of 1980 the level of unemployment, without seasonal adjustment, has reached two million, the index of industrial production has fallen to 1968 levels, and inflation is still oscillating between 15 and 20 per cent (that is, 50–100 per cent higher than when the government was elected). Only fierce internal divisions within the Labour Party seem to be cushioning the Conservative government from a quite cataclysmic loss of popular confidence and support; and certainly all the signs are that unless (as seems unlikely) investment and employment recover rapidly in 1981 and 1982, the Thatcher government must approach the next General Election with its popular credibility largely gone, and subject as a result to heavy internal pressure to change policy to avoid heavy electoral defeat.

With this in mind it is perhaps permissible to speculate tentatively about likely developments in British politics in the second half of the 1980s. One possible line of development lies with the Tribunite wing of the Labour Party. It is just possible that the tensions implicit in the competitive restructuring of British capitalism could give extra political weight to (and even make electorally popular) the Labour Left's 'alternative economic strategy' – a strategy which seeks to avoid the costs of that restructuring by creating a wall of import tariffs, strengthened trade-union rights and state-directed investment. Yet there is enough evidence in the Labour Party's past to suggest that even if this is so, the Labour Left will probably fail to win the bulk of the leadership of the parliamentary Labour Party to more than a verbal concession to that view, and to suggest that in power a future Labour government will retreat quickly to a more normal tripartite industrial strategy. There is enough evidence from the past too to suggest that, even if the Labour Left is more successful inside the Labour Party in the 1980s than in the past, industrial (and especially financial) capital faced with such a programme will react quickly against it – both conspiratorially (via the export of capital, speculation against sterling and investment strikes) to build a quick association in the public mind between the alternative economic strategy and industrial calamity; and automatically, as a strengthened labour movement blocks those intensifications in work routines and increases in unemployment which alone can permit the restoration of profitability and private capital accumulation, with a resulting slow shift of capital away to foreign competitors with more compliant labour organisations (or with no labour organisations at all). The fear of both the conspiratorial and the automatic reactions should be enough to blunt official trade-union radicalism at the critical moment, and to leave Labour Party leaders and the bulk of the trade-union bureaucracy isolated between a rank and file radicalised by high expectations and a capitalist class made apprehensive by Labour's radical rhetoric. If the revolutionary Left can build on that opportunity to demonstrate the limits of Labour Party radicalism, then a socialist solution may then emerge as a genuine possibility; but if they fail, the only beneficiaries of Left Labour sabre-rattling in the 1980s should be, as in 1979, a revitalised Tory monetarism or some even more authoritarian form of right-wing political movement.

But if the Labour Centre and Right emerge as dominant under the next Labour government, then presumably the drift to a corporatist integration of the trade-union leadership will continue, limited only by the residual (but also ultimately inevitable) rank-and-file backlash as the true meaning of that incorporation for employment, wages and work practices becomes clear. It seems to me that there are many British Leylands to come in the deepening crisis of the 1980s, many more winters of discontent at the end of Labour periods in power. And this in its turn would be enough to give Tory monetarism a fresh lease of life in the 1990s, as in their next period of opposition the Conservatives exploit the visibility of trade union defensive action in order to argue for yet tougher labour laws and yet greater dismantling of the social services. And with neither the Thatcher government of the early 1980s nor with Tory monetarists to come can the Left expect as easy a victory as the unions won over Edward Heath in 1971–2. The crisis of British capitalism is now more severe, and the confidence of the Tory neo-Liberals more entrenched; and in those circumstances the lesson to be taken from the events of the past ten years appears to be that only very strong and determined (and explicitly political) trade-union defensive action will be able to force 'U turns' on these monetarists, at the very time when the deepening threat to jobs in manufacturing industry here leaves workers so vulnerable that there is every danger that that resistance will be slow to come and hard to sustain.

Be that as it may, there is no avoiding the conclusion that the question of the character and intensity of the trade unions' industrial and political response to Tory monetarism will be the crucial issue for British politics in the 1980s. The deepening recession has the propensity both to erode that response (through the debilitating effect of actual or threatened unemployment) or to radicalise workers subject to job insecurity, falling living standards and intensified work routines. Which reaction will prevail is, and must be, an open question, one whose resolution will be intimately connected with the kind and quality of political leadership that emerges from union activists and socialist militants in the mass of the labour movement over the next few years. Past history suggests that the labour movement may be strong enough (and ultimately sufficiently militant industrially) to block any easy reduction of its control over work processes and income levels, but insufficiently radical politically even to defend the social wage effectively, let alone to push for a total transformation of property relationships. And if that is so, the 1980s could witness only a repetition of the politics of the decade just completed, an oscillation between Labour corporatism and Tory monetarism that will leave British capitalism still uncompetitive and the defensive power of British workers perpetually under threat.

POSTSCRIPT

By July 1981 the recession of British industrial capital has deepened significantly. The index of industrial production has fallen dramatically since the Conservative Government's election in May 1979, back to 98 per cent of its January 1975 level by May 1981 (with the index for manufacturing industry alone down to 89 per cent). Inflation, which quickened to over 20 per cent under the first set of policy changes by the incoming government, has still not fallen to less than 10 per cent after two years of Tory monetarism. The pound, temporarily strong because of North Sea oil and high interest rates through the first 20 months of the Thatcher government, has now once again weakened significantly against the dollar; and unemployment, officially approaching the three million mark, is in reality probably nearer to four million[14]. Indeed, during July 1981 rioting in the inner-city areas of mainland Britain has brought into the public eye scenes more reminiscent of the troubles in Ulster, as the social costs of deepening recession have precipitated ugly confrontations between the young unemployed and the police.

One consequence of all that has been a continuing swing to radicalism again within the Labour Party. The Left there is in the ascendancy, as a result of a sustained campaign to change the internal rules governing party behaviour in ways that restrict the leadership's ability to retreat to the centre in any Labour government to come. For long before the election defeat in 1979, the Labour Left had come to see itself as the guardian of an alternative and socialist economic and political programme to which the Party had committed itself in 1973 but which the Labour government had failed to implement. As a result it entered the post-mortem on the 1979 defeat convinced that the key issue was not the formulation of new policy (there were policies enough already) but rather how to prevent a future betrayal of that policy by an incoming Labour government subject to conservative pressures. Convinced of its own strength in the National Executive Committee of the Party, and in the constituencies, and aware of its relative weakness in the Parliamentary Labour Party, the Left sought to alter the balance of power between those three bodies and to erode the influence of the Right and Centre at the parliamentary level. In all this it has been remarkably successful. The Left won the mandatory reselection of MPs at the 1979 and 1980 party conferences, and imposed its own procedure on the reselection process through an NEC ruling in May 1981. It broke the monopoly of the PLP on the future selection of Labour leaders, and saw even the old method of leadership selection produce Michael Foot and not Denis Healey as Jim Callaghan's successor. It perceived a new assertiveness amongst activists in the trade-union movement, and exploited this to win massive conference backing for left-wing policies, and to support first Tony Benn and then John Silkin in a fight against Denis Healey for the deputy leadership of the Party. And in doing all that, it split the Party at its right edge, driving leading right-wing parliamentary figures out into a new Social Democratic Party, there to form a coalition with the Liberals against the rising tide of Labour radicalism.

At the time of writing, the Labour Party is deeply divided. The Left itself is split, between MPs reluctant to see that division forced even further (with the subsequent defection of even more MPs into the SDP) and those MPs and activists around Tony Benn who seem determined to push the issue forward, and to consolidate the PLP's acceptance of conference policy on Europe, defence and the economy. Yet though the divisions are real enough, the whole focus of political debate within the Labour Party has shifted to the Left, and Labour's alternative economic strategy (much of it publicly confirmed in the NEC document *Labour's Alternative*, published in May 1981) is an even more radical version of the policy adopted in 1973: proposing an attack on unemployment through greater public spending on industrial reconstruction and the social wage; tight State control of economic activity through public ownership and compulsory planning agreements; a new State bank to direct oil revenues into manufacturing investment; price and import controls, a wealth tax, greater industrial democracy and a shorter working week; and the abolition of the House of Lords and withdrawal from the EC. Armed with these policies, the scene is now set for an inevitable confrontation between a future Labour government and private capital of the kind that broke the last Labour government; but this time, at least according to the Left of the Party, it is Labour radicalism and not business conservatism that will be sustained.

Labour radicals can at least draw some inspiration for this from the resilience of Thatcherite radicalism after 1974. The Heath 'U turn' has not yet been repeated by the Thatcher Cabinet, and indeed the government has deliberately deepened the recession in its single-minded pursuit of price stability and cost-effectiveness in industry. Its ability to sustain its radicalism has reflected in part the political forces within the Thatcher Cabinet, with the anti-monetarist 'wets' being few in number and the Prime Minister herself being 'not for turning' as she put it to the 1980 Party conference[15]. But the resilience of Tory radicalism also reflects the serious weakening of trade-union power produced by the recession, and is itself indicative of the degree of distance that a Thatcherite government is prepared to establish between its policies and the expressed preferences of even industrial capital: a gap which, in 1980, prompted the secretary-general of the CBI to threaten a 'bare knuckle fight' with Conservative Ministers.

The Thatcher government began radically enough. It cut direct taxation, reduced State aid to industry, and eventually introduced swingeing cuts in public spending. It began to introduce new labour legislation, slowed here only by the Employment Secretary's rearguard action against his more determined Cabinet colleagues. It allowed spending on police pay and the military to rise, against the trend for the public sector as a whole. It removed all controls on the export of capital, and it specified tight monetary targets to be used as a benchmark of its success, and sustained high rates of interest and a strong pound in an attempt to achieve those targets.

But if there has as yet been no dramatic 'U turn' on these policies, at least by mid-term the Thatcher government was showing signs of holding its fire. The public spending cuts of 1979 and 1980 were not repeated in 1981, as a coalition of spending departments blocked further Treasury retrenchment. A major legislative assault on trade-union rights has not yet materialised, and a confrontation with the National Union of Miners was quietly avoided by a government climb-down on the funding of the Coal Board. Moreover, there is growing scepticism in wider and wider parts of the relevant elites about the viability of monetarism, as both the money supply and government spending prove difficult to control and as inflation and stagnation continue unabated. The 'wets' in the Cabinet have undoubtedly been strengthened by all this, and their political weight is now being enhanced further by the electoral threat which the recession is increasingly posing to the Conservative government in the second half of its term, and by the threat to public order that the rioting of the mid-summer is now demonstrating. Edward Heath himself made a major public defence of more moderate policies in

June 1981, and the electoral importance of his message was underlined by the successful showing of the new Social Democratic Party (and the collapse of the Tory vote) in the Warrington bye-election on July 16[16]. As we go to press, with the Conservative government still locked in an acrimonious

TABLE 6.1 British Gross Domestic Product at Constant Factor Cost

(1975 = 100)	
1970	93.3
1971	93.7
1972	96.1
1973	103.0
1974	101.0
1975	100.0
1976	103.2
1977	105.1
1978	108.4
1979	109.9
1980	107.3[a]

a This figure refers to the first quarter of 1980
SOURCE *Annual Abstract of Statistics 1981* (Table 149) p. 531; for 1979–80, *The Times* (13 August 1980) p. 18

TABLE 6.2 Index of Industrial Production

(1975 = 100)	
1970	99.7
1971	99.8
1972	102.0
1973	109.5
1974	105.2
1975	100.0
1976	102.0
1977	106.0
1978	109.8
1979	112.6
1980	108.2[a]

a This figure refers to June 1980
SOURCE *Annual Abstract of Statistics 1981* (Table 802) p. 202; for 1979–80, *The Times* (13 August 1980) p. 18

battle with its own civil servants, and with increasing public discussion of internal Cabinet divisions, Thatcherite radicalism is looking less and less capable of withstanding the rise once more of the Tory moderate centre.

TABLE 6.3 Inflation

	Retail Price Index (January each year)		*% increase on year earlier* (January to January)
	a	*b*	
1970	135.5		5
1971	147.0		8
1972	159.0		8
1973	171.3		8
1974	191.8	100.0	12
1975		119.8	20
1976		147.9	23
1977		172.4	17
1978		189.5	10
1979		207.2	9
1980		245.3	18

a January 16 1962 = 100
b January 15 1974 = 100
SOURCE *Department of Employment Gazette* (December 1979) p. 1310

TABLE 6.4 Seasonally Adjusted Figures for Unemployment in Great Britain

	Numbers in June each year (to the nearest 1000)	*Annual average* (%)
1970	524,000	2.5
1971	687,000	3.4
1972	767,000	3.7
1973	546,000	2.6
1974	516,000	2.6
1975	831,000	4.1
1976	1,228,000	5.6
1977	1,285,000	6.0
1978	1,325,000	6.0
1979	1,238,000	5.6
1980	1,441,000	6.2

SOURCE *Annual Abstract of Statistics 1973* (Table 146) p. 142; *1976* (Table 155) p. 159; *1980* (Table 6.7) p. 164; *1981* (Tables 6.7 and 6.8) pp. 160, 163

NOTES AND REFERENCES

1. In 1951 the two parties had a combined vote of 27,666,143 out of a total electorate of just over 34,000,000 (82.5 per cent of whom actually voted); by 1974 the electorate had grown (to 40,000,000) but the percentage who actually voted had fallen (to just over 29,000,000) as had the combined vote of the two main parties (down almost 6,000,000 to 21,921,896).
2. One general indicator of this is to be found in the *United Nations Statistical Yearbook for 1978* According to UN figures, taking 1975 output levels as 100, the total product of the United Kingdom economy between 1960 and 1977 moved only from 72 to 105 (grew, that is, in total by 45 per cent over the period). Over the same period the Japanese economy moved from 28 to 106 (grew by 378 per cent), the West German economy moved from 57 to 109, the French from 47 to 108 and the United States economy from 61 to 111.
3. To give 1964 as one example, in that year gross fixed asset formation, as a percentage of GNP, was 17.6 per cent in the United Kingdom, but 33.6 per cent in Japan, 26.4 per cent in West Germany, 26.9 per cent in France (cited in G. F. Fay, *The Competitiveness of British Industrial Products: A Round Up* (Woolwich Economic Papers 10, 1966).
4. Between 1955 and 1968 output per worker in Great Britain increased by an annual average of 2.4 per cent. The figure for West Germany was 4.4 per cent, for France 5.1 per cent, for Italy 6.0 per cent and for Japan 8.6 per cent. See R. Guttman, 'State intervention and the economic crisis: the Labour Government's economic policy 1974–75', *Kapitalstate* (1976) p. 225.
5. The United Kingdom share of the value of world exports of manufactures was 25.5 per cent in 1950, but only 9.3 per cent by 1977. See F. Blackaby, *Deindustrialisation* (London: Heinemann, 1979) p. 241.
6. *House of Commons Debates*, 5th series, vol. 880 (29 October 1974) column 84.
7. The policy was agreed at a series of well-published meetings at Selsdon Park early in 1970, and became generally known by that name.
8. *Labour's Programme 1973* (Labour Party, 1973) p. 7; also to be found in both the February and October 1974 election manifestos.
9. See P. Jenkins, *The Battle of Downing Street* (London: Charles Knight, 1970); E. Heffer, *The Class Struggle in Parliament* (London: Gollancz, 1973); and R. Crossman, *Diaries of a Cabinet Minister*, vol. 3 (London: Hamish Hamilton and Jonathan Cape, 1977).
10. Paul Johnson, 'A brotherhood of national misery', *New Statesman* (16 May 1975) p. 652.
11. See D. Coates, *Labour in Power?* (Harlow: Longman, 1980) chapter 3.
12. There are many examples of Labour politicians experiencing problems with their civil servants. The 1964–70 Labour government provided material on this for Marcia Williams, *Inside No. 10* (London: Weidenfeld and Nicolson, 1972); for Barbara Castle, 'Mandarin Power', *Sunday Times* (10 June 1973); and for Richard Crossman in his diaries. On the 1974–9 Labour government, see Joe Haines, *The Politics of Power* (London: Hodder and Stoughton, 1978); and Brian Sedgemore, *The Secret Constitution* (London: Hodder and Stoughton, 1980).

13. A Singh, 'U.K. industry and the world economy: a case of deindustrialisation', *Cambridge Journal of Economics*, vol. 1 (1977) p. 119.
14. On the 'missing million' unemployed, see *New Statesman* (27 March 1981).
15. *The Times* (11 October 1980) p. 1.
16. The result at Warrington gave the Social Democrats 42 per cent of the votes cast, and the Conservatives 7 per cent (and a lost deposit).

7 Political Underdevelopment and Economic Recession in Italy

PAUL FURLONG

INTRODUCTION: THE INSTITUTIONAL BACKGROUND

Analysis of the response of the state to the recurring economic crises of the 1970s must begin with the assumption that there has been a perceptible response by the state which can be investigated from a politico-economic perspective. But in the case of Italy the problem immediately arises that it is not clear in what sense we can talk of the state responding even in a superficially coherent short-term manner to successive crises (in particular, inflation 1974, exchange-rate crisis 1976, continual growth in unemployment since then). Such is the fragmentation of power at the elite level and such is the relative autonomy of the various institutions one from another that long-term government plans for recovery tend either to be blocked within the administration or to find themselves emptied of real content by party-political pressures, and short-term responses from a variety of governmental sources may conflict with one another: most obviously this has occurred in the incongruity between the tight monetary and credit policy exercised by the Bank of Italy in 1976–7 and the failure to control government spending in the same period. It has been observed in the past[1] that legislative and administrative activity in Italy apparently does little that is systematic to resolve the pressing structural problems in the Italian economy. Predieri[2] for instance has argued that much of the time of the Italian Parliament is taken up with legislation which concerns relatively small-scale or even trivial issues likely to be of concern mainly to small groups of deputies or senators with particular regional or sectoral interests. Where legislation does concern macro-economic objectives of a more or less pressing nature, it has never been likely to meet sustained expert analysis from those whose business is political scrutiny, either for lack of time or for lack of interest.

Recent developments in the party-political structure of the Parliament have made the formal process of legislation for such bills increasingly hazardous. The emergence of small left-wing parties, such as the Radical Party and the New Left, not committed to the Parliamentary process has led to repeated obstructionism and filibustering sometimes abetted by the opportunism of the neo-fascist MSI. The general context of governmental instability, apparently an unchanging feature of the Italian political system, further endangers the progress of government-sponsored anticonjunctural policies. In September 1980 the Cossiga government, in office since March 1980, was unable to ensure the passage of a group of measures designed to deal with the fall in value of the lira and to control the growth of government spending. The measures were deflationary in objective, though they coupled increased taxes and charges for public services with financial help for industry. After winning a vote of confidence on the bill as a whole, the government was defeated on major clauses of the bill and resigned the next day. Though some popular explanation[3] attributed the defeat to the communist policy of firm opposition to the government and to the bill, the crucial loss of votes from the nominal government majority occurred among the so-called 'snipers' (*franchi tiratori*) on the right-wing of the dominant Christian Democrat party who apparently found the government too left-wing in orientation and who feared that it would eventually lead to communist entry into the government. This episode was unusual in that the fall of the government was directly preceded by defeat on a bill of major importance. Usually government crises are provoked by shifts in the balance of power either within one of the governing parties or between two or more of the governing parties, resulting directly in the fall of the government, in which case the crisis may never reach the stage of parliamentary defeat.[4]

In such an environment of intrigue and unpredictability the responsible institutions have to attempt to cobble together coherent policy. Apart from the problems of cabinet instability and legislative irrelevance or unpredictability, the Italian political economy is also characterised by a cumbersome and poorly trained public administration[5] that not only constitutes a severe obstacle to radical or long-term state direction of the economy but also appears to have a detrimental effect even on short-term economic activity by reason of the higher costs resulting from its inefficiency. The honourable exception to this criticism is the Bank of Italy, an institution with an international reputation for efficiency. The overall incompetence of the bureaucracy may have a direct effect on the range of instruments available to the government in macro-economic policy. The weakness of the tax-collection system among the self-employed and the inability of the government to stop the flight of capital abroad deprive the government of important policy instruments as well as depriving the state and industry of much-needed capital resources. These problems are in some sense attributable to the lack of reliable administrative implementation of agreed policies, though it should be noted that the weakness of fiscal policies of demand management owed something (until recent reforms) to the 'timeless' nature of the Italian budgetary system, which we discuss later.

The administration is cumbersome in the sense that the fragmentation of power into diverse competing ministries with overlapping responsibilities and without a strong coordinating centre is not conducive to the rapid or efficient adjustment of policy. The tradition of the Italian civil service is formalist and anti-statistical. It recruits heavily from among law graduates and provides little post-entry training in wider administrative skills. The Gaspari reforms of 1973 led to the establishment of a Civil Service College at Caserta, near Naples, for the training of prospective entrants to the higher grades, but it is as yet a poor imitation of its French equivalent, the Ecole National d'Administration, from which it draws its original inspiration. Indeed, it is not unreasonable to attribute some of the recent disparity in efficiency between the public sector in general and the private sector to the poor quality, training and pay of the recruits to the former and to the propensity of firms in the latter not only to pay more but also to seek graduates who have training overseas or who are products of the rapidly-expanding private higher-education system. Similarly, the reforms of the standing orders of Parliament in 1971 though extending the scope of consultation with the extra-governmental parliamentary parties over the parliamentary timetable have had little effect on the problems of parliamentary irrelevance or unpredictability. In general, the historic inefficiency of its apparatus and the permeation of the state by particularistic demands mean that the response of the state to economic crisis tends to be a motley chorus of apparently uncoordinated voices from which the outside observer must attempt to decipher an overall pattern and a general trend. But the institutional framework to the response of the state provides only one set of parameters for the analysis. Consideration is now given to the wider problem of political development in Italy in the 1970s, against the background of the oil-induced inflation of 1974 and the subsequent changes in economic structure.

THE LONG-TERM PROBLEMS

Italy is rightly regarded now as one of the major industrialised nations of the West, but the peculiarly rapid and unbalanced character of its industrialisation has had a marked effect on its political and economic structure. The traditional political economy in Italy is the open economy, internally and externally. One of the main objectives of the first governments of the liberal state after the unification in 1860 was the integration of Italy into European markets and the economic unification of the country.[6] But a profound dualism already existed between the relatively advanced North and the rest of the country, in particular the South, the Mezzogiorno. This dualism was accentuated rather than dissolved by the removal of tariff barriers within the new state, and the imbalance in income, productivity, growth and industrialisation has persisted. To the economic imbalance was joined a narrow political base. The new liberal state operated on a limited electoral franchise and this added to the failure to make peace with the Catholic Church over its territorial rights ensured that the state remained in the hands of an elite which never effectively established hegemony over the majority of the population.

With the advent of universal suffrage after the First World War and the problems of re-adjustment to the peacetime economy there became evident the incapacity of the traditional liberal elite either to redistribute resources effectively towards the impoverished South and the landless labourers or to control the violent insurgents of a variety of political creeds. The important political amendment made during the fascist regime was the development of the Italian economy as a state-assisted open economy; under fascism many of the large public-sector corporations which now dominate the Italian economy were established with the political and economic default of the liberal professional classes. The Italian state had been involved in the heavy industry since 1876 with the establishment of the steel works at Terni, but this had been within the context of the liberal demands that the state had the duty to provide for economic infrastructure (particularly railways) and for the defence of the nation.

The second major structural problem in Italian political economy was the weakness of the capital market. The fascist regime saw a massive extension of state control of credit and finance by means of the takeover of banks, the establishment of state-run pension-schemes (INAM, INAIL, INPS) and perhaps most significantly the establishment in 1933 of the Institute for Industrial Reconstruction, known as IRI, which became a holding company with the function of providing support for industries considered vital to the nation's interests, sometimes with the acquisition of majority shareholdings. The particular concerns of IRI were iron and steel, shipbuilding, communication and electrification. While other policies and institutions of the fascist period sank quietly into the bottomless pit of history at the end of the war, state control of long- and medium-term credit, of national insurance, and of a large sector of industrial investment remained vested in these bodies. In 1926 AGIP was established with the aim both of supporting the efforts of private industry in the exploitation of Italy's meagre oil and gas resources and of engaging directly in exploration or research for the development of such resources; after the war this merged with the parallel state-owned body in the coal industry (ACAI) into ENI providing the state with a major interest in national energy resources.

Another sector to be affected beyond the period of fascism by the fascist demands for autarky was the chemical industry, where the privately-owned Montecatini worked in close collaboration with the parastate agencies. Gregor argues that, though under earlier and better circumstances the Northern-based liberal entreprenerial elite were able to withstand fascist intervention in the economy,

> With the crisis of the early thirties the Fascists found themselves in a position of strength. Very rapidly a plethora of parastate agencies appeared that together with the syndical, intersyndical and corporative institutions already in various stages of development extended government controls over imports, exports, services, wages, prices, conditions of labour, the allocation of materials, the licensing of new plant material and the rationalisation and modernisation of existing establishments.[7]

The institutional capacity for direction of the economy was established under fascism, and fascist rhetoric certainly proclaimed the rapid progress of Italy towards the greatest possible economic self-sufficiency under the guiding hand of the Duce. We are perhaps entitled to be more sceptical about how far the 'rationalisation and modernisation' ever progressed, particularly in the context of the problem of the South. To this outstanding dualism had been added other sources of imbalance of particular importance. Italy emerged from the war not only relatively underdeveloped, with 44 per cent of the active population engaged in agriculture in 1946, but also with the historical dualism of the North–South disparity compounded by new cleavages, in particular between public and private sector, between the traditional liberal economic elite and the new political forces of Catholicism and communism, and between the large number of small artisan-type industrial firms and a few industrial giants both public and private.[8] Initially it appeared that the return to a pre-fascist political economy could be made following the inclusion of the Liberal Party in the centrist coalitions from 1947 onwards, and the policy of the liberal Treasury Ministry, Luigi Einandi, was indeed to allow reconstruction to take place through the unleashing of market forces, in particular with the removal of foreign exchange controls, the removal of trade barriers, and the relinquishing by the state of price and supply controls in certain sectors. But for several reasons this policy line did not persist.

First of all, though the economic damage suffered by Italy during the war was not as severe as that suffered by some other countries involved, notably Germany, nevertheless the base from which Italy started particularly in terms of social infrastructure was already low, and it rapidly became clear that the reconstruction with the help of Marshall Aid demanded some provision by the state of services considered crucial to industry, a demand which the ruling Christian Democrats were not averse to meeting. A second reason for the development of state intervention within the framework of the open economy was that in 1948–50 the problem of the South presented itself in a dramatic fashion. The land-hungry and impoverished agricultural labourers and sharecroppers took to seizures and occupation in the face of government failure to provide land reforms and investment. The outbreak of civil disorder on a wide scale and the potential use to be made of such political mobilisation by the Communist Party, as well as the opportunities for the Christian Democrats to develop an autonomous power-base in the area, all were pressing motives for the government to act, and resulted in the establishment in 1950 of yet another state-controlled investment organisation, the Cassa per il Mezzogiorno, with the function of stimulating industrial development in the South and providing social infrastructure in support of the proposed land-reforms.

At first the scope of the Cassa was limited to the provision of social investment to lower the costs of industry in the area, and to bring the quality of social infrastructure up to the standards of the rest of the country with the strategic aim of reducing the disparity in income per head. The Cassa from 1958 began to involve itself directly in industrial development, eventually under the Saraceno Plan of 1964 designating industrial regions and industrial poles within them which qualified for special attention. The machinery of the Cassa, in particular its control of credit in the South, together with the holding companies and credit institutions already established under fascism, and with a newly confident and resurgent private sector, formed an investment base on which the industrial development of Italy, the so-called 'economic miracle', could take place, even though it was the North which in this period had the higher growth rates (see Table 7.1).

The machinery of state intervention also developed into a political base for the governing parties and in particular the DC as a source of mass patronage, as a result of which the DC was able to establish itself independently of the Catholic Church in Italy on whom it originally relied for activists and organisational support. Nevertheless it would be wrong to ascribe the very

TABLE 7.1 Average Annual Growth Rates, GDP by Volume at Constant Prices, 1951–73

	1951–63	*1963–73*
North	5.98	4.63
Centre	5.20	4.92
South and Islands	4.91	4.65
Total	5.56	4.71

SOURCE *Tagliacarne* (1975), p. 17.

rapid post-war industrial development solely to the existence of an aggressive independent and expansionist public sector. For our purposes, it is important to emphasise that the steady and rapid growth from 1951 to 1963 has not been repeated since. It relied on a particularly favourable set of circumstances and exacerbated the already existing structural imbalances, which now hamper sustained growth. The Italian economy is now capable of achieving high rates of growth in individual years, comparable to those of the period 1952–63; but other factors prevent such growth being sustained over long periods. The 'economic miracle' was largely export-led and relied on the availability of a ready supply of cheap non-unionised labour. The relative weakness of internal demand helped ensure that balance-of-payments problems did not arise to curtail the expansionist fiscal policy of the central authorities or to dampen buoyant business expectations. The period was characterised by a shift of income away from wages towards profits and by a high rate of industrial investment both in the public sector and in the private sector. Politically, the system rested on a succession of centrist coalitions in government led by the Christian-Democrats whose Catholic inter-class origins enabled it to appeal both to industrial workers (through the Catholic-controlled trade-union confederation CISL) and to the traditional right-wing, particularly those involved in the public sector.

With the increasing integration of Italy into international markets and the development of foreign trade as a significant component of GNP the Italian economy became more vulnerable to foreign-exchange fluctuations (because of its reliance on imported raw materials) and to international trade cycles. At the same time rapid industrial development in the North fuelled by internal-immigrant labour from the South was exacerbating the traditional weakness of social infrastructure in the large cities; the shift of active population from low-productivity agriculture to high-productivity industry which stimulated the growth of the 1950s was also producing unwelcome side effects in the sprawling overcrowded urban conglomerations of the North (see Table 7.2). Though Italy had not solved with development its

TABLE 7.2 Share of Agriculture and General Government in Civil Employment

	1955	*1960*	*1975*
Agriculture	34.5	29.5	15.6
General government	7.0	7.5	11.4

SOURCE *Economic Bulletin for Europe* (1979)

questione contadina, the peasant question, it had found the problem partially transferred to the cities with the emergence of the *questione urbana*, the urban question. At the time when the economy was developing most rapidly, 1959–63, public civil consumption expenditure was no more than keeping pace with the general rate of growth, and thereafter began a relative decline (see Table 7.3).

TABLE 7.3 Social Expenditure, at Constant Prices

	Annual rates of change			*Shares in GNP*		
	1952–8	*1959–64*	*1965–71*	*1952–8*	*1959–64*	*1965–71*
Gross public consumption	4.0	3.0	3.9	11.6	10.8	10.2
Social investment	9.2	8.2	0.9	6.7	8.0	7.5
Public administration	7.3	7.5	3.0	1.5	1.7	1.6
Housing	15.1	8.4	0.4	5.2	6.3	5.9
Total social expenditure	7.0	6.3	2.7	18.3	18.8	17.7

SOURCE *OECD* (1972)

The spending of central government, whether or not it was large enough to cope with the new demands, was in any case ill-administered by the civil servants and misdirected by the politicians. It would be misleading to suggest that in the success story of the 1951–63 period the central government played a leading role. Indeed the political supremacy of the DC in this period was linked to its development away from its distinctively Catholic orientation, under which it might have adopted a more coherent reformist character, towards its modern identity as a conservative party which is also the apparently irremoveable party of government, a party whose power-base appears predominantly clientelistic. The political premisses to rapid and undirected economic growth were the exclusion of the socialist and communist parties from government and the fragmentation and internal weakness of the trade-union movement; the period might be regarded as one of tacit alliance between the newly arrived Christian Democrat politicians and the ebullient private-sector industrialists –

organised in the employer's organisation Confindustria and having a political voice in the Liberal Party. The condition of Italy in 1963 has been described as one of precocious maturity,[9] with a geographically and sectorally restricted private sector, highly capital-intensive, which relied on state participation in steel and energy and on a high level of unemployment to keep the labour market easy.

To the Christian Democrats fell the task of defusing the resulting social tensions in the South and in the Northern cities. In part this was done by the preservation of archaic small industries through government subsidy and by the development of parasitic bureaucratic agencies of notorious inefficiency. But a second string to the Christian Democrat bow was the extension of the corporate privileges of government to the Socialist Party when the centrist coalition became electorally unviable. In 1963 the first centre-left coalition including Socialist ministers was formed, but rather than providing the reformist element which the DC had lost, the Socialists, despite some early successes with education reform and nationalisation of electricity supply, and despite flirtation with economic planning, proved unable to resist the adoption of the practices of mass patronage and of political appointments throughout the public sector, by the method known as *lottizzazione* – the 'sharing out' of senior posts in accordance with the political balance within the ruling coalition. Thus there developed also the legislative activities referred to earlier, of obsession with trivial and local bills, known as *leggine*, which usually involved the disbursement of public money. This system of administering public resources might be described as a partial pluralist corporatism: corporatist, in the sense that influence is determined by membership of groups limited by residence, occupation or clientelist affiliation; pluralist, in the sense that a variety of groups has access to the decision-making process; and partial, because that access was not extended to large sectors of the population. This corporatism can be distinguished from interest-group pluralism by the relatively restricted nature of competition among the groups that have access and by the lack of free competition among all the available groups in society.

Among the excluded groups we can number areas and sectors dominated by the communist party, trade unions, the dependent agricultural labourers (braccianti) of the South, and the urban unemployed. The apparently permanent exclusion of the PCI from ministerial posts and the stability of the electoral blocs on which parties and associations rested ensured the limitations on the internal and external competition and on freedom of membership. Despite the considerable changes taking place in Italian society, the Italian electorate was relatively stable until the 1970s and preserved intact at the parliamentary level the cold-war division of Italy into two hostile competing blocks, Catholic and Communist. Underlying the apparent stability of the party-political balance there was a failure of the political system either to integrate the industrial working-class into the decision-making process (by way of the unions, the PCI, or the reformist elements within the governing coalition) or to resolve the structural problems produced or enhanced by the process of 'precocious maturity'.

The second phase of growth in the Italian economy, 1963–73, saw a much greater interaction between the public sector and the private sector than had occurred previously. Both IRI and ENI diversified and expanded very considerably at this time, and though the Italian model of state intervention which developed then has been much admired abroad,[10] the central problems of overall political direction of the large state-owned corporations have not yet been satisfactorily resolved; the dynamic expansionist technocrats of IRI and ENI have indeed proved able to provide an alternative to penetration of the Italian markets by multinational corporations, but they have also proved adept, in their different ways, not only at evading parliamentary control but also at ensuring that the traditionally trained administrators in the Ministry of State Participation exercise little positive direction. That is not to say that the public sector escapes all political control. The links of the public-sector corporations with party factions and with individual politicians are a source of their continued accrual of privileged treatment in macro-economic policy. But IRI and ENI remain quasi-autonomous political fiefs controlled by the 'new barons' of the Italian state, the public-sector managers and their political allies.[11] Though in other areas (e.g. television and radio, public-health provision, education) there has been a significant dispersion of the spoils of office, the DC has been able to keep to itself the post of Minister of State Participation and has ensured its overwhelming predominance in the control of appointments and direction of funds to industry.

The partial corporatism that we have described has developed as a complex and sophisticated means, to use Tarrow's phrase, of sharing 'public resources among a host of private claimants'.[12] It has also proved a resilient and perhaps surprisingly stable political system. Even though Italy appears since 1963 to have entered the 'stop-go' cycle familiar to students of British political economy, the levels of activity which mark the nadirs of the stop phase have been consistently higher than those achieved in the British economy in the post-war period, and average annual growth since 1963 has compared well with that of Italy's other European competitors. But a major characteristic of the economy has been its extreme volatility, both in current balance and in annual growth rates, a volatility which reflects the structural imbalances to which we have referred. Increasingly these imbalances have come to have a marked effect on the organisation of the distribution of public resources to 'the host of private claimants'. We now consider the recessions of the 1970s as heightening factors in the development of the political and economic imbalances.

RECESSION AND UNDER-DEVELOPMENT

The major effect of the oil-induced recession of 1973–4 was, in the economic sphere, to exacerbate the balance-of-payments problem as a result of the heavy reliance of Italy on oil imports. Over 80 per cent of Italy's energy needs in 1973 were met by imported oil, and we have already observed how an early effort by the fascist regime to establish autarky demanded an independent energy policy supported by AGIP and later by ENI. The response of the economy to the energy problems presented by the oil-price rises, particularly those of 1974 and 1979, was rapid, extensive and relatively successful, at least in the sense that there has been a significant fall in the propensity to consume energy since 1973 and a decrease in the ratio of energy input to industry output. But the oil deficit as a percentage of GDP was in 1978 higher than in 1973 (1.0 per cent in 1973 to 2.9 per cent in 1978) and likely to remain higher for some time to come. The government has responded with two types of energy-policy proposals, one designed to reduce household and industrial energy consumption, and the other, from 1980, to reduce the dependence on oil in the production of electricity with a 10-year investment plan for coal- and nuclear-fuelled power stations. But whatever the success of these measures, oil price rises have a reverberating effect in Italy throughout the political system. In 1974 the oil-price rises occurred just as Italy was recovering from a prolonged period of stagnation. The recession from early 1970 to late 1972 followed significant advances made by the trade unions both in wage increases and in general working conditions after the 'hot autumn' of 1969. According to some commentators[13] the pre-oil recession was only partly induced by the shorter working-week and limitations on overtime introduced in 1969, the main burden of causality being attributed to the severe decline in housing construction and the relative decline in consumer expenditure, the former in response to new laws relating to urban planning and the latter apparently in response to fears of increased unemployment and the uncertain political and social climate. Political terrorism and sporadic urban violence had developed, and the failure of the centre-left coalitions resulted in 1972 in the premature dissolution of Parliament and early elections, the first such in the history of the Italian republic.

The initial response of the centre-left governments had been, in the short-term, the adoption of reflationary monetary policies in late 1970 and the expansion of public-sector investment, and for the long-term, commitment by the government under combined Socialist and trade-union pressure to a more programmatic approach to macro-economic policy. The first Development Plan intended to cover the period 1966–70 had been hampered by delays in enactment and implementation and by unresponsiveness to its aims both on the part of the civil service and on the part of the large corporations both public and private sector. Despite the experience of the first plan, the problems of economic development were held (at least in sectors close to the Socialist Party) to be such as to demand continued strategic government intervention.[14] But both inside and outside the Socialist Party the more general problem which presented itself was the control of government expenditure, and this problem was to become urgent in the context of the very gradual and balanced expansionist approach which government authorities attempted to adopt in answer to the recession of 1977. In part the problem was the size of demands made by the constituencies of the governing parties. In the 1970s to the clamouring voices of the 'host of private claimants' were added the demands of large areas of the state industry sector which had previously been largely self-financing but which now found themselves unable to generate sufficient revenue.[15] The control of public expenditure was not helped by the timeless nature of the Italian budget, which unlike that common in other West European countries was not a projection of government spending and revenue but rather an annual photograph of government assets and liabilities which was entirely unsuited to the demands of medium- and long-term control of fiscal policy.[16]

In the light of these and other problems some attempt was made to coordinate the activities of government agencies in industry to reduce conflict of policy and duplication of effort. In 1971 authority for planning in the South was transferred to the cabinet committee for economic planning (CIPE) and a new holding company (GEPI) was established as a common subsidiary of all the major state corporations with the purpose of intervening in the private sector to aid ailing industries. The second plan, originally drawn up to cover the period 1971–5, was revised to cover 1973–7; its fundamental objectives were full employment, reduction of regional disparities and provision of adequate social infrastructure, and it was intended to provide by a series of annual plans a flexible attempt to achieve coordinated decision-making in the long-term covering the entire public sector. But the plan was perhaps the first major casualty following the oil price rises in 1973; though its targets and projections had not seemed overambitious originally, its assumptions of almost stable balance of

TABLE 7.4 Basic Economic Indicators: 1968–79

	1968	*1969*	*1970*	*1971*	*1972*	*1973*	*1974*	*1975*	*1976*	*1977*	*1978*	*1979*
Prices[a]	1.4	2.6	4.9	4.8	5.7	10.8	19.0	17.0	14.0	17.0	12.1	14.8
Unemployment[b]	3.7	3.5	3.2	3.2	3.7	3.5	2.9	3.4	3.7	7.5	7.2	7.7
Employment[c]												
in Agriculture	22.3	21.4	19.4	19.3	18.0	17.3	16.5	15.6	15.3	15.7	15.3	
in Industry	41.4	42.6	43.3	43.6	43.8	43.5	43.7	43.7	43.0	38.2	37.9	
in Services	36.3	36.0	37.3	37.0	38.2	39.2	39.9	40.7	41.7	46.1	46.8	
Origin of GDP[d]												
Agriculture	11.0	11.3	11.6	9.8	9.2	10.0	8.4		8.5	7.6	7.1	
Industry	31.0	30.3	35.1	30.8	31.3	31.6	33.5		32.8	34.7	35.4	
Construction	8.0	8.6	6.6	7.9	7.6	7.7	8.2		8.2	7.7	7.5	
Other	50.0	49.8	46.8	51.6	51.9	50.7	49.9		50.5	50.00	50.00	
Change in GDP[e]	5.9	4.7	4.9	1.1	2.9	6.0	3.7	−3.7	5.0	2.0	2.6	4.9
Current account balance of payments[f]	2627	2340	1133	1902	2043	−2662	−8017	−554	−2816	2465	6363	5900
Currency change[g]	625	625	625	581	582	582	650	653	832	882	831	

a Percentage change on previous period, retail prices. SOURCE OECD, *Economic Survey* (1970–80).
b Percentage of labour force unemployed. SOURCE *Economic Bulletin for Europe* (1979).
c Percentage of labour force in employment. SOURCE OECD, *Economic Survey* (1970–80).
d Percentage of GDP, at factor costs. SOURCE OECD, *Economic Survey* (1970–80).
e Annual volume change in GDP at 1970 prices (1970–9). 1968 and 1969 at 1963 prices. SOURCE OECD, *Economic Survey* (1970–80).
f In millions of US dollars. 1979 forecast. SOURCE OECD, *Economic Survey* (1970–80).
g Units for US dollars, average daily. SOURCE OECD, *Economic Survey* (1970–80).

payments, buoyant world trade and mild price inflation were rendered unrealistic (see Table 7.4), though it should be observed that the welcome it received in the Christian Democrat Party had never been more than lukewarm. The plan was finally published as a consultative document only and never received official governmental or parliamentary ratification.

But by summer 1973 the recovery seemed well under way, fuelled mainly by the growth in domestic demand and in investment (see Tables 7.4 and 7.5). But the responses of the economy to changes in governmental policy were already showing some of the anomalies, delays and distortions that were to characterise the Italian economy after the oil price rises in early 1974. A primary source of the inflationary pressure was the increase in costs to industry following the three-year wage settlements of 1969 and 1972, though it should be noted that the major concern of the unions at this stage and later has been to preserve employment and enhance job security. In part this might be attributed to the protection of wages against cost-of-living increases by means of their linkage to a retail-prices index. We discuss later

TABLE 7.5 Allocation of Resources: 1969–78 at Constant Prices

	Private consumption		*Public consumption*		*Gross fixed investment*	
	% share of GNP	*% change on previous year*	*% share of GNP*	*% change on previous year*	*% share of GNP*	*% change on previous year*
1969	63.4	+5.7	13.4	+3.1	20.5	+8.2
1970	64.0	+3.5	12.6	+6.7	21.1	+15.0
1971	64.0	+7.1	14.2	+21.2	19.9	+1.6
1972	64.3	+3.3	14.7	+4.6	19.3	+0.4
1973	64.3	+6.2	14.6	+3.3	21.1	+9.9
1974	63.1	+2.5	13.2	+2.1	22.0	+3.7
1975	65.0	−1.3	16.0	+2.8	20.6	−13.0
1976	63.5	+3.5	15.4	+2.6	20.0	+2.3
1977	63.3	+2.3	15.6	+2.2	19.7	N/A
1978	63.2	+2.9	16.4	+3.5	18.8	−0.4

SOURCE ASI (1972–9)

Note to Tables 7.4 and 7.5 Figures relating to the period after 1974 are new series. In 1978 ISTAT, from whom the above figures are ultimately derived, changed their method of national account aggregating in an attempt to rectify the apparent under-estimation by previous methods of one particular sector of the accounts. The new method was applied initially to national accounts from 1975 onwards. The sector concerned was, in the production accounts, the value added per employee for firms with less than 20 employees. In the old series 1975 accounts this provided 32.5 per cent of total value added in manufacturing industry; in the new series the value added by this sector is nearly 60 per cent. The net effect of this and other revisions is an 8.3 per cent increase in the level of GDP at current prices in 1975, new series over old series. See OECD, *Economic Survey: Italy* (1980) Annex A; and *Annuario Statistico Italiano* (1979) p. 370 footnote, for further details.

this system, known as the *scala mobile*. Inflationary pressures also occurred through increases in the cost of raw materials. The balance-of-payment problem emerged also with the increased propensity to import in the economy and the initial depreciation of the lira after its floating in early 1973. Retail-price inflation in 1973 was 10.8 per cent, and Italy was in current-account deficit at the end of 1973 for the first time for a decade; though growth was also vigourous, the oil price rises of 1974 caught the economy at a particularly difficult time, rendering more acute both the rate of inflation and the current account deficit, and somewhat more tardily reversing the upward trend of economic activity. Industrial production increased by 9.4 per cent in 1973 and by an annual rate of 11.3 per cent in the first half of 1974. Thereafter it declined as restrictive government policy began to take effect, decreasing by an annual rate of 14.0 in the second quarter of 1974.

In 1973 the government's preoccupation had been the control of price inflation with if possible the maintenance of steady growth. In 1974 the moderately restrictive policy of late 1973 changed to one of severe restriction. Discount rate was raised to 9 per cent on 18 March 1974, limits on exports and imports of bank notes were introduced on 22 March, and on 6 April 1974 growth of bank credit was limited for the period from 31 March 1974 to 31 March 1975 to 15 per cent for certain sectors and 12 per cent for others. On 2 May an import deposit scheme was introduced requiring importers to deposit for 180 days in non-interest-bearing accounts with the Bank of Italy the equivalent in lire of 50 per cent of the value of their imports of certain goods in excess of one million lire. On 6 July 1974 a set of deflationary fiscal measures originally promulgated as a decree law were passed by Parliament; among the measures were the application of a 'once-for-all' surtax (*una tantum*) on the top bands of personal income, higher corporation tax, raising of VAT on luxury goods and meat, increased tax on petrol, and increased electricity and public transport charges. The economy went into comparatively severe recession in the third quarter of 1974 which deepened still further in 1975, though this did not have a marked effect on employment. At the beginning of 1975 the authorities relaxed the tightness of their monetary grip and raised credit ceilings, and in August 1975 a two-year reflation programme was introduced.

But inflationary pressures continued to push prices up. The balance-of-payments problem persisted and indeed the combined effect of inflationary expectations, rapid growth in the last quarter of 1975 and external deficit resulted early in 1976 in the collapse of the lira and the closing of the official foreign exchange markets for a period of just over two months, from 21 January to 1 March 1976. 1976 has been described by one British commentator as a 'disaster year for the Italian economy',[17] and from the external observer's viewpoint such a judgement might not be surprising; if 1975 provided internal macro-economic problems, the problems of 1976 were of an international complexion, demanding repeated recourse by the central authorities to new policy packages aimed at the control of domestic demand and the stabilisation of the lira. The period 1977–80 was one of gradual recovery from gross external deficit with the authorities being careful to limit growth with the aim of ensuring a steady slow reflation.

But despite the caution of macro-economic policy the process of recovery was again halted in 1980 by the international recession, and inflationary pressures appeared to be building up in the summer of 1980 which together with the sharp rise in unemployment levels in the period 1977–80 threatened once again the precarious stability of the Italian political economy. Thus the period 1973–80 can be characterised as one of considerable volatility, with three major downturns in activity (1974, 1976 and 1980) occurring to halt the underlying processes of growth in the Italian economy. Though the dynamism of the economy has not shown signs of weakening in the long-term, it is no longer possible under existing international arrangements for rapid growth to be sustained over long periods. The vulnerability of the balance of payments to oil price rises, the weakening of the trade-off between export surpluses and domestic unemployment, and the persistent upward pressure on prices from wage costs and from the very large public-sector deficit all militate against sustained high rates of growth in the Italian economy.

Nevertheless, in some respects the response of the state to the economic crises of the 1970s was considerably more coherent and better-directed than might have been expected, and the period 1973–9 in retrospect might be viewed as one of unusual harmony and coordination between the warring groups in Italian politics. Whether directly as a result of economic and social crises or more indirectly because of electoral and other political pressure the partial corporatism of the Italian political system has developed in two specific ways. First, the rigid exclusion of the Communists and of the trade unions from participation in governmental decision-making has weakened so that both groups were for a time (1976–9) at least partially and informally allowed some consultative function. Secondly and paradoxically, the fragmentation of governmental decision-making was affected by the consequent need to consult among a larger number of political groups, with positive though temporary effects on the willingness and capacity of senior cabinet-ministers both to reach agreements with the secretaries of the political parties, the trade unions and Confindustria, and to implement those agreements.

The traditional and unbending refusal of Christian Democrat leaders to consider in any public or explicit manner the inclusion of the PCI in government first began to undergo changes in nuance and in degrees of rigidity with the challenge posed by the PCI strategy of historic compromise,[18] which occurred at the time when the failures of the traditional governing coalitions in social and economic policy were exacerbated both by the oil crisis and by the crisis of the Christian Democrat party. As we have seen, one effect of the oil crisis was to reverse a trend of growth and to force the economy back into recession and inflation, with consequences for the capacity of the government to resolve the developing crises in the inner cities or to control the offshoot of that crisis, the resurgence of political violence. For the Christian Democrats, their identity as a conservative party dominated by factionalism and held together by clientelistic political affiliation, though well-established by 1974, was not readily recognised by their leaders. The Divorce Referendum in 1974, at which the anti-divorce lobby was defeated, may be interpreted as an attempt by the 'old guard' led by the party secretary, Fanfani, to re-establish the link between the conservative party of government and the Catholic social organisations and electorate. The clear defeat for this attempt has led to a re-appraisal both by the Christian Democrats and by the Catholic hierarchy of their traditional relationship.

Two major political scandals also came to the surface at this time and, unusually for this political system, did not lose their momentum in the labyrinthine processes of Italian law: the first related to the indirect involvement of senior Christian Democrat and Social Democrat (PSDI) politicians in the attempted coup d'etat of December 1970, and in the growth of right-wing terrorism; and the second related to the sale of Lockheed military aircraft to the Italian armed forces. In both these cases, for differing reasons, the traditional capacity of the governing parties to close the affected area from public scrutiny did not work, and this, with the apparent immobilism of the state in crucial policy areas and with significant sociological changes occurring in the structure of the electorate (the impact of the 18–21 year-old cohort in particular) led to significant changes in electoral alignment virtually for the first time since 1948. In the regional elections of 1975 the PCI gained 32 per cent of valid votes (27 per cent in 1970) while the DC declined from 38 per cent to 36 per cent; shifts of this magnitude had been extremely unusual in Italian elections, but were partially repeated in the parliamentary elections in 1976 and again in 1979 in the opposite direction (see Table 7.6).

It appears now not only that the electorate in general is extremely volatile but also that the long-standing mistrust of the PCI by significant sections of

TABLE 7.6 Parliamentary Elections 1972, 1976, 1979: Chamber of Deputies[a]

	1972	*1976*	*1979*
DC	38.8	38.7	38.3
PCI	27.2	34.2	30.4
PSI	9.6	9.6	9.8
MSI	8.7	6.1	5.3
PSDI	5.1	3.4	3.8
PLI	3.9	1.3	1.9
PRI	2.9	3.1	3.0
PR	–	1.1	3.4
Other Left	1.9	1.5	1.4
SVP	0.5	0.5	0.6

a Figures are percentages of valid votes
SOURCE 1972 and 1976: ASI (1973, 1977); 1979: *Corriere della sera* (6 June 1979)

the population has been replaced by a much more flexible attitude. The PCI fought the 1976 elections successfully on the strategy of the historic compromise and as the party 'of clean hands' – the party of administrative efficiency and honesty. Though disagreement certainly occurred over economic policy and over the anti-terrorist policy, the primary issue dominating the 1976–9 legislature was the inclusion or not of the PCI in the government. In the new legislature the DC and PCI between them had 73 per cent of the votes and 78 per cent of the seats, and though a centre-left coalition was numerically possible, the refusal of the PSI to return to such a formula ensured that for the time being the PCI must be accommodated in some form. The policy measures proposed by the PCI in their campaign emphasised the need to reorganise the public sector and to control inflation by eliminating 'the parasitisms, distortions and structural weaknesses that weigh on the productive system and weaken Italy's international position'.[19]

Primary importance was to be attached to the overhaul of public finances, increasing state revenues by firm action against tax evasion, eliminating waste in the social-security system and stopping the rise in public indebtedness. The electoral manifesto also stated

> It is radically mistaken to attribute the present difficulties of the Italian economy to the wage increases that have occurred over the past few years . . . and to seek a solution in wage restraint. Only if action is undertaken to remove the real causes of inflation and the deficit in our foreign accounts, to overcome the structural weaknesses in the Italian economy and embark on a new type of economic and social development, will the trade unions be able to further develop a line that concentrates

demands not on monetary wage increases but on expansion of investments and employment and new social reforms.[20]

It is symptomatic of the strength of the divisions between the Italian parties that though some of the PCI economic policies were later adopted – in particular, reform of the tax-collection system, unification of the social-security system and investment subsidies for small firms – it remained difficult for Christian Democrat politicians to admit to the extent of the agreement between the parties. There were also serious divergences over policy and over method: in particular, the PCI demanded much more rigorous control over the public sector in industry, and refused to take part in the system of *lottizzazione*, but demanded the application of managerial criteria in public administrative appointments. The first government after the 1976 elections had only DC ministers but relied on the agreed abstention of the four parliamentary left-wing parties (PCI, PSI, PSDI, PRI). Any more positive degree of recognition of Communist legitimacy might have been unpalatable to some Christian Democrats, and the parliamentary attitude of the PCI was described in the jargon of Italian politics not as 'confidence' but as 'non-no-confidence' (*non-sfiducia*).

With these suspicious beginnings, the government lasted until January 1978. Policy for the government was determined at least nominally at regular meetings of the five secretaries of the governing parties with the Prime Minister, Giulio Andreotti. The cooperative attitude of the PCI undoubtedly made it much easier than it would otherwise have been for the government to implement its policy of austerity – which demanded, as we have seen, high unemployment, tight credit and a very gradual reflation. But it became clear that if 'austerity' meant to the PCI equality of sacrifice with the aim of establishing a new productive base for the economy, for the other governing parties with the exception of the PSI the aim and scope of the policy was totally different, and for the DC in particular it was to keep their multifarious constituencies intact through the long-drawn-out crisis.

In January 1978, in the face of increasing activist dissatisfaction with the lack of positive change of direction by the government, the PCI withdrew from its position of non-no-confidence and demanded ministerial posts in government. The next government was approved by Parliament on 14 March 1978 the day on which Aldo Moro, the DC elder statesman who had been largely instrumental in its formation, was kidnapped by terrorists. The coalition, dubbed a government of national unity, was led by Andreotti and had only DC ministers again, this time – one small step forward for the PCI – with the external support of the four left-wing parties. But this was as far as the PCI were to get in this legislature. The Andreotti government lasted ten increasingly bad-tempered months until January 1979, when the PCI again demanded ministerial posts and were refused. Parliament was again dissolved early and at the elections both DC and PCI lost votes, the latter rather more heavily than the former. The PCI, which had called itself in this period *partito di lotta e di governo* – the party of struggle and of government – had not in fact been allowed to try the two roles together.

For the trade-unions confederations the experience of participation has been similarly chequered. The three major confederations (CGIL, CISL, UIL) appear largely to have overcome their historic differences and though there is still rivalry and muted hostility between them the consistent coordination of national and local policy has enabled them to speak authoritatively to national and local government and to employers, with some positive results. Their problems have arisen not so much from interconfederation rivalry as from the increasing volatility of the shop-floor membership, the growth of autonomous trades unions, and the persistence of traditional suspicion on the part of employers. The close links between the confederations and the political parties (in particular between CGIL and PCI) has made possible concerted action on the range of topics, though overall the concern of the confederations with protection of employment and the reviving of the economy conflicted sharply with the monetarist orthodoxy of the Bank of Italy and the balance-of-payments concern which dominated the DC finance ministers.

Perhaps the single most significant gain made by the Left during this period was the agreement reached on 25 January 1975 between the employers' confederation, Confindustria, and the trade-unions confederations relating to the 'scale mobile', the wage-indexing mechanism. Originally introduced in 1956, the mechanism provided for the automatic increase in the individual's wage by a fixed amount. The increase occurred once for each one-point rise in a specially constructed price index, and varied in accordance with the individual's wage category. The value of the increase had been established in 1956 at 1 per cent of the then wage, and remained unchanged for nearly 19 years, having a median value of about 490 lire. From 1956 to 1974 wages rose on the whole rather faster than prices, so that the percentage of the price rise compensated for grew progressively smaller. Despite other compensating factors such as the effect of the rise in the price index on the frequency with which points were accumulated, in 1974 the indexing mechanism was accounting for only about 50 per cent of the rise in prices in that year. The original aim of the mechanism, in the days of relatively low inflation and weak unions, had been to avoid the occurrence of lengthy strikes over pay increases and to provide the workforce with some means of ensuring adequate recompense for inflation without recourse to trade unions. It was with similar aims that Confindustria agreed in January 1975 to the re-adjustment of the increase and of the price index to take account of inflation.

The agreement initially applied to the industrial sector only but was later extended to other sectors, and its amendment was implemented progressively from 1975 to 1977 so that in 1977 the indexing mechanism accounted for 100 per cent of the annual price rise. The agreement also provided for a single amount in increase for each wage category, equivalent to the amount for the top of the wage scale, and for an increase in all wages of 12,000 lire, compensating for earnings lost as a result of the mechanism in the past. Ugo La Malfa, secretary of the Republican Party and deputy prime minister, criticised the agreement severely on the grounds that it had been made without reference to the government's economic strategy and that it would provide for increases of earnings well in excess of the government's intentions for the economy as a whole. The agreement was a clear indication of the frustration of employers and trades unions with the tightness of the government's monetary policy. For Confindustria, led by Gianni Agnelli, chairman of Fiat, the agreement was claimed to represent an attempt to establish constructive labour relations with the aim of increasing productivity, and in this sense it certainly marked the beginning of a new and more cordial relationship between Confindustria and the trade unions. But underlying the development in relations with the unions and the open disagreement with the government was the belief of the employers that the mechanism would push up domestic demand and allow the employers to recoup their costs in higher prices, as they had been able to do in 1973. Agnelli in response to government criticism demanded reflation of the economy, increased export credit and help for small industry.

The agreement was followed on May 1975 by the ratification by Parliament of adjustment of the Cassa Integrazione Guadagni, a system of earnings guarantee which provides for government compensation for short-time working. Under the Cassa Integrazione benefits are paid to workers at 80 per cent of gross pay for all hours not worked up to a total of 40 hours (the previous scheme had applied only to a limited number of hours). Firms calling for the assistance of the Cassa Integrazione have to pay the fund 8 per cent of the benefits due to the workers, and the fund is also financed by a contribution from firms of 1 per cent of their annual wage bill and by a government subsidy of 20 billion lire a year. Though the employers' contribution is sizeable, the new Cassa Integrazione made it much easier than was previously the case for employers to lay off workers, since the extraordinary intervention of the Cassa Integrazione could be extended up to 12 months or in some cases indefinitely. The Cassa Integrazione in practice rapidly became a half-way house to outright redundancy, for which reason its intervention has tended to be resisted by the workers. The attitude of the confederations, though tempered by considerable grassroots dissatisfaction, was based on the belief that the restructuring of the Italian economy was politically and economically feasible.

At the CGIL Congress in January 1978, Luciano Lama, secretary-general of CGIL and close ally of the PCI secretary Enrico Berlinguer, suggested that workers should be prepared to make 'substantial sacrifices' to aid the restructuring of the Italian economy. Though there was some suspicion that Lama's new cooperative attitude was a political 'bribe' to encourage DC acceptance of the PCI into the government, the overall stance of all three union confederations was undoubtedly undergoing considerable changes, at least at the leadership level. The immediate recompense that the unions have demanded in return for a more flexible attitude towards redundancy is greater public investment to depressed areas, greater public expenditure in social services and tougher government action against tax evaders. But such policies do not now appear high on the government's list of priorities.

Overall, it appears that the governments of the day took some time to appreciate the effects of the oil-price rises on the balance-of-payments problem; as a result they continued for some time to pursue an inconsistent course between sharp deflation and hasty expansion. The budgetary expansion that took place in the autumn of 1975 was clearly a pre-election move designed to please wide sectors of the electorate. After improving pensions and lowering discount rate to 7 per cent, the government announced a medium-term reflation programme aimed at satisfying the criticisms both of Confindustria and of the trade unions. After the unhappy experience of exchange-rate depreciation in 1976 which followed this reflation, subsequent governments (under IMF credit conditions) have ceased trying to make concessions to all parties and have aimed at solving the problem of inflation before seeking to reflate the economy. In this sense the need to impress the international business community has taken precedence over the satisfaction of sectoral interests such as those of the private high-technology sector and the industrial trade unions: the only sectoral interests that have continued to receive government favours are those of the public-sector corporations and the bureaucracy, the maintenance of whose privileged position in no small part explains growth of PSBR in this period.

After the parliamentary elections of June 1979 it appears no longer possible for the PCI to accept anything less than a clear change of direction in economic policy as well as ministerial posts, and the DC are not likely to concede these points now, having refused them after the 1976 elections when the PCI was in a stronger position. The crisis management policy is firmly established; it involves tight credit control through the Bank of Italy, increasing of revenue to the state through higher charges for public services and tax reform, high unemployment and the bailing-out of selected sectors of the economy through public-sector intervention. It is significant however that the government felt compelled to intervene to protect employment when in the summer of 1980 Fiat threatened to make 25,000 workers redundant in Turin and elsewhere. The case provoked mass mobilisation by trade unions and a month-long strike at the Mirafiori factory in Turin, when the unions adopted the policy unusual in Italy of mass pickets at the gates of the factory. With the agreement of the PCI the government hurriedly passed through Parliament a bill providing for about £760 million in credit and grant-aid to Fiat and other sectors of the car industry, to encourage the adoption by FIAT of a softer line on the redundancy.

We have emphasised throughout this essay the autonomy of many sectors of political society from the state; the ineffectiveness of the aid and the distance between the mass of factory workers and their union representatives were well-indicated when on 14 October 1980 the so-called 'march of the forty-thousand' demanding the right to return to work took place in Turin, an apparently spontaneous demonstration by car-workers against the strike.[21] The union confederations settled the dispute the following day. In the short-term the episode confirms that the opportunities for conciliation between conflicting political groups in Italy are now diminishing. In the long-term, the episode might represent part of a reversal of the processes of political development which have been taking place in Italy over the last decade.

CONCLUSION

I have argued in this paper that the response of the state to the consequences of the recessions of the 1970s has been coherent with the pattern of public policymaking which has developed in the post-war Republic. This pattern emerged and established itself in the late sixties after the advent of the Socialists into the government, and consists broadly in the aggregation of conflicting demands and their partial satisfaction in accordance with the existing distribution of power. Occasional attempts to impose an overriding strategy on macro-economic policy (for instance, in the first and second Development Plans) have failed to find implementation, either because of the hostility of influential political actors to important sections of the strategy, or because of particularistic demands which effectively empty the strategy of content, or because of the incapacity of the central authorities to adapt the plan to rapidly changing economic circumstances. It is therefore difficult to categorise the responses of the state in terms such as monetarist, neo-liberal, Keynesian reflationary or deflationary, since the response has at times been all of these at least in intention. The instruments available dictate emphasis on monetarist policies, firstly because the Bank of Italy is a uniquely efficient (though autonomous) politico-economic institution and secondly because the alternatives are either subject to particularistic pressure from within the governing parties or largely escape coordinated governmental control.

The reform of the tax system undertaken in 1979 may eventually provide the government with fiscal instruments of macro-economic policy. The dominant political party, inter-class, internally divided, and clientelist in operation, increasingly appears to be allying itself with the private- and public-sector industrialists: but the response of these is not always coherent either, and to some commentators the apparently irresistible growth of party-controlled patronage has seemed like 'the capture of willing victims'. Though the economy shows persistent vigour and dynamism even under the most difficult circumstances, that vigour and dynamism are purchased at the price of political and economic structural weaknesses which have been rendered acute by the disturbances in international economic organisations and operations in the 1970s.

POSTSCRIPT

Since October 1980 the pattern established in the 1970s and described in the preceding pages has continued to show itself, with one major development, in the form of a government headed by the secretary of the Republican Party (PRI), Giovanni Spadolini, which in June 1981 ended 35 years of Christian Democrat monopoly of the Prime Ministership. The collapse of the Forlani government which preceded Spadolini was occasioned by revelations of the existence of a secret masonic lodge, headed by an obscure right-wing international arms dealer named Licio Gelli, of which senior civil servants, officers of the armed forces, judges and politicians appeared to have been members. The response of the DC to the loss of the Prime Ministership was to engage in a bout of vigorous internal recriminations, mainly directed at the party secretary Flaminio Piccoli. With a national assembly planned for October 1981 and a special congress in February 1982 the DC appears set for a period of reorganisation but it is difficult to predict what balance of power will emerge. Piccoli is one of the senior politicians in the majority *Doroteo* faction and his anticipated removal from office may well cause his faction to split into several small groups led by individual senior ministers. The omens for Spadolini are not good for the period after the congress, for one of the historic leaders of the DC, Senator Amintore Fanfani, has declared that the major priority must be to avoid early elections. This clearly means that early elections are a real possibility, in which case the DC will have as an immediate tactical objective the regaining of the Prime Ministership at the earliest possible moment to ensure that they have control of the government during the electoral campaign. After that of his own party, the strongest support for the new Prime Minister comes from the Socialist Party, whose leader Bettino Craxi was immediately responsible for precipitating the collapse of the previous government and for whom the establishment of a government led by a non-Christian Democrat represents an important tactical objective achieved. The Socialist aim of establishing themselves as the third force in Italian politics is also brought closer by their improved relationship with the small Social Democrat Party (PSDI), with whom they established a formal policy agreement in October 1980, but one of the prices for this is that their relations with the increasingly-isolated PCI are not good. The significance of these developments for the political economy is their effect on governmental stability and capacity for long-term policy-making. At present, it must be observed that the new confidence and belligerence of the PSI have not yet made a significant difference to their electoral standing, but granted that the problem of internal dissent within the governing parties is not resolved, the prospects for governmental stability appear to depend either on the entry of the PCI into the government or on a fundamental electoral re-alignment.

The most serious obstacle to the formation of coherent policy responses to economic crisis is not governmental instability as such, but rather the incapacity of governments to control the relatively-independent arms of the state. Against the institutional background which we described above, the Prime Minister is often a weak and ineffective figure, unable either effectively to co-ordinate his ministers or to impose policy on the state and para-state agencies. It is therefore not to be expected that a change of Prime Minister, even from a member of the DC to a member of another party, would by itself produce radical changes in direction of policy or in methods of control, particularly since the supporting coalition remains the same.

The economic problems faced by the Spadolini government are also the same, as the Italian economy has continued its erratic course, veering from high demand and high output in January–May 1980 to severe recession in the first half of 1981. As a result of the high exchange-rate of the dollar and the increasing cost of oil to Italy, the relatively favourable trade balance of 1980 was changed to a record imbalance in May 1980; in coherence with the established policy of giving priority to external balance, the emergency measures introduced by the Forlani government included yet another import deposit scheme and a severe credit squeeze. As self-proclaimed 'good Europeanists' the Italian government was highly offended when these crisis measures were attacked by the EEC Commission as contrary to EEC trade policy; the EEC Commission in the same report fired some well-aimed salvoes at Italian procedures and administrative structures relating to public sector financing, in particular at the practice whereby the Bank of Italy took up any government stock not bought at issue by the money-market. Though the trade imbalance was quickly corrected, other problems of economic balance remained: inflation in the summer of 1981 was running at an annual rate of over 20 per cent and the budget deficit, of which the annual target was £16 billion (37,500 billion lire), was £9.3 billion (21,000 billion lire) in the first half of 1981. Spadolini on taking office in June 1981 announced his government's determination to deal with the 'four emergencies' facing the country (moral, social, economic and 'international'); his economic policies were not markedly different in appearance from those of the previous government, and it remains to be seen whether he will be able to translate the five phases into implemented policy. His particular emphasis, in line with the PRI policy of firm control of government spending, was on the reduction of public expenditure mainly through cuts in spending on health, welfare and education. He was able to secure agreement between Confindustria and the trades unions to reduce the high cost of the index-linked wage increases ('scala mobile'), and ended the rivalry within the public sector petrochemicals industry by returning Montedison, formerly partly-owned by a state-holding company, entirely to the private sector. With such policies he has been able to re-create to some extent the close links between public sector, private sector and trades unions, which appeared to have been damaged by the Fiat strikes of the summer of 1980 and the passivity of the then government in the face of labour unrest and high unemployment.

Underlying Italy's erratic economic performance is of course the problem of Italy's very high dependence on oil for energy. In 1980 51 per cent of Italy's total energy needs were met by imported oil, and 67 per cent of its electricity supply was fuelled by oil. The large scheme of investment in nuclear energy referred to above has been through several changes of minister and faced strong pressure from the unions and from local government authorities. In August 1981, by agreement between the government, ENEL (the public-owned electricity supply company), the unions and local government, a less grandiose scheme was put forward, involving four new nuclear power stations instead of ten. Even granted that the policy would work if implemented, the perennial problem remains of getting it implemented. In a phrase which may be held to apply in general to Italian policy-making, a former government minister described the policy document as 'a purely verbal agreement which suffers from continual exceptions when the necessity arises of dealing with concrete cases'.[22] The flexibility of ministerial policy in meeting local demands is part of the process of partial corporatism that we have described; while it helps account for the extraordinary vigour of Italian industry, also, as we have argued above, it makes the response of governments to macro-economic problems fractured, spasmodic and in practice unpredictable.

NOTES AND REFERENCES

1. For instance, in G. F. Poggi, 'Potere politico e potere economico in Italia', in *Il Mulino* a.xxiii, no. 233 (May–June 1974) pp. 349–62.
2. A. Predieri, *Il processo legislativo nel Parlamento italiano* (Milan: Giuffré, 1975).
3. For instance, in *The Times* (Tuesday, September 30 1980) p. 13.
4. For detailed analysis see G. Galli, *Dal bipartitismo imperfetto alla possibile alternativa* (Bologna: il Mulino, 1975) pp. 43–65.
5. Public administration in Italy has on the whole resisted well not only the reforming attempts of politicians but also the investigative efforts of academics; some useful material is available in P. Ammassari *et al.*, *Il burocrate di fronte alla burocrazia* (Milan: Giuffré, 1969); and G. Berti, 'La riforma dello stato', in L. Graziani and S. Tarrow (eds), *La crisi italiana* (Turin: Einaudi, 1979) pp. 447–96.
6. On post-unification political economy see L. Cafagna, 'Italy 1830–1914', in C. M. Cipolla (ed.), *The Fontana Economic History of Europe*, vol. 4, pt.1. *The Emergence of Industrial Societies* (Glasgow: Fontana/Collins, 1973) pp. 279–328; also A. Caracciolo; (ed.), *La formazione dell'Italia industriale* (Bari: Laterza, 1969).
7. A. J. Gregor, *Italian Fascism and Developmental Dictatorship* (Princeton: Princeton University Press, 1979) p. 155. For a balanced view of the question of economic development and rationalisation under fascism, see V. Castronovo, 'Il potere economico e il fascismo', in G. Quazza (ed.), *Fascismo e Società Italiana* (Turin: Einaudi, 1973) pp. 47–88.
8. On the problems of post-war reconstruction, see S. J. Woolf (ed.), *The Rebirth of Italy* (London: Longman, 1972); and V. Castronovo (ed.). *Italia contemporanea 1945–75* (Turin: Einaudi, 1976).
9. In M. Selvati, 'The Impasse of Italian Capitalism', in *New Left Review*, no. 76 (November–December 1972) pp. 3–33.
10. For instance, in M. Shonfield, *Modern Capitalism* (Oxford: Oxford University Press, 1965); and S. Holland (ed.), *The State as Entrepreneur* (London: Weidenfeld & Nicolson, 1972). See also M. V. Posner and S. J. Woolf, *Italian Public Enterprise* (London: Duckworth, 1967); and R. Vernon (ed.), *Big Business and the State* (London: Macmillan, 1974).

11. On the development of the public sector elite, see E. Scalfari and C. Turani, *Razza padrone: Storia della borghesia di Stato* (Milan: Feltrinelli, 1974); G. Tamburrano, *L'iceberg democristiano* (Milan: Superco Edizioni, 1975); and R. Orfei, *L'occupazione del potere: i democristiani 1945/75* (Milan: Longanesi, 1976).
12. S. G. Tarrow, *Between Centre and Periphery: Grassroots Politicians in Italy and France* (New Haven: Yale University Press, 1977) p. 64.
13. For example, in OECD, *Economic Survey: Italy 1972* (Paris: OECD, 1972) pp. 6–11.
14. Influential representatives of this view may be found in G. Amato, *Economia politica e istituzioni in Italia* (Bologna: Il Mulino, 1976); and G. Ruffolo, 'Project for Socialist Planning', in S. Holland (ed.), *Beyond Capitalist Planning* (Oxford: Basil Blackwell, 1978) pp. 69–84.
15. In 1970, for instance, IRI was 25.5 per cent self-financing in capital requirements; by 1979 this proportion had decreased to 7.8 per cent. See *IRI: Annual Report 1970* (Rome: IRI, 1971); and *Financial Times* (30 October 1980) p. 3.
16. For technical and political reasons it is extremely difficult to estimate the overall public-sector deficit; IMF estimated this provisionally as 16 per cent of GDP in 1975. Despite efforts at reforming the budgetary system and tightening control of public sector, transfer payments and subsidies to the autonomous agencies continue to present considerable problems. See Stephanie K. Holmans, *The Italian Public Expenditure System*, Government Economic Service Working Paper no. 3 (May 1978); and R. Onofri, 'The Italian Budgetary System', in *Review of Economic Conditions in Italy*, no. 2 (1979) pp. 289–306.
17. Rupert Cornwell, in '*Financial Times* Survey: Italy', *Financial Times* (Monday, 9 April 1979) pp. 17–28.
18. The Communist version of this much-misunderstood term may be found in E. Berlinguer, 'The Historic Compromise', in D. Sassoon (ed.), *The Italian Communists Speak for Themselves* (Nottingham: Spokesman, 1978) pp. 141–58.
19. Election programme 1976, p. 150; Sassoon (1978) pp. 159–68.
20. Sassoon (1978) p. 162.
21. For detailed description of and comment on these events, see *Corriere della Sera* (15–20 October 1980); and *L'Espresso*, no. 43, a.xxvi (26 October 1980) pp. 260–75.
22. R. Prodi, 'La posta in polio? Il futuro del Paise', p. 7, in *Corriere della Sera* (11 August 1981).

8 Spain: the End of the Miracle

JOSEPH HARRISON

During the international depression of the 1930s, commentators south of the Pyrenees continued to assert that Spain, because of her relative economic backwardness together with the effects of a sustained drive towards autarky over the previous quarter of a century, remained virtually isolated from the worst consequences of the greatest crisis which the capitalist system had ever experienced.[1] In a recent survey article two leading Spanish economic historians contend that 'The most serious problems facing the [Spanish] republic were not to come from coincidental external circumstances [but from] longer standing, basic internal problems such as agriculture . . . It is from here that originate most of the strains and stresses that were to explode in a bloody civil war'.[2]

The triumph of the reactionary forces led by General Franco in 1939 heralded a renewed and more emphatic phase of autarky which was enthusiastically embarked upon by the new regime's quasi-fascist political and economic advisers.[3] External pressures reinforced this chosen policy after the Second World War since the former ally of Nazi Germany was practically excluded from the world trading community. Deprived of essential raw imports, industry languished, while agriculture also suffered from a variety of shortages, most notably tractors and fertilisers. According to one estimate, industrial production did not rise above 1929 levels until 1950; agricultural production until 1958.[4]

The provision of United States aid after 1951, however, at last enabled the Iberian power to overcome many of the previous bottlenecks to economic growth by initiating a policy of import substitution.[5] Yet the main turning point on the road to economic (if not political) liberalism was the Stabilisation Plan of 1959 which was designed to put an end to the perennial balance-of-payments problems and incipient inflation which marked the intervening years. The Plan's success owed much to the financial support provided by the International Monetary Fund (which had blackballed Spain in the past) as well as by the United States.[6]

The next decade and a half brought unprecedented rates of growth, enabling Spain to claim the title of most rapidly expanding economy in Western Europe. Between 1961 and 1973 the rate of growth in real Gross National Product averaged 7.3 per cent per annum, never falling below 4 per cent. While official sources seeking to divert attention from the lack of basic political freedoms in Spain's one-party state, attributed the so-called Spanish 'miracle' to the system of indicative planning introduced by the Franco regime in 1964 in the aftermath of the Stabilisation Plan, others maintained that the much-trumpeted economic growth could be explained by three basic factors, all of them external, viz. foreign investment, emigrant remittances from Spanish labourers working abroad, and earnings from tourism. Income from these sources was sufficient to cover Spain's traditionally huge balance-of-trade deficit and allowed for the continuation of import substitution aimed at bringing about a modernisation of the industrial sector.

Foreign investment played a major role in the development of a number of high-technology industries, not least chemicals, transport, electrical engineering, food processing and metallurgy. Between 1959 and 1975 Spain received 773 billion pesetas of investments from abroad, four-fifths of which originated in the United States, Switzerland (almost certainly including Spanish funds in Swiss bank accounts), Germany, France and the United Kingdom (see Table 8.1).[7]

Remittances from Spaniards working in northern Europe, mostly in

TABLE 8.1 Inflow of Long-term Investment into Spain, 1959–75

Year	*Amount (millions of pesetas)*	*Year*	*Amount (millions of pesetas)*
1959	3,894.6	1968	38,430.0
1960	7,011.6	1969	43,424.5
1961	10,284.6	1970	60,953.9
1962	7,534.4	1971	65,361.8
1963	14,257.8	1972	85,248.6
1964	17,022.6	1973	105,430.2
1965	20,284.8	1974	107,779.9
1966	25,056.0	1975	127,169.8
1967	34,341.3		

SOURCE Juan Munoz *et al.*, *La internacionalizacion del capital en Espana, 1959–75* (Madrid 1978) p. 68

France, Germany and Switzerland, amounted to $913 million in 1973. However, the onset of the European recession of the mid-70s constituted a setback to this source of income. By 1975 Spanish migrant workers were sending back no more than $700 million.[8]

There is little doubt that the main stimulus to the economy in these years was provided by the spectacular increase in tourism.[9] Between 1959 and 1973 the number of foreign visitors to Spain increased more than eightfold from 4.2 million to 35.6 million while receipts soared from $129 million in 1959 to $3,404 million in 1975 (see Table 8.2). By the early seventies earnings from tourism alone more or less covered Spain's balance-of-payments deficit, a factor which was dramatically reversed after 1974 when OPEC began to raise the price of oil on the world market.

A clear indication of the intensity of economic development in the decade and a half before the oil crisis is shown by official data on the employment of

TABLE 8.2 The Contribution of Tourism to Spain's Balance of Payments, 1959–79

Year	*Tourists ('000)*	*Receipts of foreign currency from tourism ($ millions)*	*Balance of trade deficit ($ millions)*
1959	4,194	129	253
1960	6,113	297	57
1961	7,445	385	279
1962	8,668	513	634
1963	10,931	679	1,004
1964	14,102	917	1,056
1965	14,250	1,157	1,737
1966	17,251	1,293	1,964
1967	17,858	1,210	1,745
1968	19,183	1,213	1,548
1969	21,680	1,311	2,333
1970	24,106	1,681	2,360
1971	26,759	2,054	2,025
1972	32,513	2,488	2,911
1973	34,560	3,239	4,405
1974	30,343	3,167	8,340
1975	30,122	3,506	8,572
1976	30,015	3,090	8,749
1977	34,259	4,181	7,635
1978	39,971	5,488	5,583
1979	38,892	6,466	7,215

SOURCE Ministerio de Informacione y Turismo; Ministerio de Commercio, *Balanza de Pagos de España*; Banco de Bilbao, *Informe economico, 1979* (Bilbao: 1980) p. 181

the active labour force by sector (see Table 8.3). In relative terms, between 1960 and 1973 (the year the crisis began) the number of Spaniards working the land fell from 40.5 per cent to 25.2 per cent. Encouraged to leave by the planners, five million agricultural workers and their dependents quit the countryside for the industrial towns and the tourist regions during these years. In 1965 the factory finally overtook the farm as the leading employer of labour.

TABLE 8.3 Occupation of the Total Active Labour Force According to Census Data, 1950–78 in percentage terms

Year	*Agriculture*	*Industry*	*Services*
1950	47.6	26.6	25.9
1960	40.5	30.3	29.2
1964	34.8	33.5	31.7
1971	27.5	35.6	37.0
1973	25.2	36.1	38.8
1975	22.9	36.8	40.3
1978	20.2	37.4	42.5

SOURCE Instituto Nacional de Estadistica; Banco de Bilbao, *Renta nacional de Espana y su distribucion provincial, serie homogenea, 1955–75* (Bilbao: 1978) p. 33

In sharp contrast to the reformist Republicans of the thirties, the Franco regime with its close links with landed, business and financial interests, made little attempt to tackle the basic structural problems of the economy such as the need for agrarian reform and the introduction of a progressive taxation system. Moreover, the prevailing goal of growth at any cost exacerbated already glaring regional imbalances within the economy. For example, at the end of the Dictatorship in 1975 the three Basque provinces of Vizcaya, Alava and Guipuzcoa along with Barcelona and Madrid, which together contained 30.2 per cent of the Spanish population, produced 39.1 per cent of the nation's wealth. At the other end of the scale, the five agricultural provinces of Jaen, Lugo, Badajoz, Granada and Caceres, with eight per cent of the population, produced only 4.8 per cent of the national income.[10]

THE OIL CRISIS

Because of her amicable relations with the Arab states, Spain was exempted from the boycott imposed by the oil producers in 1973. Even so, she did not escape the huge increase in oil prices which ensued. In 1974 the nation's bill for imported oil rose by 225.9 per cent. The share of oil costs within Spain's total imports shot up from 11.0 per cent in 1973 to 24.3 per cent in the following quinquennium (see Table 8.4). In 1979 petroleum imports cost Spain $6,231 million while preliminary estimates for 1980, carried out in the wake of the increases which followed OPEC's Venezuela meeting over Christmas 1979, suggested a doubling of that total to $11–12 billion.[11]

TABLE 8.4 Spain's Petroleum Imports, 1973–8

Year	*Millions of tons*	*Amount Millions of pesetas*	*Percentage of total imports*
1973	41.4	61.8	11.0
1974	43.9	198.5	22.34
1975	41.3	204.3	21.92
1976	49.0	299.8	25.64
1977	45.9	339.3	25.13
1978	45.1	356.5	26.51

SOURCE Servicio de Estudios del Banco de Bilbao, *Situacion*, vol. 7, no. 4 (April 1979)

Among western industrial nations Spain was to prove the least equipped to adapt to the sharp rise in oil prices. Her industrial expansion of the sixties and early seventies was founded almost entirely on the availability of abundant supplies of cheap oil for use as a fuel. Moreover, Spain needed oil to meet the requirements of her expanding export industries. For example, at the end of the 1970s the nation had become the world's leading supplier of cement, the production of which is very energy intensive. This was also the case with the manufacture of the Ford Fiesta, the first Spanish-produced car to penetrate the European market. In addition, owing to the absence of an adequate infrastructure of railways in the peninsula, the transport of manufactured goods depended to a large extent on the petrol-guzzling heavy lorry.[12]

Throughout most of the late seventies the energy sector was plunged into a state of near chaos. In 1974 Spain depended on oil for as much as 69 per cent of her total energy requirements; by 1978 this had only been reduced to 66.82 per cent. The bulk of this oil had to be imported. Domestic production of 1.4 million tons in 1978 accounted for a mere 3.1 per cent of national needs, while 45.1 million tons were imported.[13] Moreover, the outlook for the future appears bleak. The ten-year energy plan (*Plan de Energia Nacional*) announced in 1977 estimated that at best reliance on oil could be reduced to 59 per cent of total requirements by 1987. The PEN also recognised that domestic discoveries of oil off the Mediterranean coast and in the Bay of Biscay offered little possibilities. Onshore prospects appear even flimsier.

By the end of 1974 the oil crisis had put an end to a decade and a half of economic progress. In the following year the rate of growth of GNP dwindled to 1.1 per cent. Industry declined by 2.5 per cent, with a drop in industrial investment of nine per cent. Over the next three years (1976–8) growth rates recovered a little, with GNP rising from 2.9 per cent in 1976 to 3.1 per cent in 1978. Nevertheless, these figures represented only about one-third of the growth levels of the 'miracle' years and one-half of the prevailing rate in the EC countries. Thereafter in 1979, following a new round of OPEC price increases in June, the growth rate fell again to 1.4 per cent compared with previous government hopes of between 2.7 and 4.5 per cent, while all the signs point to a growth rate of minus one per cent in 1980. Consequent upon the return of migrant workers from north of the Pyrenees, unemployment more than trebled in the period 1974–9. At the end of the seventies, 10.14 per cent of the labour force (1.33 million) were out of work according to official figures; only Portugal had a higher unemployment rate in Europe. In addition, the jobless total was becoming increasingly disturbing in the southern regions of Andalusia and Extremadura owing to the declining opportunities presented by emigration.

As oil prices soared so too did Spain's trade deficit. A shortfall in the balance of trade of $3,545 million in 1973 was almost doubled to $7,069 million in 1974. Two-thirds of this was accounted for by the oil-price rise. In the same period a surplus on current account of $557 million was converted into a deficit of $3.3 billion.

TABLE 8.5 Some Indicators of Economic Activity, 1973–9

	1973	*1974*	*1975*	*1976*	*1977*	*1978*	*1979*
Level of unemployment ('000)	361.3	431.4	619.7	730.1	831.8	1083.3	1334.2
Rate of increase of GNP (%)	8.5	5.4	1.1	2.9	2.6	3.1	1.4
Rate of increase in investment (%)	14.3	6.7	−3.9	−2.0	−1.2	−4.7	−1.9
Cost of living increase (average annual rate) (%)	11.4	15.7	17.0	17.7	24.6	19.8	15.7
Balance of payments per current account (millions of dollars)	557	−3278	−3477	−4300	−2512	1400	400

SOURCE Banco de Bilbao, *Informe economico 1979* (Bilbao: 1980) p. 92

During the next three years (1975–7) the increased oil prices continued to pose a threat to the economic stability of Spain as the country embarked on the slow and painful transition from dictatorship to parliamentary democracy. In 1978, however, Spain seemed to have turned the corner. After running an overall balance-of-payments defecit of $13.6 billion during the preceding four years, a healthy surplus of $1.4 billion was achieved. Three factors appear to have been responsible for this development. Firstly, exports were given a boost by the devaluation of the peseta by 20 per cent in July 1977. Secondly, receipts from tourism in 1978, which stood at $5,500, broke all existing records. Thirdly, the general recognition of Spain's new-found political stability led to a doubling of foreign investment in that year. Direct foreign investment in 1978 rose by 97 per cent over the previous year to $1,220 million (see Table 8.6).

TABLE 8.6 Balance of Payments per Current Account, 1973–9 (millions of dollars)

	1973	*1974*	*1975*	*1976*	*1977*	*1978*	*1979*
Jan	692	211	−2,326	−2,857	−4,271	−2,384	1,617
Feb	720	2	−3,570	−2,482	−4,804	−1,896	1,692
March	639	−163	−3,729	−2,641	−4,748	−1,576	1,922
April	679	−665	−3,643	−2,555	−4,881	−1,063	1,823
May	691	−1,186	−3,372	−2,721	−5,033	684	1,931
June	789	−1,648	−3,292	−2,894	−5,386	279	1,609
July	548	−1,972	−3,275	−3,288	−4,738	509	1,068
Aug	767	−2,081	−3,199	−3,551	−4,089	702	509
Sept	702	−2,266	−3,208	−3,748	−3,735	1,143	120
Oct	730	−2,635	−3,170	−3,728	−3,437	1,262	117
Nov	609	−2,885	−3,121	−3,787	−3,263	1,399	
Dec	570	−3,249	−2,927	−3,996	−3,023	1,674	

SOURCE Banco de Espana

Most disturbing of all to successive governments, the full impact of OPEC's decisions was reflected in the sharp upward movement in the cost of living. At the time of the *Pacto de la Moncloa*, an agreement drawn up between the Suarez government and the main opposition parties in the autumn of 1977, inflation in Spain was running at 15–16 per cent above the EC average. Yet government perseverance with stabilisation measures soon attracted the approbation of a number of international bodies, not least the OECD and the International Monetary Fund. After reaching the unacceptably high level of 37 per cent in the summer of 1977 the rate of inflation was brought down to a more manageable 16 per cent at the end of the decade.[15]

As Spain entered the 1980s one of the main planks of government policy was to ensure that any future increase in oil prices was not reflected in wages and internal prices. Unfortunately, the further round of oil-price increases announced by individual OPEC members after the Venezuela meeting did not augur well. One respected Spanish authority on the oil industry recently estimated that each 30 per cent increase in the price of crude oil to Spain resulted in a one per cent fall in GNP.[16]

THE POLITICAL TRANSITION

In a recent work on the political economy of *Franquismo*, the Spanish economist Jesus Gonzalez portrays Franco's Spain as an authoritarian regime based on an oligopoly of political families.[17] The role of the *Caudillo* under this system of limited pluralism was that of undisputed and charismatic arbiter. With the worsening of the economic situation in the late fifties, he authorised a fundamental change of direction in Spanish political economy, transforming a system characterised by state intervention into one dominated by the market. This he achieved by permitting the political ascendancy of a new breed of economic liberals closely associated with the Catholic lay groups *Opus Dei*. Other ingredients necessary to complete the transformation were a willingness to overcome the stubborn resistance of the isolationist bureaucracy and a forthright diplomatic offensive to gain foreign support. Throughout the sixties and early seventies *Opus Dei* ministers, chief among them Lopez Rodo and Lopez Bravo, saw that by convincing the ageing dictator of the political benefits of their mish-mash of economic policies, power was theirs.

The oil crisis hit Spain amidst the death throes of the dictatorship. At the end of his life Franco became preoccupied with ensuring his own succession. The Organic Law of the State of 1967 made certain that the functions of head of state and president of the government (prime minister), previously carried by the *Caudillo* himself, were to be separated. In 1969 the Cortes accepted the name of Juan Carlos de Borbon y Borbon as Franco's successor as head of state, while in the summer of 1972 the ailing dictator decreed that his trusted friend Admiral Luis Carrero Blanco, patron of the *Opus Dei* clan, would automatically become prime minister in the event of his sudden death. Yet these carefully-laid plans were upset in December 1973 when Franco's heir apparent was assassinated by Basque extremists belonging to the terrorist group ETA, an event which presaged the political demise of the liberal technocrats. Carrero Blanco was replaced by the former Interior Minister and hardliner Carlos Arias Navarro who stated his desire to move towards greater political freedom; a promise which in the event fell short of permitting the legalisation of political parties of any shade. He responded to the demands of the newly emergent opposition groups with widespread arrests, torture and executions. Throughout 1974 and 1975 the clandestine trade unions resorted to the strike weapon in support of their claims for recognition and at times paralysed entire provinces. The Basque Region, scene of the most bitter hatred towards the oppressive centralising regime, was plunged into a state of *de facto* civil war.

Within the Francoist political elite demands for democratisation were at that time championed by Manuel Fraga, who had served as Information Minister and Ambassador to London; yet the so-called 'liberalisers' were bitterly opposed by a group of old-style fascists, bureaucrats, soldiers and policemen collectively dubbed the 'bunker' by the Left. Yet, such was the ineffectiveness of the reformist elements within the regime that the varying strands of opposition within Spain and in exile became committed to the concept of 'democratic rupture' (*ruptura*). This was the tactic adopted by the inter-class political alliance in Catalonia formed in November 1971 known as the *Assamblea de Catalunya* and later taken up by the Communist-led *Junta Democratica* formed in the summer of 1974 and the Socialist-Christian Democratic *Plataforma de Convergencia* created in the following year.

When Franco died in November 1975 the thirty-seven-year-old Prince Juan Carlos assumed the role of head of state. Arias Navarro meanwhile, frustrated by the 'bunker' in his attempts to get through his aforementioned programme of minimalist reforms, finally resigned in July 1976. This cleared the way for the King to appoint Adolfo Suarez as his prime minister.

The choice of Suarez, the former head of the Francoist single party, *the Movimiento*, and one of only three candidates put to the King by the Franco-appointed Council of the Realm, was greeted with astonishment and amazement by democratic elements. The recently founded liberal newspaper *El Pais* featured a prominent article written by the ex-Francoist Ricardo de la Cierva who exclaimed, 'What a blunder! Only a miracle can save the situation.'[18] Nevertheless, so effective was the combination of Juan Carlos and Suarez in the essential preliminary task of dismantling the Francoist state without provoking serious political upheavals that in January 1980 *The Economist* nominated the King for the Nobel Peace Prize.[19]

Even so, the democratisation of Spain turned out to be a protracted and difficult process. Both government and opposition feared that if Suarez and the King moved too quickly they would trigger off a counter movement spearheaded by Francoist elements within the armed forces.[20] There is little doubt that the inherent weakness of the two men's positions in the early days gave rise to timid and occasionally irresponsible government. In the economic sphere, for example, lack of a coherent policy culminated in the rampant inflation of summer 1977. Their political record at this stage, however, is more impressive. Against considerable odds, in the winter of 1976 they forced a Political Reform Act through the last Cortes of Franco allowing for a bicameral parliament consisting of a Congress of Deputies of 350 members elected by proportional representation and a Senate of 207 members partly elected and partly nominated by the King. In December 1976 this Act was overwhelmingly approved by referendum.[21]

To justify its claim to be staging free elections in June 1977 the Suarez government abolished the *Movimiento* while at the same time legalising the majority of political parties, including the Communists. It also allowed the outlawed trade-union movement to operate freely and permitted freedom of speech and assembly during the electoral campaign. The legalisation of the *Partido Comunista Espanol* in April 1977 shortly after the dismantling of the *Movimiento* came close to provoking a *coup d'etat*. Political tension mounted at that time, enflamed by the resignation of the Navy Minister, Admiral Pita de Veiga. Throughout 1978 the work of the newly elected Constituent Cortes was dominated by the drafting of the 169-article Constitution which finally received the overwhelming approval of the nation in the referendum of 6 December 1978. The aim of Suarez and the King consisted in consolidating the authority of the democratic apparatus without alienating powerful vested interests hitherto favoured by the now defunct Franco regime. Hence a kid-glove approach was deemed the only viable way of dealing with the underworked and massively incompetent bureaucracy while the government also prevaricated on its proposals foı fiscal reforms.[22]

Following the approval of the Constitution, Suarez sought a renewed mandate from the electorate in March 1979 as a result of which his party, the *Union del Centro Democratico* a ragbag of ex *Franquistas* with Christian and Social Democrats, achieved a near majority of the seats in the Lower House over the Socialists (*Partido Socialista Obrero Espanol*) and the Communists. In sharp contrast, the municipal elections of April 1979 brought the victory of the Left as the result of an electoral pact drawn up between the PSOE and the PCE. Shortly thereafter Suarez surprised his critics in Catalonia and Euskadi (the Basque Region) when he sanctioned a further referendum in those regions in October 1979 which offered substantial amounts of autonomy. Once this had been approved the government was at last free to devote greater attention to the outstanding problems of inflation, unemployment, the energy crisis and Spain's application for membership of the European Economic Community, although first indications are that, prior to the government reshuffle of September 1980 at least, they had manifestly failed to do so.

ECONOMIC POLICY

As we have seen, the full impact of the oil crisis was felt in Spain during 1974 and was further underlined by the country's disastrous growth performance in the following year. However, the difficulties involved in the political transition meant that neither of the first two administrations of the new monarchy felt capable of coming to grips with the immediate problems of the economy, let alone tackling the profound structural problems that needed to be solved in order to bring about lasting recovery.[23]

It was all too apparent that tough measures were required to deal with the deteriorating situation. The economist and future deputy Jose Ramon Lasuen reflected the despair of many when he declared, 'Spain has the least possibility of growth and the greatest likelihood of inflation in the OECD'.[24]

After the elections of June 1977 premier Suarez assumed responsibility for drawing up a wide ranging agreement (*the Pacto de la Moncloa*) which took advantage of the framework of parliamentary consensus which then existed in the Constituent Cortes. Over the next two years the Moncloa pact, which established norms for wage and price increases plus a calendar of institutional and economic reforms, appeared to bear fruits. Above all, inflation was brought under control. However, in June 1979 the hopes of the policymakers were once more dashed when OPEC announced a 20 per cent increase in oil prices thereby inaugurating a further period of economic recession. In July the government raised the prices of petroleum products, transport and electricity by about one-fifth which was soon incorporated in the price of foodstuffs and other products. The annual report of the OECD, published that month, contained a short typewritten note which proclaimed

> Overall, although it is not possible to present a new set of forecasts, real GDP growth is now likely to be significantly below the 4 per cent forecast earlier; consumer price increases may be appreciably higher than 14 per cent; and the current balance of payments should be unfavourably affected by the oil price increase and by the likely slower growth in exports of goods and services than foreseen earlier.[25]

The prevailing mood of pessimism was reinforced in December 1979 when OPEC members began to announce further increases in oil prices. These coincided with a number of independent and official forecasts of Spain's growth for that year which ranged between 1.5 and 2.0 per cent. The government responded early in the new year with an announcement of further increases in the price of petroleum products which varied from 14.3

per cent for 98 octane petrol to 110 per cent for military aviation fuel.[26] This pessimism has, as we have seen, been borne out in the country's disastrous growth performance in 1980.

PLAYING FOR TIME

In its survey of Spain published during the run-up to the elections of June 1977, the *Economist* summed up the handling of economic affairs by the Arias Navarro and Suarez governments as 'surprisingly lackadaisical'. Before October 1976 the prices of petroleum and electricity were permitted to be increased much less than in other European countries. Of the ten leading western industrial nations, Spain was the only one in which petroleum consumption had actually risen since 1973. While the consensus of cabinet opinion was that tough economic measures could not be enacted until after parliamentary elections many economists accused the politicians of failing to comprehend the urgency of the situation.[27]

Arias Navarro, confronted with a division within his cabinet between *aperturistas* (liberalisers) and the 'bunker' of hardline *franquistas*, decided upon a policy of minimal reforms. In an attempt to convert a growth rate of 0.7 per cent (that of 1975) into a more respectable level of 3–4 per cent, Arias and his Economics Minister Villar Mir sought to encourage a rapid increase in foreign investment. During his much publicised visit to the United States in the spring of 1976, the premier's frequently repeated message was '*Espana es un buen negocio*' (Spain is good business), a line later to be repeated by his successor Adolfo Suarez.[28]

Early in 1976 Arias Navarro sent to the Cortes a reflationary package of measures contained in the *proyecto de ley de actuacion economica*. The latter included proposals aimed at more progressive taxation, increased budgetary revenue, price controls for certain foodstuffs and support for private investment to create new jobs. To nobody's surprise these proposals remained a dead letter. Even if they had been approved by Franco's last parliament there was no adequate political and administrative mechanisms which would permit their enforcement. For its part, the 'Left' saw the whole operation as a device for gaining time.[29] The same accusation can undoubtedly be levelled against the Stabilisation Plan of October 1976 issued by the first Suarez government. With somewhat greater conviction than his predecessor, Suarez proclaimed his administration's intentions of combatting both unemployment and inflation while simultaneously putting forward proposals for modest taxation and budgetary reforms. Yet, such measures were certainly incapable of achievement without the cooperation of both the employers and the trade unions. The latter, however, although increasingly tolerated, remained outlawed by the State, while management's only experience of negotiations with the labour force was through the outmoded corporatist vertical syndicates. In order to reach any meaningful and lasting agreement a new social and economic climate was required.

THE MONCLOA PACT AND BEYOND

The *Pacto de la Moncloa*, a political document which combined a mild monetarism with protestations of social justice, was signed by the government and the opposition Socialist and Communist parties in October 1977. Neither the employers nor the unions took part in the negotiations although they were expected to carry out its recommendations. The agreement was drafted in the wake of the June elections at a time when the foreign trade deficit was deteriorating rapidly (see Table 8.6) and speculation against the peseta was rife. It followed the decision, taken in July 1977, to devalue the peseta by 20 per cent. At the heart of the pact was a 22 per cent wage ceiling which, it was hoped, the unions would accept in return for a number of institutional and economic reforms. Since inflation was running well ahead of that figure what was implied was at best a stagnation in purchasing power. In an attempt at equity it was proposed that lower-paid workers should benefit most. Only the public sector was directly involved although it was intended to exert some control over private companies in receipt of state subsidies. For the private sector as a whole, however, the upper limit of 22 per cent was purely indicative with the vaguest of threats that firms which paid over the odds could find themselves temporarily out of favour with the administration. Meanwhile, the government's part of the bargain was a declaration of intent to reduce the level of inflation to 15 per cent by the end of 1978 compared with an average weight of 19.8 per cent in 1976. In the event, this objective was only narrowly missed: inflation in 1978 was brought down to 16.5 per cent, a fall of nearly ten points on the 1977 level of 26.4 per cent.[30]

To combat inflation the government chose to pursue a restrictive monetary policy. At the beginning of 1977 the money supply in its widest sense, M3, was restricted to allow for a 21 per cent increase over the next twelve months. This increase was thought to be compatible with a 3 per cent growth in GNP coupled with a 17 per cent rise in the cost-of-living both of which, in the event, proved to be wildly optimistic (see Table 8.5). By the summer of that year inflationary tendencies within the economy appeared to warrant a further tightening up of the money supply. The new (post Moncloa) policy fixed the increase in M3 for 1978 at 17 per cent, with a margin of error of 2.5 per cent.[31]

Also incorporated into the package, partly to sweeten the pill for the unions, were proposals to attenuate the effects of unemployment through budgetary expenditure, a commitment to fiscal reforms and proposed changes in housing, urbanisation, social security and energy policy. In spite of the refusal of the government to consult them during the drafting of the Moncloa pact, the unions nevertheless saw fit to a recommend wage restraint to their memberships as a means of containing unemployment and strengthening Spain's fledgling democracy against its detractors. For its part, the main employers' grouping, the *Confederacion Espanola de Organizaciones Empresariales* (CEOE) reluctantly accepted the 22 per cent wage ceiling although many of its supporters throughout the regions regarded this figure as excessive.

However as unemployment began to escalate in 1978, pressure from the employers led the government to drop quietly a number of the more controversial proposals contained in the reform. Before long, agreement on a more far-reaching package to replace the stop-gap Moncloa pact was out of the question. Suarez therefore elected to act alone. After securing approval of the Constitution by the referendum of December 1978, the government announced its intentions of imposing a statutory incomes policy, with an 11–14 per cent wage band to come into effect in January 1979 for the next twelve months. With elections arranged for March 1st 1979 Suarez calculated that neither the Socialists nor the Communists would want to run the risk of being labelled irresponsible during the campaign and would consequently refrain from an out-and-out criticism of the government's proposals. Meanwhile, as an incentive to the trade unions, an indexation clause was inserted in the measure to the effect that if the rate of inflation exceeded 6 per cent in the first six months of 1979 a cost-of-living increase would be triggered off immediately. Despite the moderate stance taken by the leadership of the PSOE and the PCE, both parties manifestly failed to dampen down the demands of their respective unions, the *Union General de Trabajadores* (UGT) and the Workers' Commissiones (*Comisiones Obreras*). This failure was reflected in the high incidence of labour disputes during the election period. In the first quarter of 1979, 2.5 million Spaniards went on strike over the proposed wage ceiling while a total of 76 million man hours were lost.[32]

After the victory of Suarez's UCD in the March elections both union movements, but especially the Socialist UGT, witnessed a pronounced decline in their influence. This decline coincided with a growing preference on the part of the government to leave industrial relations to the two sides of industry, interfering only in cases of deadlock. In such circumstances a legally binding system of arbitration, inherited from the Franco dictatorship, was called into operation.

After two years of harmonious and joint initiatives, the spring of 1979 saw the emergence of a serious rift between the UGT and the Workers' Commissions. Such a development did not go unnoticed by the government. Prime Minister Adolfo Suarez, who had aroused considerable hostility within the ruling UCD for previously consorting with the Communists took advantage of the new situation to exclude the Secretary General of the PCE, Santiago Carrillo, from all future negotiations. At the same time, he persisted in his consultations with the Socialist leader Felipe Gonzalez. Behind this dividing tactic lay the realisation that PCE, with its static 9 per cent share of the vote in 1977 and 1979, posed little threat to the UCD which, with the support of regionalist votes, ought to be able to count on a parliamentary majority. The main Communist threat was posed by its control over the powerful Workers' Commissions.

No less significantly, early in 1980 the employers of the CEOE appended their signature to a two year bilateral agreement on industrial relations with the UGT which the Workers' Commissions, who did not take part in the discussions, refused to ratify. Despite official denials by both organisations there appears to be little doubt that the object of this exercise was to strengthen the minority UGT at the expense of its Communist counterpart.[33]

Yet even before this split came into the open, other voices on the Left argued forcefully that the Moncloa agreements brought no benefits at all to the working class. Thanks to the moderation of the unions, they contended, capitalism was put back on its feet at the expense of employment.[34]

After the OPEC oil-price increases announced in June 1979, which effectively raised Spain's energy costs by 70 per cent in the space of six months, the government at last unveiled its new economic programme known as the *Programa Economico del Gobierno* (PEG). In common with the *Pacto de la Moncloa* the PEG comprised essentially short-term measures. Yet the new agreement differed from the former in two vital respects. Firstly, while the Moncloa pact was multi-party the PEG was the product of UCD thinking alone. Secondly, the PEG broke new ground in that it set out how the government proposed to liberalise the economy as a prelude for Spain's eventual entry into the European Economic Community.

In line with diminished expectations, the programme envisaged a growth rate of no more than 2.6 per cent (soon to be scaled down even further) and a two-point increase in inflation, resultant upon the recent OPEC announcement. The PEG also reaffirmed the government's commitment to the primacy of monetary policy as a means of regulating the economy. Yet, in a further note of realism, it was proposed that the money supply be allowed to grow by 19 per cent in the following year.

THE NATIONAL ENERGY PLAN

Despite Spain's massive dependence on imports of fossil fuel, which accounted for over two-thirds of its primary energy needs, it took fully eighteen months before the Cortes approved the National Energy Plan (PEN). The bill, covering the period 1977–87, was subjected to frequent delays and amendments before it finally became law in the summer of 1979.

The main bone of contention was the paramount emphasis in the bill on expanding nuclear capacity. Notwithstanding the OPEC price rises, opposition to the proposals remained particularly strong in the peripheral areas of the Catalonia and Euskadi while neither the PSOE nor the PCE supported the Plan.

The PEN ratified the completion of seven nuclear plants already under construction along with three others which had received outline approval. It also set a target of 10.500 MV of nuclear generating capacity by 1987. In defence of its nuclear programme the government argued that it would provide a much-needed and immediate boost to the construction and capital goods industries and lead to the creation of thousands of new jobs. Meanwhile, the nuclear power companies let it be known that $800 million of contracts had been frozen in the long delay. In order to maintain a margin of flexibility the PEN proposed that arrangements be made to increase the consumption of both coal and oil by 40 per cent and 20 per cent respectively. In addition, the government declared its intentions of stimulating research into other sources of energy. Trials began in the province of Almeria into the possibilities of harnessing solar energy, a field in which Spain leads the world. Research is similarly under way into making greater use of the country's geothermal and biomass resources.

The energy option most favoured by the opposition Socialist and Communist parties is to increase the output of coal in the Peninsula. At present 7–10 million tons of coal are imported annually. The PEN contains proposals to double coal production to 40 million metric tons by 1987. At the same time it is hoped that the contribution of natural gas to total energy consumption can be raised from 2 to 6 per cent. Great hopes have been shown in the deposits of gas lying in the province of Cadiz and Jaca although it is acknowledged that transportation costs are likely to be high.

Whatever the result of the multifarious investigations at present under way, much will depend on the government's ability to overcome the mounting tide of opposition towards nuclear power which persists throughout the Peninsula. One setback in this direction was provided by the announcement of radiation leaks from the pressurised water reactor on Three Mile Island in the United States. This writer witnessed a demonstration of tens of thousands of angry Basques who marched through the streets of Bilbao in April 1979 protesting against the construction of a similar plant at nearby Lemoniz. The fact that planning permission for the plant had been granted by the 'occupying' Franco regime guaranteed the support of practically the whole spectrum of political opinion in Euskadi.

SPAIN AND THE EC

Another item on the government's agenda as Spain entered the 1980s was the country's application for membership of the European Economic Community. Although outline agreement has been reached for Spain to become a full member of the Community on January 1st 1983 difficulties remain over the length of the transitional period. While the Spanish government estimates that it will require at least ten years for her farmers and industrialists to adapt to competition from her would-be partners, Brussels would prefer a transitional period of no more than five years, in deference to the interest of the existing members.

If Spain does eventually join the Common Market in January 1983 it will be almost twenty-one years since Franco's Foreign Minister Fernando Castiella first put forward his request for an associate agreement with the Community in February 1962. Castiella, who was widely regarded as the most liberal member of the Franco administration, sought to obtain full membership of the EC after a period of preparatory association. At that time Spain counted on the political support of a number of Conservative and Liberal parties in Europe, not least the French Gaullists and the Italian Christian Democrats. Yet subsequent events did much to discredit Spain's democratic credentials in the eyes of Community members. Among other unfavourable development, the Franco government chose to exile the Christian Democratic leader Jose Maria Gil Robles after he had jointly proposed a motion in favour of political liberalisation in Spain at a meeting of the European Movement at Munich in the spring of 1962. In the following year Julian Grimau, a member of the Central Commitee of the Spanish Communist Party, was court-martialed and summarily executed. Although negotiations started with the European Commission in December 1964, at the instance of the latter, discussion was restricted to economic subjects. These negotiations proved to be protracted, largely as a result of disquieting political events in Spain. Eventually, an agreement on associate membership acceptable to both sides was reached in July 1970. Yet once again Community members were to show their disapproval of the absence of fundamental political rights in Spain. In particular they were publicly to attack the attitude of the Franco regime towards its political dissidents. When members of the Basque terrorist group ETA were court-martialed in Burgos at the end of 1970 Franco was compelled for reasons of foreign policy to commute their death sentences to life imprisonment.

Moreover, within the Community a series of critical changes took place in the early seventies which meant that Spain's agreement had to be renegotiated. In 1972, the Dahrendorf Report prepared the guidelines for a common policy towards Mediterranean countries as a whole, while in January 1973 the composition of the EC was altered by the enlargement of the original 'six' to include the United Kingdom, Ireland and Denmark. Later, as a result of the oil-price increases, discussions on olive oil, citrus fruits and wines became deadlocked as Europe was plunged into economic crisis. Neither Spain nor the Community were prepared to make concessions given the uncertainty of the moment. In addition, with Labour and Social Democratic governments in power in Britain, Denmark and West Germany, little sympathy was shown towards the increasingly intolerant Arias Navarro administration especially after the execution of the anarchist Puig Antich in 1975.

However, the simultaneous collapse of the dictatorial regimes in Portugal, Greece and Spain in the mid-seventies and the emergence of democratic alternatives found a corresponding willingness of behalf of the 'nine' to further enlarge the membership of the Community. For his part, Prime Minister Suarez demonstrated the overriding commitment of his government towards EC membership after the elections of 1977 when he appointed his senior colleague and close friend Leopoldo Calvo Sotelo as minister in charge of Spain's relations with the Common Market, where he remained until the cabinet reshuffle of September 1980. This commitment reflected Spain's increasing commercial links with the Community. In 1978, for example, 48 per cent of Spain's exports went to the EC as against 10.1 per cent to the United States and 10 per cent to Latin America.

Even though the political path to entry has been smoothed over, a variety of economic obstacles remain. On the agricultural side, Spanish producers of olives, oranges and lemons as well as livestock farmers face fierce competition not only from existing members but also from Greece, which is set to join the EC in January 1981, ahead of the two Iberian States. The Spanish fishing fleet faces disaster, while the problems of industry could also prove intractable. A recent study showed that 53 out of 94 leading industrial products elaborated in Spain will be adversely affected by the country's entry into the Community. These items include special and laminated steels, containers, electronic equipment, car parts and tractors.[25] Despite the avowed liberalism on the new economic programme (PEG) Spanish manufacturers remain thoroughly permeated with protectionist sentiments and nowhere is this more emphatic than in Catalonia.

CONCLUSION

Throughout the middle years of the 1970s the Spanish authorities were inhibited in their ability to tackle the worst effects of the economic recession by the instability of the political situation. The death of General Franco, whose authoritarian regime had presided over unprecedented rates of economic growth for a decade and a half, prefaced a slow and difficult transition from dictatorship to parliamentary democracy. Gradually, however, Spain's new King Juan Carlos and his prime minister Adolfo Suarez dismantled the Francoist state and paved the way for a sustained attack on the conjunctural crisis provoked by the Arab states' increase in oil prices in 1973–4. The Moncloa pact between the government and the main opposition parties, enacted in the autumn of 1977 shortly after the first free elections for forty-one years, enabled the authorities to bring down inflation from 37 per cent to 16 per cent within the short space of two years. At first the government's restrictive monetary policy, which did little to stop the sharp rise in unemployment, could count on the support of the main trade unions who sought to stabilise the nascent democracy against its enemies. From the middle of 1979, however, the political consensus began to break down. In an attempt to gain entry into the EC the Suarez government enacted a neo-liberal economic policy (the PEG) and began to put a distance between itself and the Spanish Communist Party. At the same time new increases announced by OPEC members in the second half of 1979 appear to have nipped Spain's modest recovery in the bud. Much now depends on the fortunes of the Ten-year Energy Plan, finally approved in 1979 despite strong opposition in the country to strong emphasis in the PEN towards nuclear power.

POSTSCRIPT

On 23 February 1981, the day that Leopoldo Calvo Sotelo was to have been confirmed in office as Spain's Prime Minister in succession to Adolfo Suarez, the world was suddenly and dramatically reminded of the fragility of the new democratic institutions south of the Pyrenees when a band of marauding civil guards, under the command of Lieutenant-Colonel Antonio Tejero, stormed the Cortes in an attempt to overthrow the elected government. While early reports, particularly those filtering abroad, portrayed the attempted *coup d'état*, which was put down in less than 24 hours, as the dying throes of *Franquismo*, it soon became apparent that the so-called *Tejerazo* had been greeted with widespread enthusiasm in nearly all sections of the Spanish military and would have long-lasting implications for the political life of the nation.

Despite the failure of the plot, which public opinion polls showed had the backing of no more than four per cent of the population, and the massive street demonstrations in the wake of the attempted *coup* in support of Spain's fledgling democracy, there is little doubt that the Army has hijacked the Spanish Cabinet and that now all political decisions of any substance require the *placet* of the armed forces. The Spanish population meanwhile lives under a *coup* psychosis, attributing all kinds of disparate developments to the influence of the Generals.

Nowhere is the new-found influence of the Spanish military more obvious than with regard to the handling of terrorism and the regional question. The new administration of Senor Calvo Sotelo, while falling short of declaring a state of alarm in the Basque region, soon announced that the government was working in close collaboration with the Army to stem the new wave of violence launched by the terrorist organisation ETA in the desperate hope of provoking a second *coup* which would somehow incite the Basque people into taking up arms against the repressive state. Men and *matériel* were quickly dispatched to the region, while frontier patrols were strengthened to prevent the free movement of *etarras* between Euskadi and their safe houses in the Basque départements of southern France. The Catalans too, despite their previous good relations with the Suarez administration, were told in no uncertain terms to moderate their demands for greater regional autonomy and were rudely informed that Castilian speakers in the Principality were suffering from a similar degree of cultural oppression that native Catalan speakers claimed to be experiencing under the Franco regime.

With the military firmly entrenched at the right hand of the politicians, Spain's democracy is at present conditional – conditional upon further obeisance to the authoritarian demands of the armed forces. Such a situation is now fully realised by the Left, as it was by the King from the very beginning. Both the Socialists and the Communists, whom most political commentators concede behaved with commendable responsibility and moderation before the *pronunciamiento*, now see the task of the opposition as that of maintaining the politicians in power. Socialist demands soon after the *coup* for a coalition government met with short shrift from the ruling UCD while few believe that, all things being equal, should the Left win the elections of 1983 the Army would tolerate an administration led by Felipe Gonzalez, let alone one with Communist participation. As for King Juan Carlos, in spite of silly rumours that he failed to move against the February plot with sufficient speed, there can be no doubts about his commitment to democratic rule, and he has risen in stature in the eyes of all true democrats, even the nominally republican Left. As Commander-in-Chief of the Armed Forces it was King Juan Carlos' determined refusal to succumb to the military threat, by placing his own life at stake, that finally cleared the tanks from the streets of Valencia on the morning of 24 February and persuaded vacillating military governors to reject the appeals of the rebels.

However, given that Spanish politics is now all about survival this does not augur well for finding a solution to the pressing economic problems which continue to confront the country in the aftermath of the oil crisis. While the level of inflation has been stabilised at around 15 per cent, unemployment is still rising rapidly. Figures for February 1981 show that the jobless total has now reached 1.50 millions, 11.68 per cent of the active population. In the construction industry, moreover, three out of ten workers are unemployed.

Nor has the Spanish administration had much success in reducing the nation's dependency on imported fossil fuel. At present, about two-thirds of the earnings from Spanish exports go towards the imports of oil and petroleum products. Even so, visitors to Madrid in the winter never fail to be amazed when they discover that the government has again issued orders to public buildings in the capital to turn off their oil-fired central heating for long parts of the day in order to reduce the high level of atmospheric pollution.

Finally, those who look for salvation in Spain's eventual entry in the European Economic Community have had little to cheer them. Even in the most optimistic circles January 1984 is now seen as the earliest possible date for Spanish entry, although as yet there is no definite timetable. Soon after the abortive *coup* the Spanish press speculated that the Eurocrats in Brussels were none too impressed by Spain's inability to consolidate democratic rule, thereby prejudicing an early entry into the EEC. Such rumours were soon refuted in official quarters, though few Spaniards took these denials seriously. As for the military men and their vociferous supporters on the extreme Right, entry into the EEC is far from their minds.

The author wishes to thank John Reeder, Jesus Gonzalez and Pedro Schwartz for their help and encouragement.

NOTES AND REFERENCES

1. See especially Servicio de Estudios del Banco de Espana, *Ritmo de la crisis economica espanola en relacion con la mundial* (Madrid: 1934) p. 354.
2. Josep Fontana and Jordi Nadal, 'Spain, 1914–70', in Carlo M. Cipolla (ed.), *The Fontana Economic History of Europe*, vol. 6, ii (London and Glasgow: 1976) pp. 485–86.
3. See Manuel-Jesus Gonzalez, 'Neomercantilismo en Madrid: dos economistas de postguerra', *Informacion Comercial Espanola*, 517 (1976), 125–43.
4. Pedro Schwartz, 'Politics First: The Economy After Franco', *Government and Opposition*, 11 (1976) p. 85.
5. On this period see Joan Clavera *et al.*, *Capitalismo espanol: de la autarquia a la estabilizacion, 1939–59*, 2 vols (Madrid: 1973); and Manuel-Jesus Gonzalez, *La economica politica del Franquismo: 1940–70: dirigismo, mercado y planificacion* (Madrid: 1979).
6. See Charles W. Anderson, *The Political Economy of Modern Spain: Policy Making in an Authoritarian State* (Wisconsin: 1970) pp. 130–1.
7. Juan Munoz *et al.*, *La internacionalizacion del capital en Espana, 1959–77* (Madrid: 1978) pp. 68, 124–30.
8. Cited in Richard Comyns Carr, 'Spain's Economy: the Miracle and After', *National Westminster Bank Quarterly Review* (Nov. 1979) p. 67.
9. This point was made emphatically at the time by Professor Jose Luis Sampedro, 'Le plan de developpement espagnol dans son cadre social', in 'L'Espagne a l'heure du developpement', *Revue Tiers Monde* (Paris: 1967) pp. 1033–41.
10. Banco de Bilbao, *Renta nacional de Espana y su distribucion provincial, 1975* (Bilbao, 1977), pp. 34, 45.
11. *El Pais* (8 Jan. 1980).
12. See 'Despues del petroleo, que?', *Economia y Dialogo* (Madrid: 1979) pp. 8–9.
13. Ibid., p. 11; see also Servicio de Estudios del Banco de Bilbao, *Situacion*, vol. 7, no. 8 (Aug.–Sept. 1979), pp. 41–8.
14. *El Pais* (6 Sept. 1980).
15. Ibid. (6 Jan. 1980); Organisation de Cooperation et de Developpement Economiques, *Etudes economiques: Espagne* (Paris: 1979) p. 5.
16. Emilio Sanz Hurtado quoted in *Economia y Dialogo*, p. 13.
17. Gonzalez, *La economica politica del Franquismo, passim*.
18. Cited by Ray Allen in 'All the Spains', *The Economist* (3 Nov. 1979).

19. *The Economist* (5 Jan. 1980). In contrast, since the 1979 elections Suarez, looking tired and ineffective, has lost the initiative and has faced successive political crises within his own party.
20. An opposing view, i.e. that the Left consistently overestimated the effectiveness of the military as a political force and therefore failed to press for greater concessions, is argued by Julio Rodriquez Aramberri, 'Political Transition in Spain: an Interpretation', *The Socialist Register* (London: 1979) pp. 172–203.
21. On this transitional period see Stanley Meisler, 'Spain's New Democracy', *Foreign Affairs*, 56 (1977–8), pp. 190–208.
22. See Robert Graham, 'Free from the Past', *Financial Times* (13 Dec. 1978).
23. Organisation de Cooperation et de Developpement Economiques, *Etudes economiques: Espagne* (Paris: 1978) p. 25. See also *Financial Times* (13 July 1977).
24. Cited in 'The New Spain', *The Economist* (2 April 1977).
25. OECD, 'Service de l'Information, Paris, le 6 juillet', in *Etudes economiques: Espagne* (1979).
26. *El Pais* (9 Jan. 1980).
27. *The Economist* (2 April 1977).
28. See Jose Luis Garcia Delgado and Julio Segura, *Reformismo y crisis economica: la herencia de la dictadura* (Madrid: 1977), pp. 89–132.
29. Ibid., p. 112.
30. See the self-congratulatory pamphlet published by the Ministero de Economia, Direccion General de Prevision y Coyuntura, *La economia espanola en 1978: el proceso de ajuste* (Madrid: 1979) p. 31.
31. OECD, op. cit., p. 22.
32. See the *Financial Times* Survey (20 Dec. 1979).
33. For details of the agreement see *El Pais* (6 Jan. 1980).
34. See for example Rodriguez Aramberri, op. cit., pp. 191–2.
35. Michael Noelke and Robert Taylor, *La industria espanola cara al Mercado Comun: el impacto de la adhesion*, cited in *El Pais* (11 Jan. 1980).

9 The European Community and the Economic Recession: 1973–9

EMIL KIRCHNER

In attempting to assess a European Community-wide approach to the recession in the mid-1970s, it is first necessary to identify the nature and background of this recession. This involves a brief summary of the economic and social situation of the Community in the mid-1970s; dealing particularly with the impact of the international monetary and energy crises on basic economic variables. We shall then examine perceptions and reactions of the main EC political actors to the crises.[1]

THE IMPACT OF THE RECESSION ON BASIC ECONOMIC VARIABLES IN THE EC

Unemployment trends

One of the most visible impacts of the 1974–5 recession in the EC was the swelling of unemployment figures as shown in Table 9.1. By the beginning of 1980, the figure had risen steadily to double that of 1974 thus exceeding the six million mark. Unemployment among young people in the Community has grown particularly since 1974. By 1974 there were 824,000 unemployed under the age of 25 (30.7 per cent of total unemployed); by 1977 the figure had reached two million (37.4 per cent of total unemployed). Another feature of the employment situation is that with the growing participation of women in the increased labour force in the 1970s female unemployment has risen from 33 per cent of the total in 1973 to 41 per cent in 1977 and 44.6 per cent in March 1980.[2]

TABLE 9.1 Rate of Unemployment, Registered Wholly Unemployed in the Civilian Labour Force

	1960–70	*1971–2*	*1973*	*1974*	*1975*	*1976*	*1977*	*1978*	*1979*	*1980*[a]
B	2.2	2.5	2.9	3.2	5.3	6.6	7.8	8.4	8.8	8.8
DK	1.2	1.2	0.7	2.0	4.6	4.7	5.3	5.6	5.3	6.0
France	1.4	1.7	1.8	2.3	3.9	4.3	4.9	5.3	6.1	6.6
Germany	0.8	0.8	1.0	2.2	4.2	4.1	4.0	3.9	3.4	3.8
Irl	4.7	6.0	6.0	6.3	8.8	9.6	9.4	8.8	7.9	8.1
Italy	5.7	5.0	4.9	4.8	5.2	5.6	6.4	7.1	7.6	8.1
Lux.	0.1	0	0	0	0.2	0.3	0.5	0.8	0.7	0.8
NL	0.9	1.8	2.3	2.9	4.1	4.3	4.1	4.1	4.2	4.4
UK	1.9	3.4	2.5	2.4	3.8	5.3	5.7	5.7	5.3	5.7
EC	2.1	2.6	2.5	2.9	4.4	4.9	5.3	5.5	5.6	6.0

a Average January–April

SOURCE *Eurostat* (series) and *Annual Economic Review* (1978–9), Commission of the EC SEC (78) 4033 Final (19 October 1978) table 3.2

On the structural side, the demand for labour was buoyant in the service sector, sluggish in industry, and still more so in agriculture because of restructuring.

Economic growth rate developments

Another significant impact of the 1974–5 economic crisis was a drastic fall in economic growth rates. Between 1958 and 1972 the member states had experienced a period of sustained expansion. Certainly there were slow-downs (in most countries in 1961–2, 1966–7 and 1971–2) in which the rate of growth briefly faltered but generally remained positive. In 1974 and 1975, however, the Community countries experienced the lowest growth rates in the post-war era. Despite a substantial recovery in 1976, as illustrated in Table 9.2, the growth rate reverted in 1977 to figures generally about half the average of the 1960s and increased only slightly in 1978 and 1979, reaching 3.3 per cent.

Inflation

It is difficult to grasp that inflation can occur in a period of recession, and thus unemployment. But as a report of the Economic and Social Committee points out

TABLE 9.2 Increase in the Volume of Gross Domestic Product (%)

	1960–70	*1971–2*	*1973*	*1974*	*1975*	*1976*	*1977*	*1978*	*1979*
Belgium	4.9	4.8	6.5	4.7	−2.1	5.7	1.3	2.0	2.7
DK	4.9	4.0	5.2	0.6	−1.2	6.3	1.8	0.0	2.8
France	5.6	5.7	5.4	2.8	0.3	4.6	3.0	3.0	3.2
Germany	4.7	3.5	4.9	0.5	−2.1	5.6	2.8	2.7	4.2
Irl	4.2	4.9	4.6	2.1	1.2	2.9	5.5	6.0	3.0
Italy	5.6	2.3	6.9	4.2	−3.5	5.7	1.7	2.2	4.8
Lux.	3.3	5.4	11.3	5.0	−11.0	2.9	1.3	2.5	2.6
NL	5.4	4.2	5.9	4.2	−0.9	4.5	2.4	1.9	2.2
UK	2.8	2.6	6.6	−0.6	−1.6	2.6	0.7	3.2	0.4
EC	4.6	3.8	5.8	1.7	−1.6	4.7	2.2	2.6	3.3
US	3.8	4.3	5.4	−1.4	−1.0	6.0	4.9	3.5	
Japan	10.7	8.1	9.7	−1.2	2.3	6.0	5.0	5.7	
OECD	5.3	4.6	6.0	0.1	−1.0	5.2	3.6	3.5	

Note EC totals based on 1970 exchange rates, OECD totals for 1960–70 based on 1963 exchange rates and 1970 exchange rates thereafter. The price base is 1970, except for 1978 and 1979, which are based on the prices of the preceding years

SOURCE *Annual Economic Review* (1978–9), Commission of the EC (October 1978) table 2.1; and Annual Report 1979 of the European Investment Bank, p. 10

the best interpretation may be that the inflationary pressures of the seventies originated mainly on the international commodity markets. These pressures then hit national production costs, directly in the case of imported commodities and indirectly in the case of wages and interest rates. The net impact of the ensuing pressure was probably to exacerbate inflation rather than reduce it.[3]

Increases in oil prices and rises in other imported raw materials led to a sharp upturn in consumer prices; averaging 13 per cent in 1974 and 1975 respectively, compared to an average of 3.5 per cent per year between 1958 and 1967 (see Table 9.3). The international monetary crisis has not helped either. The US Dollar has consistently dropped in value whilst remaining the principal means of payment in world trade. The slow-down in inflation in 1978 was general throughout the Community, with the exception of France and has been closer to the OECD average (about 7 per cent) than at any time since the oil crisis. After falling for three consecutive years consumer prices rose again to 9 per cent in 1979 and were still increasing in 1980.

TABLE 9.3 Increases in Consumer Prices (Implicit Price of Consumer's Expenditure) (%)

	1960–70	*1971–2*	*1973*	*1974*	*1975*	*1976*	*1977*	*1978*
Belgium	3.1	4.8	5.7	12.3	12.1	7.7	6.6	4.0
DK	5.5	5.4	8.2	15.3	8.4	9.3	10.9	9.0
France	4.2	5.7	6.8	13.4	11.7	9.9	9.1	9.2
Germany	2.9	5.8	7.6	7.0	6.3	4.4	3.9	2.5
Irl	4.6	9.2	12.4	15.2	21.8	17.0	13.9	8.0
Italy	4.0	6.2	12.2	21.0	17.6	17.9	18.0	12.5
Lux.	2.5	4.7	5.5	9.5	10.7	9.8	6.7	3.1
NL	4.2	8.3	8.9	9.7	10.3	9.2	6.7	4.4
UK	4.0	7.6	8.2	16.4	23.3	15.5	14.3	8.6
EC	3.7	6.3	8.7	12.8	12.8	10.0	9.1	6.9
USA	2.6	3.9	5.4	10.8	8.2	5.8	6.5	7.5
Japan	5.6	5.4	11.0	21.5	11.0	9.3	8.1	4.0

SOURCE *Annual Economic Review* (1978–9), Commission (October 1978) table 4.1

Industry adjustments

Until 1973 the six original members of the Community experienced rapid economic growth, thereby abandoning certain traditional industries in favour of new technologies. The high growth industries were common to all countries: chemicals, oil and energy products other than coal, electrical and electronic equipment. Italy and the Netherlands caught up in steel production, Italy gained in the textile field, France in agricultural and industrial machinery, Germany in transport construction and both Germany and Britain developed powerful food processing industries.

Since 1973, steel, textiles, clothing and paper, together with industrial construction, building materials and ship building, have suffered severe setbacks in all countries geared up by factors like new competition from developing countries, and the competitive vigour of the US and Japan.[4] During this period, the food-industry sector moved to the top of the growth table. The equipment products industries (capital goods and consumer durables) and chemical industries were least affected by the crisis, thanks largely to orders from the developing countries, the USSR and OPEC.

Consumption and investment patterns

As indicated in Table 9.4, in 1974–5 there was clearly a lower contribution from consumer demand throughout the EC relative to the 1960–70 decade.

TABLE 9.4 Private and Public Consumption in Gross Domestic Product (% shares: current prices)

	1960	*1965*	*1970*	*1973*	*1974*	*1975*	*1976*	*1977*	*1980*
Belgium									
private	68.7	62.6	59.4	59.8	59.1	60.6	61.3	60.0	59.7
public	12.4	12.8	13.4	14.5	14.6	16.5	16.5	15.3	15.4
DK									
private	65.9	62.6	57.4	54.3	54.6	55.7	56.1	56.2	55.8
public	12.3	15.1	20.0	21.0	23.0	24.7	24.0	24.0	24.0
France									
private	61.4	61.0	60.2	60.1	61.2	62.0	62.3	62.1	61.9
public	13.0	13.1	13.4	13.2	13.6	14.4	14.6	14.9	14.9
Germany									
private	59.8	59.1	57.7	57.7	58.2	61.3	60.9	61.3	61.1
public	10.7	12.7	12.1	13.2	14.1	14.6	14.0	13.9	13.8
Ireland									
private	80.5	75.9	70.9	64.6	68.3	64.6	63.6	63.2	63.2
public	12.4	13.3	14.8	16.1	18.1	19.5	19.5	19.2	19.2
Italy									
private	65.9	64.9	65.0	65.1	65.6	67.3	65.7	65.8	65.1
public	12.2	14.5	12.7	14.0	13.5	13.8	13.2	13.7	14.2
Luxembourg									
private	56.2	61.1	51.9	47.5	45.8	58.2	59.2	60.0	58.8
public	9.6	10.6	10.0	10.3	10.7	14.2	14.4	15.3	15.4
NL									
private	58.3	58.9	56.7	55.4	55.2	57.4	56.5	57.2	57.6
public	13.4	15.5	16.3	16.3	17.0	18.4	18.3	18.5	18.6
UK									
private	66.1	63.7	62.0	62.3	63.2	61.5	60.5	60.0	61.1
public	16.5	16.8	17.7	18.4	20.2	22.1	21.8	21.0	20.2
EC									
private	63.2	61.8	60.4	60.0	60.6	61.9	61.4	61.5	61.3
public	13.2	14.1	14.1	14.6	15.4	16.3	16.0	15.9	15.9

SOURCE *Annual Economic Review* (1978–9), Commission of the EC (October 1978) tables 8 and 9 of Statistical Annex

Public consumption rose until 1975 and, with the squeeze in public expenditures, slightly declined thereafter.

However, the fall in private investment (as demonstrated in Table 9.5) and stock decumulation probably contributed more to the recession than the weakness of household demand.

The principal factors behind the low rates of private investment since the 1974–5 recession are generally considered to include the depressed level of profits, continuing high levels of capacity under-utilisation, uncertainties

TABLE 9.5 Fixed Investment in Gross Domestic Product (% shares: current prices)

	Belgium	*DK*	*France*	*Germany*	*Irl.*	*Italy*	*Lux.*	*NL*	*UK*	*EC*
1960	19.3	19.4	20.1	24.3	14.3	22.3	21.3	19.3	16.4	20.6
1965	22.4	21.7	23.3	26.1	21.3	19.0	29.2	25.0	18.3	22.3
1970	22.7	24.7	23.4	25.6	22.6	21.3	23.7	25.7	18.7	22.8
1973	21.5	25.4	23.8	24.5	25.3	20.8	25.2	23.0	19.7	22.8
1974	22.7	24.7	24.3	21.9	26.1	22.4	24.4	21.8	20.7	22.4
1975	22.6	22.1	23.2	20.8	23.4	20.6	27.8	21.0	20.0	21.4
1976	22.0	24.2	23.3	20.7	24.5	20.0	26.9	19.7	19.2	21.1
1977	21.6	23.3	22.6	20.8	25.9	19.8	28.0	20.8	18.2	20.9
1978	21.4	21.9	22.1	26.4	27.2	18.9	27.6	21.0	17.8	20.7

SOURCE *Annual Economic Review* (1978–9) Commission of the EC (October 1978) table 10 of the Statistical Annex.

created by fluctuating exchange rates, the effect of high nominal rates of interest on the cash-flow implications of borrowing and a general lack of confidence in demand management policies.[5]

THE PROBLEMS POSED FOR THE MAIN POLITICAL ACTORS AND THEIR POLICY PRESCRIPTIONS

The following section looks at the problems the economic crisis of 1974–5 posed for the Council of Ministers, which represents national governments as the institution in which most important EC decisions are finalised. It also examines the policy prescriptions put forward by the Council of Ministers to cope with the crisis. A similar analysis will be made of perceived problems for the Commission, which alone initiates and implements Community policy, and its policy prescriptions. Finally, pressure groups representing trade unions, industry and employers at European level will be considered in this way.

The Council of Ministers

The main problems the economic crisis posed for the Council of Ministers were how to cope with: (a) the political implications of a levelling-off of and or drop in standards of living in the EC with regard to, first and foremost, the occurrence and outcome of national elections, and second, the pursuit of wider Community goals;[6] (b) the high rates of youth unemployment and its potential for spillover into political unrest; (c) the EC's vulnerability vis-à-vis the countries which supply raw materials, especially oil; (d) the spate of protectionism introduced by non-EC countries such as the USA and Japan; (e) the gradual loss of EC competitiveness on the world market; (f) the accumulation of petro dollars by OPEC countries, i.e. how these dollars could be recycled and invested into Community countries with the necessary political security; (g) the repercussions of measures governments were taking or wanted to take individually (either in the field of energy or giving aid to ailing industries) which were undermining common-market principles.

The extent to which a common approach to these problems was both necessary and possible was a debating point within the Council of Ministers. On the one hand, the percentage of intra-Community trade (slightly over 50 per cent) and the existence of certain common policies (like coal and steel) suggested joint action. There was also an incentive to capitalise on the size of the Community in negotiations with outside countries to secure raw materials and deal effectively with import and export policies. On the other, the lack of Treaty provisions in certain key areas of the economy (economic, monetary and energy) and the reluctance, though with variations, of governments to transfer competences in these areas to the EC institutions, brought into question the need and extent of common action.

In addition, the EC collective spirit to deal with the economic crisis of 1974–5 was affected by the scars the Copenhagen Summit Conference had left,[7] the interruptions caused by changes in leadership in Germany, France and Britain in 1974, the bilateral, competitive bidding over oil supply in 1974–5,[8] the strains which had resulted from British membership renegotiations (1975), and the differences over which forum (OECD or UN – both non-EC) should be selected in coordinating a common oil-supply policy for the main western oil-consuming countries.[9]

Yet, while accepting the different economic situations of the EC countries, member governments nevertheless saw scope for joint action. The view that national solutions offered scant protection became more and more paramount. By 1977, it was felt pertinent to create conditions in which an economic policy should be pursued which would encourage growth and the creation of jobs, combat inflation and, at the same time, promote active policies. These should contribute to the necessary adjustment of the affected regions and sectors so as to safeguard the Community's competitiveness, encourage the development of fresh demand, and avoid the harmful effects resulting from unemployment. Member governments also acknowledged that more efforts should be devoted to the establishment of a coordinated energy policy.

The Commission

The main problems the economic crisis posed for the Commission were similar to those mentioned for the Council of Ministers above. This is understandable, given that the Commission shares, at least in theory, the executive function with the Council of Ministers, which means, for example, that without a Commission recommendation there can be no Council decision.

The gravest problem for the Commission arose from the resurgence of national interest in EC affairs. With national governments seeking individual measures against the economic crisis on the one hand, and insisting on economic coordination among the nine governments on the other, the role of the Commission, as the exponent of Community interest, was curtailed.

This coincided with the continual debate on whether various systems of regional and industrial aid run by EC members were compatible with EC competition law. The Community's founding Treaties gave the Commission the power to prohibit and to penalise agreements between enterprises which constitute an abuse of economic power, as well as to monitor public aid which distorts the free play of market forces in the Common Market to the detriment of other companies.[10] The difficulty for the Commission, and the subject of debate, is to decide which aids do or do not contravene Community rules on fair competition. As a general reference, the Commission has taken the view that aid should be authorised when it is necessary (and the need has been clearly demonstrated) to correct severe regional imbalances, to help accelerate industrial growth or change, to permit certain industries to be run down without too much social distress, or to neutralise, at least temporarily, distortions of competition due to outside factors.[11] Thus the Commission's approach is to allow aid for struggling industries but, at the same time, to ensure that national aid does not simply transfer the ills of one country to a Community partner, i.e. investment assistance should not expand capacity since over-capacity is prevalent in all crisis sectors.

However, the Commission is actively encouraging member states to promote development of the data processing, electronics and aerospace sectors; but urges that expansion programmes should be coordinated at Community level.

In a four-page memorandum on Community structural policy in the industrial sector, the German government in 1978 expressed a view which was very much in line with that of the Commission, and going even further in insisting on liberal and anti-protectionist policies.[12] It pointed out that an accumulation of sectoral measures would seriously compromise overall economic potential and thought it essential that intervention should not go beyond what was strictly necessary. In other words, aid should be used to promote structural change rather than to preserve inefficient structures. Similarly, the German government indicated that it agreed to measures regulating imports in the textile and steel sectors with considerable reservations, and urged that the degree of liberalisation of world trade must be maintained and increased.

There are member governments, like the French and British, who do not share the same liberal and anti-protectionist attitude of the German government and have subsequently brought pressure on the Commission to fall more in line with their outlook.

While generally in line with the policy prescriptions of the Council of Ministers (as expressed above) the Commission put extra emphasis on the following:

(a) to complete the establishment of the Common Market and Customs Union, i.e. removal of barriers to the free movement of persons, goods, services and capital;
(b) to safeguard Community principles, as particularly enshrined in the competition sector, to secure and supply energy resources by means of diversification of domestic and foreign energy sources, and to create a unified market for energy;
(c) to respond to the specific problems of particular sectors and to help to launch the new technologically advanced industries;
(d) to move more quickly towards economic and monetary union.

European pressure groups

Although there is a reluctance by the Council of Ministers to deal directly with European pressure groups, the latter, at least the larger ones, manage to submit statements and arrange visits with the President chairing the Council of Ministers, especially before European Council meetings. They also try to influence the Council of Ministers via their national affiliates.[13]

For reasons of space, consideration will only be given to the Union of Industries in the European Community (UNICE), which is the main spokesman for industry and employers' organisations at European level, and the European Trade Union Confederation (ETUC), which encompasses trade unions across Western Europe.

UNICE

Between 1976 and 1977, UNICE suggested three main headings for priority actions.[14] These were to align economic, monetary and social policies; strengthen the Common Market and put it on a more solid basis; and strengthen the position of the Community in the world.

UNICE insisted that a main objective of economic policy was to create a favourable environment for private business growth, to promote innovation and investment and to increase productivity and competitiveness. These objectives should be carried out by general policies rather than by specific government interventions to assist failing industries or companies. In addition, UNICE recommended improvement of the employment situation and inflation control (through strict monetary policies, a slow-down in growth of public spending, and moderation in the wage-income trend). It also called for a better adjustment of supply and demand in the labour market by means of training policy and a suitable degree of labour mobility. There should be a concentration of efforts for the benefit of the least favoured regions of the Community.

Under the second heading, UNICE urged the elimination of technical obstacles to trade, the improvement of standardisation and the abolition of frontier controls. A reciprocal opening of public supply contracts should gradually be introduced. With regard to energy policy, UNICE proposed: to introduce free movement of energy products within the Community, to harmonise as far as possible energy-saving policies, to encourage research and development into new sources of energy and to secure fair allocations of energy available in the event of crisis.

Concerning the third heading, UNICE made the following proposals: a mutual dependence relationship and cooperation with the oil producing countries should be built up; efforts should be introduced to guarantee access to the raw materials of developing countries and the atmosphere for investment in developing countries should be improved.

ETUC

Responses of the ETUC to the economic crisis of 1974–5 were taken from their Second Statutory Congress in 1976, which centred on the following points:
(a) The restoration of full employment, the protection of employment, incomes and purchasing power with special attention to youth unemployment.[15]
(b) The improvement of social and working conditions through such measures as raising wages, reducing working time to 35 hours per week, increasing holiday entitlement to five weeks annual holiday, extending the school-leaving age to 16 years, lowering the retirement age, harmonising (in

an upward fashion) the pension rates and generally adjusting these to wage development.[16]

(c) The improvement of employment services and coordination at European level; setting up of regional tripartite committees for analysis of active intervention in employment policy; improvement and coordination of the work of the Community financial instruments and greater participation of trade-union representatives in the policies of these instruments.

(d) The development of a European zone with stable rates of exchange extending, for example, agreements such as the 'snake' agreement to other countries which are not included at present (1976).

(e) The organisation of sectoral meetings in certain industries on a parity basis centring on employment problems which could later become joint committees or possibly lead to the conclusion of European collective bargaining agreements.

(f) Reduction of dependence on imports for the supply of energy to Europe; introduction of optimum conservation measures, use of nuclear energy and developments of new technology.

The ETUC was (and still is) particularly keen to try to offset unemployment by providing more jobs through work-sharing, reduction of working time and related measures. UNICE, in turn, was (and still is) equally adamant in rejecting the idea that such measures should become Community-wide agreements. Dissatisfied both with the attitude of UNICE and the Council of Ministers on these issues generally, and the outcome of the Tripartite Conferences on Employment in particular since 1977,[17] the ETUC has organised action days and information campaigns, such as in November 1978 and April 1979, in order to make its views known to the public.

THE POLICIES AND SOLUTIONS FORMULATED BY THE EC IN THE 1970s

The Community approach towards coping with the economic crisis of 1974–75 falls into four main headings:

(a) The coordination of national economic and monetary policies of EC countries;

(b) The selective intervention in the EC economy as a whole through EC financial instruments;

(c) The development of a coordinated energy policy;

(d) The advancement of a Community industrial policy.

It is worthwhile to point out that in implementing the Treaties, the Council and the Commission issue regulations, directives, decisions, resolutions, recommendations and opinions. Regulations are of general application; they are binding in every respect and have direct force of law in every member state. Directives are binding on the member state to which they are addressed as regards the results to be achieved, but leave the mode and means to the discretion of the national authorities. Decisions may be addressed either to a government, an enterprise or to a private individual; they are binding in every respect on the party or parties named. Resolutions, recommendations and opinions are not binding.

THE COORDINATION OF ECONOMIC AND MONETARY POLICY

The Council of Ministers sets aside one day per month for consideration of economic and monetary problems and devotes three meetings a year to consideration of the economic situation. The Council lays down guidelines for economic policy, including quantitative guidelines for national budgets. There are a number of Committees, such as the Economic Policy Committee, advising the Council and Commission on economic and monetary policies.

At least every five years the Council adopts a medium-term economic policy programme (MTEPP) on, for example, unemployment, economic growth and inflation rates, volume of investment and balance of payments. These objectives, however, constitute no more than guidelines.

THE EUROPEAN MONETARY SYSTEM (EMS)

At its meeting in Bremen on 6–7 July 1978, the European Council proposed that closer monetary cooperation be established between the member states of the Community by setting up a European Monetary System (EMS).[18] The two principal architects, Chancellor Schmidt and President Giscard d'Estaing, saw it as a fundamental element in a more comprehensive concept aimed at lasting growth and stable prices, a gradual return to full employment and a reduction in regional disparities.

On 5 December 1978, the European Council decided to introduce the EMS from 1 January 1979 and declared itself resolved to ensure the lasting success of the EMS by policies conducive to greater stability at home and abroad for both deficit and surplus member countries of the Community. The Council also resolved to consolidate the EMS by setting up, two years after the start of the scheme, a European Monetary Fund (EMF) implying the full use of the European Currency Unit (ECU) as a reserve asset and a means of settlement. Due to implications of the common agricultural policy, the EMS came into force in March 1979–ten weeks later than originally planned.

The ECU will be used as the denominator for the exchange-rate mechanism, as a divergence indicator, as the denominator for operations in both the intervention and credit mechanisms and as a means of settlement between the monetary authorities of the EC. The ECU is a monetary unit based on a basket of national currencies identical to those used to calculate the European unit of of account.[19]

The EMS exchange-rate mechanism differs from that of the 'snake' insofar as the EMS has been approved by all the member states (although the UK does not participate for the time being in the intervention mechanism) and is, therefore, a Community mechanism. Adjustments of the central rates may be carried out under a common procedure in which all countries participating in the exchange-rate mechanism and the Commission will be involved.

Participating states place 20 per cent of their gold and dollar reserves into the European Monetary Cooperation Fund and receive a supply of ECUs to regulate Central Bank interventions.

The European Council of December 1978 also adopted measures to assist the least prosperous Community countries. It requested the Community institutions and the European Investment Bank to make special loans available for a period of five years to such countries effectively participating in the exchange rate and intervention mechanism. (See section on Community loans below.)

In the judgement of the Commission and the Monetary Committee on the first year of operation of the EMS,[20] the system operated 'correctly'; the technical mechanisms introduced proved to be well adapted;[21] the consultations, vital for the smooth management of the system, took place in good conditions. They also pointed out two main shortcomings. First, the ECU was hardly used as a settlement instrument, and the interventions on the markets were not adequately carried out with Community currencies (but mainly with US dollars). On top of this, and most important of all, the countries running deficits in the system had recourse to sources of capital outside the Community rather than using the EMS credit mechanisms. Second, the rates of inflation all diverged excessively, indicating that the coordination aspects was not operating as hoped.

On the last point it can be added that oil-based inflation is mainly to blame, not the EMS itself. But the EMS has proved unable to halt the trend, even though member countries have succeeded in harmonising their stability policies in one respect. Everywhere bank rates have been increased, which is seen as an earnest attempt by member countries to tackle inflation.

The argument most frequently used against the EMS is that the economic performance of the EC member states varies so much that any system for maintaining stable exchange rates cannot survive.

The Social Free-Market Economy Working Party of Heidelberg goes even as far as arguing that it is pointless to begin with exchange rates rather than with domestic financial stability (money and cyclical policies of each individual country). Their claim is that flexible exchange rates will continue to be appropriate until such time as countries have come so close together that rates remain stable anyway.

It is still somewhat premature to give a verdict either way. A real test of the EMS will occur when the second stage comes into operation, which looks less and less likely to happen as scheduled on 1 January 1981. What must be settled with the establishment of the EMF, which is to mark the second stage, is the question of what powers are to be attributed to this Fund. This involves the limits and conditions in which the EMF can create ECUs,[22] the coordination of exchange-rate policies with regard to the dollar, and the role the EMF should play in conducting the economic and monetary policies of the EC countries. Since the final decision over the establishment of the EMF will commit part of the member countries' national gold and foreign exchange reserves, Chancellor Schmidt and President Giscard d'Estaing did not with to deal with these questions until after their respective national elections in 1980 and 1981. It is reasonable to assume that the EMS will continue to improve gradually and that the existing mechanisms will be strengthened, as well as being accompanied by increased coordination of national policies.

THE COMMUNITY'S FINANCIAL EFFORTS

One of the most immediate Community responses to the economic crisis of 1974-5 was to make more Community resources available to stimulate economic growth, to promote vocational training and retraining of workers, to aid ailing industries, to alleviate problems of economic divergence, and to help in research and development of new energy sources and technology. In the following, these financial efforts will be traced by making a distinction between Community grants and loans. Community grants involve the European Social Fund (ESF), the European Regional Development Fund (ERDF) and the Social Fund of the European Coal and Steel Community (ECSC). Community loans include the European Investment Bank (EIB), loans sponsored under the Euratom and ECSC Treaties respectively, and the New Community Instrument (NCI).

The following review will concentrate on the financial aid provided by these Community instruments. With the exception of NCI loans, descriptions, working methods and allocations to individual countries (until 1976) of these instruments are well documented in the ESC publication on *Action by the European Community through its financial instruments*.[23]

Community grants

The European Social Fund (ESF)

The ESF has existed since 1962 and underwent a major reform in 1971. The ESF can be used when the employment situation is, or risks being, affected by measures taken in the framework of Community policies. It can also finance preparatory studies or pilot projects dealing with new training methods.

In 1979, the ESF had a budget of 767 million EUA, representing a 35 per cent increase over 1978. As shown in Table 9.6 the two biggest recipient sectors of the ESF have been regions and young people, comprising nearly 90 per cent of the total in 1979. However, the former, whilst increasing in absolute terms by 66 per cent between 1978 and 1979, has been decreasing as a percentage of the total ESF outlay since 1976. The latter has been steadily increasing both in absolute and relative terms over the same period. On 27 November 1978, the Council adopted a Regulation specifically designed to provide more ESF aid for vocational training of unemployed young people under the age of 25. Funds for projects assisting the young unemployed increased by almost 70 per cent between 1978 and 1979.[24] The handicapped sector ranks third, followed by the agricultural and textile workers. A fifth, and very rapidly growing sector is women. The financial impact of programmes for women has doubled between 1978 and 1979. Approximately 1 million workers have benefited from measures subsidised by the ESF in 1978 alone.

Requests for intervention can emanate from private organisations (companies, associations, etc.) as well as from public authorities. But it is up to national governments to send these requests to the Commission. The ESF takes upon itself half the cost of projects undertaken by public authorities. Projects undertaken by private organisations receive a subsidy equivalent to that from the relevant national authorities.

The European Regional Development Fund (ERDF)

The object of the ERDF is to correct the principal regional imbalances within

TABLE 9.6 Aid by the European Social Fund and the European Regional Development Fund

ESF: Distribution of Grants by Sector, 1972–9 (in million u.a.)

Types of intervention	*1972–5 Community* million u.a.	%	*1976–9 Community* million u.a.	%
Agriculture	81.9	9.8	82.8	3.46
Textiles	15.4	1.85	82.94	3.5
Agriculture & textiles	16.9	2.02	15.45	0.65
Young people	35.1	4.19	720.00	30.2
Women				
Handicapped				
Migrants	52.9	6.33	151.4	6.35
Article 4	202.2	24.18	1055.7	44.16
Regions				
Technol. Advance Enterprises	528.4	63.19	1162.00	48.61
Handicapped	105.6	12.62	172.8	7.22
Article 5	634.0	75.82	1334.8	55.84
Total	836.2	100.00	2390.5	100.00

SOURCE 1972 6 figures, ESC, 'Action by the EC through its financial instruments' (p. 78, Brussels, 1979); 1977, 1978, 1979 figures, General Reports, EC Commission, pp. 125, 129, 115, respectively

ERDF: Distribution of Grants by Sector and Country 1975–9 (in million u.a.)

Types of intervention	*Industry Crafts Services* million u.a.	%	*Infrastructure* million u.a.	%	*Hill farming area infrastructure* million u.a.	%	*Total* million u.a.	%
Belgium	10.59	1.17	20.9	1.21	3.07	2.89	34.56	1.23
Denmark	4.33	0.47	29.87	1.71	–	–	34.20	1.20
Germany	101.29	11.2	78.25	4.53	–	–	179.54	6.0
France	165.96	18.33	255.74	14.65	13.66	12.80	435.35	15.1
Ireland	83.71	9.25	81.83	4.7	16.45	15.42	181.99	6.5
Italy	246.76	27.27	829.6	47.5	59.13	55.46	1135.49	41.0
Luxembourg	–	–	2.6	0.15	–	–	2.60	0.08
Netherlands	5.52	0.61	35.87	2.05	–	–	41.39	1.3
United Kingdom	286.89	31.7	410.06	23.50	14.32	13.43	781.27	28.3
Total	905.05	100.00	1744.72	100.00	106.62	100.00	2756.39	100.00

SOURCE 1975–6 figures, ESC, 'Action by the EC through its financial instruments' (p. 45, Brussels, 1979); 1977–9 figures, 'Europe', Selected Statistics (2 Jan. 1978) p. 15; (9 Jan. 1980) p. 13; 1978 figures, EC Commission, 'ERDF: 4th Annual Report' (1978) p. 79

the Community arising from agricultural poverty, industrial change and structural under-development.

The ERDF was established in March 1975 and by the end of 1979 had made grants totalling 2,826 million EUA. According to the figures provided in Table 9.6, nearly two-thirds of that total went into infrastructure investments. The overall allocation of the ERDF increased by 72 per cent between 1978 and 1979. However, while infrastructure investments were augmented by 90 per cent in the same period, industry and service-sector investments only obtained a 42 per cent increase.

On 6 February 1979, the Council agreed on new rules for the ERDF, dividing it into two parts: the largest part continues to operate under a system of national quotas and a new quota-free section.[25]

Under the quota section, applications for Fund assistance are made by governments. It can help finance two types of investment in member states' aided areas:

(a) industry and service-sector investments, which create new jobs or are necessary to guarantee existing ones. Fund aid can go up 20 per cent of the investment cost or 50 per cent of national public aid, but is also related to the number of jobs created;
(b) infrastructure investments which contribute to the development of the regions concerned – normally up to 30 per cent of the cost of the investment but in exceptional circumstances can be 40 per cent.

The quota-free section is seen as the beginning of an instrument of Community regional policy, rather than a mechanism which simply provides support for national regional development measures. It will be used to finance, jointly with the national authorities and in close coordination with the Community's other financial instruments, specific Community regional development measures. However, until 1980, expenditure was limited to 5 per cent of total ERDF resources; the Commission, encouraged by the European Parliament, had suggested 13 per cent.

The current ERDF Regulation expires at the end of 1980. The contribution of regional policy to the objective of convergence in the Community will be a main item in drafting a new Regulation. Mr Gioleti, the Commissioner responsible for regional policy, felt in January 1980 that the main problem for regional policy was 'one of co-existence of regions at different levels of development, rather than one of catching up'.[26] He thought the problem of co-existence between countries with different economies would be accentuated with EC enlargement.[27]

ECSC Fund

The ECSC Fund for the readaptation of workers in these industries was established in 1951. It has provided aid totalling nearly 200 million EUA between 1975 and 1979, distributed nearly equally between the coal and steel industry sectors. Germany and France were the main beneficiaries in the coal and steel sectors respectively, but the United Kingdom took top honours for the two sectors combined. Statistics provided by the Community indicate that 140,000 workers (58,000 in coal and 82,000 in steel) benefited from the Fund between 1975 and 1979.[28]

The granting of aid is conditional on payment by the state concerned of a contribution of not less than the amount of the aid. Aids are granted by the Commission on application from the ECSC member countries. There is no national quota system relating to this Fund.

The Guidance Section of the European Agricultural Fund (EAGGF) provides individual grants to help modernise the structure of agricultural production and distribution. In addition, grants are made, via the national authorities, for schemes designed to encourage the amalgamation of very small farms, the formation of cooperatives, training in modern management and production techniques and early retirement for those wishing to leave farming. All in all, the resources available to the Guidance Section of the EAGGF have increased substantially and now run to around 500 million EUA per year, with a much higher proportion going to the less prosperous areas within recent years.

Community loans

European Investment Bank (EIB)

The EIB, an autonomous public institution within the Community, was established by the EEC Treaty (Articles 129 and 130). Its principal task is to contribute, operating on a non-profit-making basis, to the balanced development of the Common Market. For this purpose, the Bank operates by granting long-term loans to guarantee to undertakings, public authorities or financing institutions, investments for developing less developed regions or regions undergoing redevelopment, or investments which are in the common European interest, i.e. the development of investments benefiting small and medium-sized undertakings and support for investments in the energy sector. Although initially limited to the European territory of the member states, the scope of the Bank's activity has gradually been extended under

TABLE 9.7 Loans by the European Investment Bank, New Community Instrument and the ECSC[a]

Financing of Projects	EIB Loans by Sector and Country: Total 1975–9 (in million u.a.) Prod. Sector	Infra-structure	Energy	Total	NCI Loans by Sector and Country (loans allocated by mid-1980) (in million u.a.) Infra-structure	Energy	Total
Belgium	26.6	–	122.7	149.3	–	–	–
Denmark	51.3	62.4	67.7	181.4	–	–	–
Germany	15.5	–	217.00	232.5	–	–	–
France	53.1	668.2	375.3	1096.6	–	–	–
Ireland	119.9	312.6	112.6	545.1	62.0	24.7	86.7
Italy	774.3	1322.9	820.4	2917.6	39.6	45.6	85.6
Luxembourg	–	–	–	–	–	–	–
Netherlands	–	–	30.4	30.4	–	–	–
United Kingdom	461.6	981.9	967.9	2411.4	25.9	79.4	105.3
Non-Member Countries[b]	–	–	88.2	88.2	–	–	–
Total	1502.3	3348.0	2802.2	7652.5	127.5	149.5	277.0

a Industry, agriculture and services
b Austria and Norway
SOURCE EIB and NCI figures were taken from 'Tendances et Perspectives économiques à court terme: Les instruments d'emprunts/prêts dans le cadre des instruments financiers de la Communauté', no. 6 (July 1980) Commission of the European Communities.

ECSC Loans and Types of Interventions 1954–78 (Community)

Types of Interventions	1954–75 million u.a.	%	1976–8 million u.a.	%
Iron ore mines	25.75	0.98	75.1	2.5
Conversion	327.33	12.49	245.2	8.5
Iron and steel industry	1550.50	59.16	1736.9	59.7
Coal industry	421.58	16.09	710.7	24.5
Thermal power stations	111.52	4.25	44.7	1.54
Workers' housing	173.27	6.61	81.3	2.8
Retraining-resettlement	7.11	0.27	0.5	–
Technical research	3.12	0.12	0.7	–
Miscellaneous	0.74	0.03	12.5	0.4
Total	2620.92	100.00	2907.6	100.00

SOURCE General Reports of the European Communities (1975–8) pp. 46, 62, 59, 62, respectively.

various association or cooperation agreements to 13 Mediterranean countries and to 58 APC countries which are signatories to the Lome Convention.

EIB loans have doubled between 1976 and 1979. As indicated in Table 9.7 the fastest growing sector has been that of energy. Over the same period, this sector was augmented by 165 per cent, and was by far the largest single item in the EIB budget in 1979, amounting to 44 per cent of the total.[29] The two biggest beneficiaries have been Italy and the UK, accounting for 76 per cent of total loans, followed by Ireland and France, drawing 20 per cent.

New Community Instrument (NCI)

In October 1978 the Council authorised the Commission, for an experimental period, to raise loans on the capital market in conjunction with the EIB, up to a maximum of 1,000 million EUA. The objective was to promote investment projects which would contribute to greater convergence of the economic policies of the member countries, and to make the Community less dependent on outside energy supplies. This instrument (known as the NCI) was also to be used in conjunction with the European Monetary System for making loans available at subsidised interest rates to less prosperous members of the Community *fully participating* in the EMS scheme. The total of loans made available at subsidised rates was fixed at 1,000 million EUA a year for five years, with an interest rate subsidy of 3 per cent. The subsidy was, however, limited to a maximum of 200 million EUA a year for five years. Loans with interest subsidy were intended for infrastructure projects and programmes.

The first instalment of 500 million EUA was authorised in May 1979. See Table 9.7 for a breakdown of the allocation made in 1979 (only three countries benefited).

ECSC loans

Under Articles 54 and 56 of the ECSC Treaty, loans are available to assist investment projects. Such projects include modernisation and conversion of steel plants, and the provision of loans, often at low-interest rates, for the establishment of new employment in areas of coal and steel production. There are also loans (at 1 per cent interest) for house building or modernisation of existing dwellings for those working in the industries.

As highlighted in Table 9.7, ECSC loans have doubled between 1976 and 1978, i.e. slightly more than the total amount provided between 1954 and 1975. The largest item (60 per cent of the total) are loans for modernisation in the iron and steel industries, followed by loans for the coal industry (25 per cent).

Euratom Treaty loans

In March 1977 the Council authorised the Commission to raise capital for lending to the finance of the construction of nuclear power stations and industrial installations for fuel recycling. The Council authorised the Commission to negotiate loans up to an initial sum of 500 million EUA, followed by a second instalment of the same amount, authorised in December 1979. By mid-1980, 385 million EUA had been lent to power-station projects in the Community.

Assessment of Community financial instruments

Community resources, as we have seen, are not negligible, but they have to cover a vast terrain and suffer from a lack of coordination. A more effective coordination should, for example, ensure that the training schemes supported by the ESF can provide the appropriate skills for the new jobs created with the aid of the ERDF, which might also, along with the EIB, help to pay for infrastructural facilities which the new factories will need.

Naturally there should also be coordination between Community and national financial instruments and related policies. There was a Council Resolution in 1977 urging such a coordination to achieve a more effective employment policy, but more precise follow-up decisions are necessary in order to introduce what the Commission has phrased as the 'deployment of integrated operations in the problem regions'.

Although the ESF and ERDF can be used as partial repayment of national aids, the Commission has consistently emphasised that the real aim of these Funds is to *supplement* rather than replace government payments. Otherwise the full impact of Community help is lost on the public. Yet, judging from the growing disparity between, for example, the volume of requests for aid and the resources available to the ESF, Community aid seems to be used as *replacement* rather than as supplement. This gap has stretched from 52 per cent in 1977 to 93 per cent in 1978, and has scarcely shown any reduction since then.[30] It is for this reason that the Commission and the European Parliament demand increases in the ESF.

The paradox, however, is that great sums of Community aid requested and granted are not called up by member governments, especially Italy. For example, at the beginning of 1979, the total proportion of ESF aid granted but not called up had grown to 300 million EUA. For the ERDF the figure was 180 million EUA and for the Guidance Section of the EAGGF, the amount was 220 million EUA. Similarly, the Commission had granted

1,350 million EUA of ESF aid in 1978, but only 569.5 million were called up. In the Guidance Section of the EAGGF the respective figures were 1,100 million EUA to 356 million EUA.[31] Laxity in the national administrations was cited as the main cause for this incongruence.

COMMUNITY REACTION TO PROBLEMS IN THE STEEL, SHIPBUILDING AND TEXTILE INDUSTRIES

There has been a serious contraction in the steel, shipbuilding and textile industries since 1974. The following is a short analysis of the problems faced and the Community measures taken in these industries.[32]

Steel

In 1974 Community steel accounted for 22 per cent of world production, employed nearly 800,000 workers and was responsible for 7 per cent of the Community's industrial production. In 1975, world crude steel production dropped by 9 per cent. Of the major steel producers in the world, the Community was hardest hit, operating at about 60 per cent of capacity in 1977, compared with the USA at 77 per cent and Japan at 74 per cent. For the Community this meant cutbacks in production (155 million tonnes in 1974 to 126 million tonnes in 1977),[33] a slump in prices (a 35 per cent drop between 1974 and 1977) a fall in employment (107,000 were made redundant between 1974 and 1978 and 100,000 were put on short time work).

In addition to structural over-capacity the industry also has a problem of low productivity. A large number of European steel plants are old and ill-equipped to face the competition from new steel producers.[34]

The Simonet 'Plan', named after the then Commissioner responsible for Industrial Affairs, which came into effect on 1 January 1977 and covered the first six months of the year, provided for a joint procedure involving 70 groups of EC iron and steel undertakings in the implementation of production and delivery programmes. This Plan relied largely on voluntary cooperation with steel producers. New proposals put forward by the Commission and adopted by the Council in December 1977, became known as the Davignon Plan, named after the Commissioner in charge of Industrial Affairs. This anti-crisis Plan extends over two phases. In the short term it aims to:

(a) put a ceiling on (already surplus) production capacities in the Community and establish compulsory minimum prices for particularly

sensitive products and recommend prices for other products; and
(b) issue controls on imports from outside the Community by, for example, adopting anti-dumping measures.

Over the medium-term, the Plan, which the Council adopted in December 1978, attempts to:
(a) prohibit national aids which increase production capacities or which distort competition within the Community;
(b) grant Community loans to encourage the modernisation and rationalisation of companies to provide a better balance between supply and demand;[35]
(c) increase Community aid for industrial conversion and diversification in the major steel-making areas;
(d) study ways of improving the share-out of available work, possibly through financial intervention from the ECSC; reducing the retirement age, reorganising shift work, reducing the length of the working week, restricting overtime, etc.;
(e) intensify the innovation and research efforts covering products and production process;
(f) conduct negotiations with other major steel producers to ensure an equitable division of the cost burden at the world level.

Voluntary (bilateral) arrangements have been concluded with a number of countries, including EFTA. All include a clause whereby these countries respect fixed prices to allow them a degree of penetration on the Community market (from 4 to 6 per cent according to products), as well as quantitative restrictions on the volume of imports authorised and, at the same time, prohibiting Community undertakings from aligning their prices with these.

For countries which have not concluded bilateral agreements with the Community, a system of basic prices – anti-dumping duties is applied. Thus, steel imports coming from such countries at unreasonably low prices will be subject to an anti-dumping duty that will bring prices up to a reasonable minimum. This minimum is being established by reference to the lowest cost of production in supplying countries where fair conditions of competition apply. The anti-dumping measures were taken in accordance with the procedures laid down by the ECSC Treaty and by the GATT anti-dumping code. The USA adopted similar measures in 1978.

The internal section of the Community's emergency plan (steel forecasting programmes, minimum prices and guidance prices), whilst working reasonably well until early 1980, was altered in some essential aspects. On 23 July 1980 the Council of Ministers suspended the anti-crisis regime of minimum prices for hot rolled coils. Over-production of these coils and slackening demand had, for several months, forced prices below the

Davignon Plan's levels. To ensure the integrity of the Plan as a whole, the Council argued, it was necessary to introduce this measure.

Hot rolled coils now join reinforcing bars and merchant bars as steel products released from the Plan's structure of price minima. However, the latter products were dropped earlier this year for quite the opposite reason, as restructuring in the industry has cut back EC output and thus raised normal market prices.[36]

On the external side, as a result of anti-dumping restrictions and voluntary agreements on export reductions, the European steel imports, which amounted to 12.4 m. tonnes in 1976 fell to about 11 m. tonnes in 1978, while exports rose by nearly 9 m. tonnes to a total of 30 m. tonnes, thus saving 55,000 jobs in the European steel industry.

Shipbuilding

Since 1975 the workforce has fallen from a Community total of 206,354 to an estimated 138–145,000 in 1979 – a loss of 50–60,000 people. Throughout the member countries the jobs of another 50,000 are at risk if orders remain at their present low level.

In December 1977 the Commission submitted a comprehensive reorganisation programme for shipbuilding, providing for the reduction of shipbuilding capacity in the Community to 2.4 million GRT in the first half of the 1980s.

A Council Directive of 4 April 1978 prohibited the member countries from granting further aid to shipbuilding which would increase capacity. Only degressive aid may now be granted to help overcome serious crises. Negotiations are to be opened with third countries, particularly Japan, to persuade them also to reduce their shipbuilding capacity.

Textiles

Another industrial sector hard hit by the economic crisis was that of textiles. In particular the import of textile products into the Community proved problematic. Negotiations in trade policy (except for Eastern European countries) is the domain of the EC rather than individual countries. The Community is a member of the arrangement regarding international trade in textiles (known as the GATT 'Multifibre Agreement' (MFA) on textile products made of wool, cotton and man-made fibres), which came into force on 1 January 1974. A common stand for the Community was particularly necessary when this Agreement had to be renewed on 1 January 1978. Community textile imports had increased considerably (about 80 per cent) since 1973, while its consumption of textile products had remained stable. This had resulted in a substantial fall in production and employment levels in Europe, and obliged the Community to resort to various safeguard measures.

In order to safeguard the Community textile industry and allow time for rationalisation and modernisation, the EC has under the MFA negotiated limitation agreements with 23 low-cost supplying countries, and devised similar arrangements with those countries with which it has preferential trade agreements, like Taiwan and Yugoslavia. These agreements, which are due to expire on 31 December 1981, cover 127 categories of textile products and include either quantitative limits (quotas) for categories of sensitive products, or a mechanism for potential limitation, which can be applied to sensitive products from present small suppliers, or to less sensitive products, which may become sensitive in time. 80 per cent of the highly sensitive commodities are being covered by these agreements.

In the spring of 1980, the Commission indicated that it would increase its aid efforts in the textile (as well as the shoe) sector by, for example, encouraging the exchange of information, supporting pilot projects and participating in the financing of market surveys. However the Commission has requested that no aid, including regional, be given to the industry branch which produces man-made fibres.

The arrangements, negotiated under the MFA have helped to lift the threat to the Community industries caused by the enormous influx of low-cost textile products from developing and other countries in the last two to three years. However, the Commission emphasises, this is only a limited reprieve. The agreements are due to expire in 1982 and the interval, the Commission insists, must be used to adapt to new conditions of both Community and international competition. Unless this is done, the textile agreements will merely have provided a false sense of security.

Energy policy

EC proposals in the energy sector centred basically around five aims:[37] (a) to develop a coordinated energy policy; (b) to emphasise methods of conserving energy; (c) to expand existing energy resources and invent new ones; (d) to secure reactor safety and nuclear waste disposal; and (e) to promote supplies of external energy resources.

EC efforts to introduce a coordinated energy policy have involved the gathering of information on trends in the energy market and procedures for monitoring oil imports quarterly. Arrangements have been made for compulsory storage of oil derivatives corresponding to 90 days consumption. Stocks must also be kept at electricity power stations to ensure at least one month's operation. In addition, during supply shortages, the Community can make intra-Community trade in oil and oil products subject to a special surveillance. Finally, the Community agreed in 1974 to reduce energy consumption by 15 per cent by 1985 and dependence on imported energy from 63 per cent in 1973 to between 40 and 50 per cent in 1985.[38]

With regard to the rational use of energy and energy-saving measures, a number of directives have been adopted by the Council of Ministers, covering the performance of heat and hot-water generators, the rational use of energy in industrial enterprises, building insulation and electrical apparatus.[39] The EC complements and supplements these efforts with contributions from its financial instruments towards methods of energy conservation and development. On 13 May 1980, the Council approved a programme of energy saving, designed to meet the reduced ratio goal of 0.7 between energy consumption and economic growth.

Attempts to expand existing energy resources and to invent new ones have taken the following forms. Besides research contributions in the fields of nuclear fission and fusion,[40] the Community has helped to sponsor research into the production and use of hydrogen, the use of solar and geothermal energy, as well as the liquefaction and gasification of solid fuels. Community aid is also provided for the development of new technology for finding and exploiting hydrocarbons. Similarly, there is EC support for projects for uranium prospecting in the member states. In 1978, energy research and development accounted for nearly 70 per cent of the total Community research and development budget: 105 million EUA for nuclear energy, 37 million EUA for fossil energy and 28 million for new energy sources.[41]

The Commision's R&D budget provides a 96 per cent increase for 1980–3 in reactor safety research. Steps were also taken for expanding Community collaboration in the management of nuclear waste and the nuclear 'Trilogy' strategy was adopted, including closing the fuel cycle through the processing of fuels and development of the fast breeder option. The Commission also organised two sessions of public hearings during 1977 and 1978 to enhance public awareness of the facts relating to nuclear-power development.

A number of attempts have been made to secure external supply of energy resources. One such attempt was the Euro-Arab dialogue which originated in initiatives taken after the Copenhagen Summit Conference in December 1973. Under the Lome Convention (first signed in 1975 and renewed in 1979) provisions exist whereby the Community will develop the mining and energy potential of the ACP countries; and thus, indirectly, increase the supply potential for the EC. Some ACP countries, like Nigeria, are also important oil exporters to the Community. Additional endeavours have been made through bilateral agreements such as with Tunisia and Algeria.[42] There have also been efforts to conclude outline agreements on uranium supply. An agreement of this kind has already been concluded with Canada (January 1978) and another is being negotiated with Australia.

Against these achievements, however, a communication from the Commission to the Council COM (80) 235 in May 1980 highlights why even more vigorous Community actions are needed in the energy field. The Commission points out that for 1979 oil consumption was some 25 million tonnes above the target of 500 million tonnes and oil imports at 475 million tonnes were slightly up on the 1978 level. Whilst coal consumption increased by 9 per cent, coal production remained virtually static at 239 million tonnes; indicating that there is little likelihood of meeting the Community's production target of 270 million tonnes in 1985. The Commission also stated that in the Community, the annual rate of ordering of nuclear power stations achieved during the last three years needs to be doubled over the coming three years if nuclear power is to make its due contribution to our energy needs in 1990.

Feeling that member states' measures to achieve Community energy independence are still too divergent,[43] the Commission therefore, in mid-1980, re-emphasised the need for the Community to agree as soon as possible on an energy planning framework for the period up to 1990, including guidelines on increased energy efficiency, reduced oil consumption and levels of other fuels (notably coal and nuclear). It also called for increased energy investment, a continuing campaign of public education about energy problems, and improved relations with other industrial countries, oil producers and non-oil developing countries. Finally, the Commission was of the opinion that a Community energy policy would have to aim at a progresseive harmonisation of prices and taxes. And just for good measure the Commission has floated the idea of a Community tax on imported oil, i.e. a tax of £2.56 per tonne as EC revenues.

One can conclude, therefore, that the large number of attempts introduced, a fair number with success, have not added up to a coherent energy policy at Community level. Good intentions from the member states are not enough to put Community policy into practice. Much more commitment is needed to meet the energy challenge jointly in the 1980s.

THE ADVANCEMENT OF COMMUNITY INDUSTRIAL POLICY

The EC has taken a number of measures since 1974–5 in order to promote the development of an industrial policy at Community level in general, and to pursue a more effective employment policy in particular. Some of these measures will be examined below.

The completion of the Common Market

It is hoped that steps towards the completion of the Common Market will give new opportunities to EC industries. Efforts are being concentrated on the elimination of technical barriers to trade, i.e. abolition of all trading difficulties resulting from national provisions covering the quality, composition, packaging or inspection of goods. This is particularly important in the pharmaceutical industry where large-scale obstacles still prevail. The Commission also urges that public markets be opened up (that contracts from authorities in the nine be open to Community and not just national suppliers). This would be particularly relevant to the telecommunications sector.

Another area in which the Community has tried to contribute towards the completion of the Common Market is through the harmonisation of company law. Directives passed so far aim to standardise the requirements for setting up limited companies, to ensure 'transparency' of the accounts and to keep shareholders and workers better informed. Progress is only slowly forthcoming and many proposals are outstanding, such as on the structure of limited companies. This proposal has run into difficulties since it involves harmonising the application of a two-tier structure (management committee and supervisory council and promoting worker participation in the management of companies, an innovation about which certain member states are somewhat reticent.

However, the Community has been more successful in the legal protection of workers' rights, particularly in cases of collective dismissals (Directive of February 1975) and mergers (February 1977).

The development of 'growth' industries

According to Mr Davignon, Commissioner responsible for Industrial Affairs,

> The Community should not become a hospital for sick industries. Community action to help growth industries is as important as the strategy

> to restructure industries in trouble. In the aerospace industry, in data processing and in other areas opening up markets and pooling industrial capacity it will be necessary to reach the scale required by international competition.[44]

There cannot be much doubt that cooperation is needed among EC countries or companies if the challenge of international competition is to be successfully met. To promote cooperation in this field, which is important for the maintenance of employment levels in the Community, the Commission put forward proposals in 1976 and 1977 on data processing designed, with the help of central funds (a Community Leasing Fund), to encourage greater collaboration between companies in the Community in the standardisation of their products.

A Working Group on Standards has already been set up to develop a standardisation policy for the Community. In spite of the successful initiatives of *industrial* undertakings on the Airbus project, much more remains to be done in the field of advanced technology in terms of coordination, cooperation and pooling of resources, if the Community industry is to stay competitive.

CONCLUSION

Community institutions do not have the same flexibility as national governments to adapt to situations of economic crisis. Inadequate treaty provisions, conflicting national interests and competence challenges between national and Community authorities are just some of the underlying causes. This is particularly visible in the Community's response to energy problems.

In spite of a number of important decisions taken by the Council of Ministers since 1974–5, such as on emergency measures, neither a 'coordinated' approach nor a common energy policy have been forthcoming. No doubt, natural-energy resources, levels of energy efficiency, the ability to finance investment (at the same time as financing oil imports) and the political priorities accorded to the energy problem, all vary widely. One of the main reasons for the absence of a common policy, however, is that such a policy would need to cut across nationalised industries and fiscal policy, and would challenge the national energy interests across the board. As Evans correctly points out, this would mean 'tampering with one of the tap roots, not only of national sovereignty but the independence of some of the most powerful elements in the structure of industrial society'.[45]

In contrast, however, to the rather slow progress in the energy sector, there have been more successful Community attempts in a few other areas. Two attempts, in particular, stand out: cooperation in the monetary field, and measures in the steel and textile industries. Of these, the former have global implications for the EC countries' economies, and the latter serve selective industries. Although in time the EMS will become very important for a Community monetary policy, especially after the establishment of the EMF, for the time being the measures taken in the steel and textile industries can be seen as the more dominant Community method of coping with the 1974–5 economic crisis. This, however, is more the case with the steel industry, where both internal and external measures were adopted, than with the textile industry, which centred more on external factors.

The reason that measures in the steel and textile sectors became the dominant focus in the Community response can be explained by the following factors. Both industries occupy a central role in the economy of the member states. For example, the textile and clothing industry provides approximately 10 per cent of industrial jobs, and accounts for some 8 per cent of the Community's industrial activity. The Community is also the world's leading exporter of textiles and clothing.

It is the agreed role of the ECSC Treaty to have a common control over the steel sector. Under this Treaty, the Commission has responsibility for restrictive practices (state aid) to the coal and steel sector. It also has powers (and with the consent of the Council) if the industry is confronted 'with a period of manifest crisis' to take binding action on the establishment of production quotas or other measures to maintain viability. It would have been difficult to undertake effective reorganisation independently in a depressed world and European steel market with 35 per cent of Community steel production capacity unused.

The Simonet and Davignon Plan made reorganisation of the steel sector acceptable because (a) it offered a system whereby the difficulties, costs and sacrifices would be adequately distributed among the member states; (b) it was based on agreement with the major steel producers in the Community (grouped in the Eurofer 'Club') and had therefore obtained a broad consensus of the major actors involved; and (c) it centred on *temporary* measures aiming to adapt the Community steel industry to the demands of international competition.

A common stand in the renewal of the Multifibre Agreement, negotiated by GATT, was essential for the Community in 1977 in order to reduce the ever-growing level of textile imports from non-Community countries.

There has so far been no massive public finance mechanism within the Community, but the Community finds itself on the threshold of at least having the means for implementing structural reforms in, for example, the steel and textile industries.[46] European Parliament insistence on increases in the non-compulsory part of the EC budget and the introduction of Community backed loans, such as the NCI, have definitely strengthened Community financial means.

In the meantime, the extent of the economic problem facing the EC has not lessened. On the contrary, it has seemingly become greater. Growth rates in EC industrial production in the last seven years have been only one-ninth of what they were between 1963–73. Forecasts of most economic indicators for the second half of 1980 are pessimistic.[47]

Yet even if there was an economic upsurge, doubts are being expressed as to whether renewed economic growth can, in fact, absorb all the unemployed. By 1985 there will be an extra 9.7 m. people on the Community job market. However, economic growth and automation often mean less jobs.

Since 1978 there has been a trend within member countries to adopt tight monetary policies. The establishment of the EMS in 1979 is an indication that this is becoming a Community-wide approach and one which, according to the latest declaration at the Euro-Council meeting in Venice in June 1980, will prevail for some time to come. The underlying argument is that as long as oil prices increase drastically a tightening is necessary. However, with unemployment still on the increase and signs of another recession looming, it would seem reasonable to expect a relaxation of the grip on monetary policy and a consideration of policy alternatives. One such alternative consideration would be work-sharing methods for reducing unemployment.

So far, rather than forcing the issue at Community level, the Council, in a Resolution of 22 November 1979, is merely encouraging member governments to examine various forms of work sharing and is calling for further examination at Community level of prospects for a reduction in annual working time. It thus seems at least for the moment to be content with the stalemate situation which has arisen over the pros and cons taken by the ETUC and UNICE respectively on the introduction of such schemes at Community level.

But then one must ask whether Community legislation would be the right procedure anyhow on an aspect which is usually part of collective bargaining. As the Commission has pointed out, in its working paper on work-sharing in October 1979, the success of work-sharing schemes will depend on normal agreement procedures between workers and management.

Interest groups fully participated in the anti-crisis plan for steel, mainly because there were provisions in the ECSC Treaty calling for their participation in decision making. In other instances, like the Community

Tripartite Conferences on Employment, consultation and participation has not resulted either in concrete Council decisions or in binding collective agreements between the two sides of industry. True the employers are most adamant in rejecting Community-wide collective agreements, but empirical evidence suggests that trade unions too have not sufficiently transferred orientation and competences to the European level in order to facilitate the conclusion of such agreements.[48]

It is, therefore, only in isolated instances, like the coal and steel sector, and to some extent in the agricultural field,[49] that one can observe signs of corporate interventionism.

The Council of Ministers' consent to Community-wide approaches or policies is essential, as witnessed in the establishment of the EMS. The preparatory work of the Commission in general and its powers held in such areas as coal and steel and competition policy also make it a political actor of considerable importance in EC decision-making. European interest groups have not taken up corresponding roles to such practices as the social contract (as, for example, arranged between the British Labour Government and the TUC between 1974–8). This is largely due to the fact that important policy sectors, like economic, monetary, fiscal, etc. remain the domain of member government.

What, then, does the future hold? While it is true to say that no government is capable of coping with the ongoing economic crisis sufficiently it must also be realised that successive shocks have accentuated the inability of the member states' to overcome the challenge with which they have been confronted. The fact that there are big differences in the abilities of the EC countries could mean that 'the respective interests of each country in continuing the work on building Europe will be very much at variance. This could risk dislocating Europe into several speed systems', as is sometimes muted under the notion of a two-tier system.

Another major factor for the future involves the willingness of governments to forego parts of their sovereignty in favour of Community authority.[50] Yet due to the overall economic squeeze and certain governments' preferences to take a particularly tough stand on EC affairs, a situation is building up in which large parts of the population are becoming increasingly disenchanted with the Community and, subsequently, might demand, through the election box, disengaging rather than integrating government EC policies. Against these must be held events on the international scene, such as the constant rise in oil prices, and the situation in Iran and Afghanistan, which might strengthen integrative and cooperative ties.

If an overall Community strategy to cope with the economic problem is to be developed, it is simply not enough to remove customs duties. Nor is it sufficient to concentrate EC efforts on the two extremes of the industrial spectrum (advanced industries, on the one hand, and 'problem sectors', on the other). What is needed is the establishment of a comprehensive industrial structural policy. As a starting point, this would not necessarily have to take the form of specific Community measures and the subsequent transfer of far reaching competences to the EC institutions. Rather, steps can be taken to improve further national policy coordination, involving the activities of the EC institutions, the national administrations, and the participation of the two sides of industry.

Progress has been made in this direction in the last two years, but there is still a long road ahead.

NOTES AND REFERENCES

1. The term EC signifies the combination of the European Economic Community and Euratom set up in 1958, and the European Coal and Steel Community established in 1952.
2. There is a decline in the male labour force due to prolongation of education and earlier retirement. See *Annual Economic Review 1978–9,* Commission of the EC, SEC (78) 4033 final (Brussels) 19 October 1978.
3. The report goes on to state that 'recession boosts inflation by increasing idle capacity, thus pushing up fixed costs per unit output. Unit labour costs are pushed up because labour is shed at a slower rate than the fall in production . . . wages show a markedly counter-cyclical pattern with wages rising sharply during recessions and less vigorously in periods of economic recovery', Economic and Social Committee: *Report on the Economic Situation in the Community* (first half of 1980), Document CES 250/80 (May 1980) pp. 14 and 15.
4. According to a Commission Report, these intermediary activities registered near or below zero growth rates between 1973 and 1977. See Commission Report on trends in sectoral structures of the European economies since the oil crisis – from 1973 to 1978, published in January 1980.
5. See *Annual Economic Review 1978–9*, Commission of the EC (October 1978) pp. 2, 15.
6. For example, Article 2 of the EEC Treaty states: 'The Community shall have as its task . . . to promote throughout the Community a harmonious development of economic activities, a continuous and balanced expansion, an increase in stability, an accelerated raising of the standard of living and closer relations between the states belonging to it', *Treaties Establishing the European Communities*, European Communities Office for Official Publications (Luxembourg: 1973).
7. See Warner Feld, *The European Community in World Affairs* (Port Washington, N. Y.: Alfred Publishing Co., 1976) p. 4.
8. A number of EC member countries had arranged bilateral deals with

oil-exporting countries. For example, Germany had concluded bilateral deals with Iran and Kuwait, enabling the Iran shares/investments in Krupp (steel company) and Kuwait the same in Daimler Buiz (automobile firm) in return for fixed quantities of oil supplies.

9. France, wanting a UN forum, is not a member of the International Energy Agency (IEA) established under the auspices of the OECD
10. Article 93 (3) of the EEC Treaty specifically requires the member states to give 'prior notice of plans to grant or alter aid'. Articles 92 and 94 of the same Treaty provide the Commission with considerable powers to monitor both industrial and non-industrial national aids to check whether it is compatible with Community interests. In exercising these powers the Commission is fulfilling its obligations under the Treaty, and the Court of Justice which can impose penalties in the event of the Commission failing its job properly, monitors the way in which the Commission fulfils these obligations (see Article 175 and 215 of the EEC Treaty). *Treaties Establishing the European Communities*, EC Office for Official Publications (Luxembourg: 1973).
11. See European Communities Commission, *Background Report*, ISEC/B56/78 (17 August 1978).
12. This memorandum was presented to the Council of Ministers on 2 May 1978. The full text of it (from which excerpts were taken) is reprinted in *Europe* (Europe Documents No. 1002): Agence Internationale d'information pour la presse (18 May 1978).
13. See Emil Kirchner, 'Interest Group Behaviour at Community Level' in Leon Hurwitz (ed.), *Contemporary Perspectives on European Integration* (Westport, Conn: Greenwood Press, 1980) pp. 192–239.
14. These actions were listed in the following UNICE documents: the memorandum submitted by UNICE on the occasion of the replacement of the European Commission (November 1976); the Annual Report of 1976 (April 1977); and 'The Position of UNICE on Tripartite Conference in Luxembourg' (June 1977).
15. In 1979 the ETUC added that it opposed any anti-inflationary policy based on general wage restriction. It also stated that public spending should be used on a planned and selective basis to develop housing, education, health and other services, to restructure industry, and to achieve regional balance. Social entitlements should be safeguarded and public services developed. See Third ETUC Statutory Congress, Munich, May 1979, and ETUC Statement of 28 September 1979.
16. In 1979 this objective was specified further by demanding a reduction in working time by 10 per cent in the near future and without wage loss, through a 35-hour week, six weeks' annual holiday, the right to retirement at 60, later school-leaving age. Certain specific questions, such as the introduction of a fifth shift, should also be dealt with on a European level (Third ETUC Statutory Congress, Munich, May 1979).
17. The Tripartite conferences owe their origin to the Community's and the member States' concern in overcoming the employment crisis since 1974–5. Ever since 1975, such a conference has been held each year. These conferences gather together representatives of trade unions and employers' organisations, as well as government representatives (Ministers of Labour and Finance) and the Commission.

18. Formerly, the term was Summit Conferences and they had been held in 1961, 1967, 1969, 1972 and 1973. In December 1974, the French Government proposed that these should be institutionalised under the name 'European Council' and be held three times a year.
19. This basket is composed of DM 0.828, UK pound 0.0885, FF 1.15, Lira 109, FL 0.286, BF 3.66, F Lux 0.14, DKR 0.217 and Irish Punt 0.00759. The weight of each currency in the basket is as follows: DM 33 per cent, UK pound 13.3 per cent, FF 19.8 per cent, Lira 9.5 per cent, Florin 10.5 per cent, Belgian Franc 9.2 per cent, Lux. Franc 0.4 per cent, Danish Kroner 3.1 per cent and the Irish Punt 1.1 per cent (12 March 1979.) 1 ECU = approx. 10.66.
20. Cited in *Europe* (28–9 April 1980) pp. 13, 14.
21. The variations in the exchange rates between the EC currencies since 1972 were never kept within such narrow limits as during the period March 1979–March 1980 (1.9 per cent average variation for 1979–80 as against 5.2 per cent for the previous six years): *Europe* (28–9 April 1980) pp. 13, 14.
22. For example, the German Government has expressed fears that without certain member states' safeguards the EMF could create monetary liquid assets which could add to inflationary pressure and render conditions or restrictive national policies null and void.
23. Published by Editions Delta, Brussels, 1979.
24. It is estimated that since 1975, the time of the Council decision enabling young people to benefit, the ESF has helped approximately 200,000 young people to find work. The European Social Fund, *European File* no. 19/79, Commission of the EC, Brussels (November–December 1979).
25. The applied quota is as follows: Italy 39.39 per cent, UK 27.03 per cent, France 16.86 per cent, Ireland 6 per cent, Germany 6.4 per cent, Netherlands 1.58 per cent, Belgium 1.39 per cent, Denmark 1.2 per cent, Lux. 0.09 per cent.
26. Speaking before the VII International Regional Economy Conference in Paris from 3 to 7 March. Quoted in *Europe* (3–4 March 1980) p. 9.
27. With Greece, Spain and Portugal the EC will have 53 million more inhabitants; 34 million of which live in regions with average incomes similar to those of Southern Italy or the West of Ireland.
28. All aid figures regarding the ECSC Fund were taken from the *General Reports* of the EC for 1975–9, pp. 123, 140, 124, 128, 114 respectively.
29. One-third of the 997 million u.a. spent on energy was largely attributable to hydroelectric and thermal power stations; another 18 per cent went into electricity transmission lines and 15 per cent to oil and gas extraction and transport projects. European Investment Bank, *Annual Report* (Luxembourg: 1979) p. 38.
30. The European Social Fund, *European File* 19/79, Commission of the EC, (November–December 1979).
31. These figures were reported in the *Stuttgarter Zeitung* in Germany, 11 July 1979.
32. Statistical data for these three industries were mainly taken from European Communities *Background Reports*, ICEC nos. B/28/79 (2 July 1979), B43/79 (2 November 1979) and B3/79 (17 January 1979); *Information*, p. 27, Commission of the EC (March 1979); 'A Steel Policy for Europe', *European File* 6/79, Commission of the EC (March 1979).
33. Production rose slightly in 1978 to 134 million tonnes, but productive capacity

in the Community stands at some 200 million tonnes. The industry needs to produce and sell 160–70 million tonnes to be profitable.

34. In 1973 – a prosperous year – it took 8.3 hours of labour to produce a tonne of crude steel in the Community, but only 5.9 hours in Japan.
35. ECSC loans should represent a quarter of the total amount of national investment, private and public, estimated at 2,000 million units of account per annum from now to 1983. The Commission has laid down a series of Community rules for aid and intervention by member states to the iron and steel industry.
36. *Financial Times* (23 July 80).
37. The Council Resolutions of September and December 1974 and of February 1975 represent the cornerstone for ensuing Community resolutions and recommendations in the energy field.
38. In March 1979, the Council decided on an immediate 5 per cent reduction in the EC's annual petrol consumption. It also intended to hold net imports for oil up to 1985 at or below 1978 levels (472 million tonnes).
39. Although not necessarily due to EC directives, it is still encouraging to note that by 1978 EC member states were successful in reducing energy consumption by about 8 per cent between 1974 and 1977.
40. One research development project of particular importance is the Joint European Torus (JET) on thermonuclear fusion established in 1977 and stationed at Culham in the UK. The Community finances at 80 per cent of JET's construction cost of 200 million EUA. It should also be mentioned that the Community (under the Euratom Treaty) has a Joint Research Centre (JRC) which employs about 2,300 people mainly at Ispara, Italy.
41. The total EC finance for R & D was 255 million EUA in 1978. For further details see 'Science, Research and the European Community', *European File* 11/79, Commission of the EC (June 1979); and *Information*, P-64, Commission of the EC (July 1980).
42. These agreements intend to foster participation by Community firms in programmes for exploration, production and processing of energy resources, and to ensure that long-term contracts for the delivery of petroleum products are properly performed. See Georges Brondel and Noel Morton, 'Energy Policy' in Peter Coffey (ed.), *Economic Policies of the Common Market* (London: Macmillan, 1979) p. 195.
43. This was the view held by Roy Jenkins, President of the Commission in a speech given in Hanover before the Forum on Energy Prospects on 17 April 1980, quoted in *Europe* (18 April 1980).
44. Quoted in *Eurofile* (March 1979) p. 6.
45. Douglas Evans, *Western Energy Policy: The Case for Competition* (London: Macmillan, 1978) pp. 39–40.
46. The overall Community budget is only 0.7 per cent of the GNP. Agricultural expenditures (guarantee section) take up the overwhelming proportion of Community expenditures (70 per cent). See Helen Wallace, *Budgetary Politics: the Finances of the European Communities* (London: Allen & Unwin, 1980).
47. In a Report of 5 March 1980 the Commission notes that for 1980 the average foreseeable growth rate has to be reduced by more than half a point and has gone down to 1.2 per cent (instead of 2 per cent as predicted in late 1979);

inflation rate has gone up two points and the foreseeable annual average is now estimated at a little over 11 per cent instead of earlier forecasts of just over 9 per cent; unemployment could be as much as 6.4 per cent of the working population, which would mean that there could be 7 million jobless by the end of 1980; and the deficit in the balance of payments on current accounts, which at the end of last year was estimated at about 4 billion ECUs, could be as much as 14 billion ECUs. Quoted in *Europe* (7 March 1980) p. 5.

48. For example, Martin and Ross in a recent survey of trade-union leaders' perceptions of the crisis in five western European countries conclude 'all the labour movements see the solutions to whatever problems result in essentially national terms . . . very little is proposed and less is done to alter the international economic environment particularly insofar as union action across national borders is concerned' (Andrew Martin and George Ross, 'European Trade Unions and the Economic Crisis', in Jack Hayward (ed.), *Trade Unions and Politics in Western Europe* (London: Frank Cass, 1980) p. 66). For a more detailed account on trade union structures and activities at European level, see Emil Kirchner, *Trade Unions as a Pressure Group in the European Communities* (Farnborough: Saxon House, 1977) especially chapter 8.

49. Two agreements have been concluded between the Committee of Professional Agricultural organisations (COPA) and the European Federation of Agricultural Workers' Union in the Community (EFA) concerning the hours of work per week and number of annual holidays in agriculture. For further details see Emil Kirchner, 'International Trade Union Collaboration and the Prospects for European Industrial Relations', in Jack Hayward (ed.), *Trade Unions and Politics in Western Europe* (London: Frank Cass, 1980) pp. 132–5.

50. As Mr Brunner, Commissioner responsible for energy questions, so aptly remarked in an interview: 'There can be no improvement in Community performance without some transfer of sovereignty. Who pretends otherwise is throwing dust in the eyes of the people of Europe.' Quoted in European Communities Commission *Background Report* ISEC/B9/79 (London) 22 February 1979, p. 5.

Index